PAPER TIGER

PAPER TIGER

AN OBSESSED GOLFER'S QUEST
TO PLAY WITH THE PROS

TOM COYNE

GOTHAM BOOKS

GOTHAM BOOKS
Published by Penguin Group (USA) Inc.
375 Hudson Street, New York, New York 10014, U.S.A.
Penguin Group (Canada), 90 Eglinton Avenue East, Suite 700,
Toronto, Ontario M4P 2Y3, Canada (a division of Pearson Penguin Canada Inc.);
Penguin Books Ltd, 80 Strand, London WC2R 0RL, England; Penguin Ireland,
25 St Stephen's Green, Dublin 2, Ireland (a division of Penguin Books Ltd); Penguin
Group (Australia), 250 Camberwell Road, Camberwell, Victoria 3124, Australia
(a division of Pearson Australia Group Pty Ltd); Penguin Books India Pvt Ltd,
11 Community Centre, Panchsheel Park, New Delhi — 110 017, India; Penguin Group
(NZ), cnr Airborne and Rosedale Roads, Albany, Auckland 1310, New Zealand
(a division of Pearson New Zealand Ltd); Penguin Books (South Africa) (Pty) Ltd,
24 Sturdee Avenue, Rosebank, Johannesburg 2196, South Africa

Penguin Books Ltd, Registered Offices: 80 Strand, London WC2R 0RL, England

Published by Gotham Books, a division of Penguin Group (USA) Inc.

First printing, June 2006
1   3   5   7   9   10   8   6   4   2

Gotham Books and the skyscraper logo are trademarks of Penguin Group (USA) Inc.

LIBRARY OF CONGRESS CATALOGING-IN-PUBLICATION DATA
Coyne, Tom.
    Paper tiger : an obsessed golfer's quest to play with the pros / by Tom Coyne.—1st ed.
    p.   cm.
ISBN 1-592-40209-7 (hardcover)
1. Golf. 2. Golfers. 3. Coyne, Tom.   I. Title.
GV965.C692 2006
796.357092—dc22   2005037751

Printed in the United States of America
Set in Adobe Caslon
Designed by Elke Sigal

For my caddy

. . . we know what we are, but know not what we may be.

—WILLIAM SHAKESPEARE

Golf is hard.

—DR. JIM SUTTIE

"This is the 7:30 tee time off tee number one. Now on the tee, from Philadelphia, Pennsylvania . . . Tom Coyne."

The scene looks vaguely familiar. In every direction, the wet-tipped morning grass, pine trees standing in careful rows, and here, in front of my feet, a square carpet of perfect green, the grass clipped tight as the scalp of a re-upped marine. The small plateau is empty save two black plastic blocks, planted in the turf across from each other in some seemingly purposeful position. A woman is standing at the edge of the short grass holding a clipboard in one hand, megaphone in the other, though she doesn't need to use it—there are only a dozen or so faces, all gathered within earshot. Most look like they're on the same team, or recently arrived from the same boarding school. All young men in saddle shoes or wingtips, khaki slacks, sweaters and vests, everyone in baseball caps. And most of them are holding long, skinny sticks in their hands, silver- and black- and green-colored rods, waving them around their bodies like drunken fencers. They all seem to be in their twenties, tall and skinny, perhaps even athletic-looking if they weren't dressed up like their fathers. They all have a look on their face like somebody pissed in their Wheaties. And they are all looking straight at me.

Tom Coyne, I think to myself, *I know that guy.* I'm half-asleep, confident that I am standing upright even though I feel nothing below my chin, and, like the rest of the crowd, probably just to blend in, I am holding one of these blue staffs with a small black bulb attached to the end of it, a sort of space-age mace, dangerous-looking, yet impossibly lightweight. I am here, but not sure how that happened, as if I've just woken up from a drunken night in a strange town, and I feel like if I just stand here long enough, frozen still on this giant raft of green—*don't move, nobody else is moving*—pose here long enough, I just might disappear.

But before I can blend away into oblivion, I feel my legs start to life, my feet begin to heel-toe their way forward—*this feels nice, I wonder where I'm going.* I reach my hand into my pocket—it looks like my hand, pale and freckled, hanging from what I have to trust is my arm (it's wearing my shirt, after all). I feel my head begin to fall toward the ground, my body bending at the waist—bad idea, whatever I was able to choke down for breakfast tries to make a quick run for it—but I stand up straight, take a deep breath, cough down what's tugging at the bottom of my throat, and when I look back down at the grass, surprise, a little white globe is floating magically above the turf.

I watch my fingers tangle around the rubber end of my stick, and I drop the dangerous end squarely behind the sphere as if I intend it harm. The little ball looks innocent enough, plastic yet precious, all lit up with hundreds of careful angles—and yet I feel nothing but resentment for this tiny jewel. It needs to be punished. It needs to be struck, this much I know, but the tool I'm holding next to it seems perfectly ill-suited for the job.

Something is about to happen. And nothing is about to happen. I become as stiff a part of the scene as those pine trees, transfixed by this milky piece of plastic at my feet. My eyes study the ball's every peak and valley, wandering up and down its curves, the same way my eyes probe that spot on the wall just above the urinal, mesmerized by every nook and cranny of the concrete, lost in the texture, comforted by the familiarity of that omnipresent booger smear—

And then it's gone. I don't see the ball leave, but I watch it rocket through the air, far and away, soon just a speck skipping down a runway of wet turf. We didn't have a lot of time together, me and my little white ball. But they were good times.

I step aside and watch as three of the young men from the crowd, apparently inspired by my display, step forward and attempt their own imitations. Hand in the pocket, bend over, pose there for a while and then give it a whack. It's an understated violence, and it seems an ineffective release, like whipping a horse with fishing line. The ball escapes with all the energy, and the young men are left with looks on their faces like they already miss their friend, like if it would come back to them, next time they would treat it better.

And apparently there will be a next time, and soon, because in a moment we are walking across a field, sacks of sticks swinging from our shoulders, a platoon of four heading out to chase down the one that went AWOL.

As we march, I start to feel my hands again, and my feet, and I'm aware that my knees are bending. I look around. Fairway. Bunkers. A flag waving in the distance as if calling us home. I know where I am, and I was right: I've been here before. But before was never quite like this.

Welcome to your dream.

If not your dream, then your father's. Or your brother's dream. Maybe your neighbor, or the quiet guy in the office down the hall, maybe they have imagined themselves to sleep with a story not too unlike the one I am about to tell you. It might be as simple as leaving early on a Friday afternoon, sneaking away from the office to soak up a few extra hours of sunshine on the back nine. Maybe instead of rewarding you with another awkward lunch, this time the boss takes you out to his millionaire country club, offers you the new driver he's been talking about since Christmas, hangs your sack of clubs on the shoulder of the greatest grizzled caddy this side of Scotland. The fantasy might be as uncomplicated as the wife canceling the trip to the in-laws so you can spend the afternoon working on your short game. Or maybe, if your dream is like mine, you quit your life and go play golf for 546 days in a row. Either way, you've seen the cover of this book and you've made it this far—which means you're somebody who isn't playing right now, but would like to be.

Because you know that golf is not a game. The cliché doesn't work—it's not life, either, because we don't spend near as much time contemplating our actual lives. Golf is as perspective-altering and priority-skewing as any opiate out there. It has laid waste to bank accounts, steamrolled marriages, demonized fathers, and alienated sons. Its brutally efficient buzz is its hook—just one good shot out of a hundred, just 1 percent of pure, *did you see that one* high—it's enough to keep millions of us jonesing our way to the weekend. That glint of golf ball climbing up the breeze, suspended there in some heavenly grip, then rolling over and careening back to the earth, settling into the fairway like it was being reunited with an old friend. No matter that your next swing is an exercise in self-flagellation, that your shank from the fairway looks like you were throwing to first base, that you four-putted from five feet and proceeded to dramatically advance the science of profanity—for one moment on that one afternoon, you had your fix. You felt it click far back in your mind, and you were off soaring with that golf ball, all warm and smiley like a kid in a Nike commercial: *Nice to meet you, golf. I am Tiger Fucking Woods.*

As a spectator sport, golf is as oft-maligned as drying paint and NASCAR, but the lucky ones among us understand why watching golf can be a regular voyeuristic thrill show. In every moment of every professional tournament, we find a little bit of our own game, a glimmer of our own potential. Consider the rival pastimes: Tennis players don't watch Agassi smoke the ball through his adversary's racket strings and think, *Yeah, I love it when I do that.* Middle-aged accountants don't look at LeBron and recall their own 360 windmill jam at last Wednesday night's pickup game. But every golfer, even the most bogey-bedraggled, has at some point amid all the punishment made a thirty-foot putt. Or hit a drive that split the fairway, chipped one up next to the hole, stuck a five-iron inside the barrel. Golf is the ultimate vicarious adventure, because no matter how good the pros get, no matter how far Tiger distances himself from the field, those snappy dressers at the Booz Allen Classic are essentially doing exactly what you did on your own course two days ago. They just do it a helluva lot more frequently.

And frequency—that's something we can manipulate, something we can develop. Consistency is a behavior. Consistency is different from being eight feet tall, different from being able to bench-press a Fiat. If you, if I can hit one respectable shot each round, then why not two? Why not ten passable passes at the ball? How about thirty, sixty good shots per round? If there were no spouse, no kids, no job, if you had the prime equipment, the top instruction, the best trainer and best coach and best shrink—if you had all their reasons, and none of your excuses, could you play with the big boys? Provided with all the trimmings and trappings of the elite players' lives, how elite might you become?

That question is at the heart of why we play, why we sleep in our cars in the parking lot, waiting for the chance to get out there and chase it around, from hole to hole and fairway to green, stalking those moments when we might be better than ourselves. It's grabbing at water, drips and drabs of the game, and one soft center click is just enough to keep us coming back, keep us believing that tomorrow all the shots will come easy. That is the dream—that someday we will really know our game, that golf won't always be lurking a few hundred more yards down the fairway.

It isn't just a dream for the helpless golfhead. Everyone who has made contact with a golf ball understands a piece of the game's spirit. It's there as your hands fall toward the ball, just before your club tears the turf, when anything might happen and you can still wonder . . . what if?

We confess it every time we tee it up, we speak it in our sleep, we feel it as we watch our ball go jumping off the screws—we love this game. What if we could give it everything, just for a little while? How much would it love us back?

Seven minutes into the 2004 Fall Qualifying School of the Canadian Professional Golf Tour, I feel my Softspikes pressing their way across the first fairway of the Royal Ashburn Golf Club, tracking my little white ball to the edge of a wet and sandy crater.

My opening drive has crept into a fairway bunker, rolling to rest on a crusty plate of sand. A clean lie, 260 yards to the green on this opening par-five, and I have arrived at my first decision of my first Qualifying School. In my gut, I want to reach for my putter—there'd at least be guaranteed contact—but the ball is sitting fine, the lip in front of me generously shallow, and the two Canucks in my foursome have already gone for the green, slapping perfect three-woods off the deck: pretty showy for eight in the morning, if you ask me.

I climb down into the bunker, guessing that a four-iron will clear the lip if I can just nip it clean. I look at my playing partners, they're all looking at me. It's that moment unique to golf when the game silently screams at you: *Your turn. Your time to go.*

I take a practice swing, feeling my chest and my elbows putting the golf club on plane, placing the club head in ideal position, just the way my swing coach taught me.

I stand behind my ball, I make my plan, I see my shot and I pick my target and I commit, just as my psychologist wanted me to. But I am not just thinking about my target alone—part of me, maybe all of me, is thinking about the last year of my life spent preparing for now. For my turn. I don't know if one year is going to be enough, but I know I am the only man on this golf course, in this country, on this whole damn continent who can say that in the past twelve months alone:

I have hit over 75,000 range balls.

I have hit over 100,000 golf shots.

I have spent 120 hours in sand traps.

I have hit 15,000 four-foot putts.

I have played 5,418 holes of golf.

I have lost 38 pounds.

I have spent 215 hours in the gym.

I have spent 36 hours on the trainer's table.

I have spent 43 hours one-on-one with the PGA national teacher of the year.

I have spent 7 days learning from a world-renowned golf psychologist.

I have digested 37 books, 24 magazines, 42 videos, 3 CDs, and 2 audiotapes.

I have gained 34 yards off the tee.

I have shaved 15 shots off my handicap.

I have reduced my stroke average from 87.0 to 72.9.

I have spent $52,000 I didn't have.

All to prepare me for here, for this spot where I can't prepare anymore.

I step toward my ball, twist my spikes into the sand. I feel the good posture in the muscles down my back—set, steady, and square.

I think about being thoughtless, I focus on being focused. There is a swing-thought lost somewhere in my head, a few quick words I might tell myself to help get me from here to my backswing to my follow-through. I worked on it with my shrink, we had settled on a phrase—something positive, simple, effective—but I can't recall it now. This morning, looking down at my Titleist 2 in the sand, I have two new swing-thoughts working.

Don't miss it.

Followed by, *Don't miss it, you asshole.*

PART ONE

Our foursome sits around a table of magically replenishing bottles of Miller High Life, adding up the damage from a game of two-dollar skins. It's my first round of golf this year, but there is still no excuse for owing Jack McDougal eighteen dollars. Jack is five feet six and a hundred pounds carrying his golf bag. He's the sort of golfer who, when you owe him eighteen dollars, you start playing tennis.

Along with my dollars, Jack takes the opportunity to remind me that I started playing golf when I was kid, while he started hacking around a mere three summers ago. He points out that while I play an authentic Callaway Big Bertha, he triumphed with its lesser-known cousin, the Callahan Big Bursar. He feels it necessary to tell me that the cigarette he smoked on the third tee was, say, enhanced, and he still proceeded to get in my pocket (the fact that I was giving Jack seven shots a side seems to have gone adrift in his short-term memory). And then, as if the High Life wasn't bad enough, Jack serves me up a "And didn't you write a book about golf?"

It hurts.

The rest of the table celebrates my every wince. Gavin and Damon, two lads from Northern Ireland and maestros of ballbusting, are positively bouncing with pleasure at the prospect of their next dig. It's three against one, but I can take it—I have to take it, the easy target, the only member of the foursome to ever take a lesson, belong to a golf club, or rationalize paying fifty bucks for a dozen balls. They take turns chopping away at my ego, passing abuse around the table as freely as they passed around their open packs of cigarettes.

"Maybe you can write another book about golf, one where you don't suck at it."

"How many times does the guy in your book three-putt?"

"Did I tell you—the other day, I met the guy who saw your movie."

And while I could throw it back, get nasty on Jack McSkinny and two tubby Irishman who were emptying beers like there were holes in their bottles, I don't. I hold my tongue in my teeth. I don't mention that Gavin hit more weak pop flies today than the Phillies' lead-off hitter, that on four different chip shots, Jack folded the dirt over his ball like he was making a turf omelet. And I don't remind Damon that on the par-three seventeenth, when I told him I'd bet him five bucks on his score for the hole—I set the over-under at 8—he thought about it longer than I expected him to, then gave me a confident nod and said, "I'll take the over."

Instead, I just smile and let them have their fun—*Hey, Coyne, that was mighty generous of you, donating all those expensive golf balls to the golfers behind us*—because with three against one, self-defense sounds the same as whining, and no one here is interested in stories about a shelf full of dusty trophies, golden golfers posed in their backswing, the tiny golf clubs meant to fit their hands snapped or disappeared a dozen years before. My name, it used to pop up in the sports section from time to time, back when I was seventeen and I could hit it as deep as anyone at my club, anyone in the section— but those stories are not entirely interesting, and not entirely true. And no tap dance of excuses—*I haven't played in six months, my cart was too slow, my ball too white, my driver's been having problems at home*—none of it matters when you're the only real golfer in the group (or at least used to be), when they know you're the only one who would actually care about losing, and you lose.

You're either a spoiled brat or a lucky bastard (probably both) when the only free clinic you were ever forced to visit was the one at your parents' country club. I reluctantly took up the game at nine years old, a Sunday participant in the junior golf clinic at Rolling Green Golf Club. One of my older brothers had already chiseled out his niche as the golfing son, and nine-year-olds don't want to do anything that their older brothers do. Unless they can do it better. The clinic quickly turned into a few private lessons with the assistant pro, then a spot on the club's nine-holer team, and in the space of a few weeks, golf had its claws in deep.

I sacrificed my starting spot on the Little League team in order to better nurture my new golf swing. I went to golf camps and took lessons by the bundle and spent ten hours a day working on my sunburn at the club, whittling my handicap down to the single digits. Each summer morning my mother would drop me off at the bottom of the driveway to the golf course, and I would sit with the other caddies in the basement of the clubhouse, listening to old men tell stories of bar fights and battlefields, hoping not to get a loop, so I could sneak out to the range and spend yet another afternoon beating balls. At six o'clock, my father would show up from the office, still wearing half his suit, sleeves rolled up as he putted on the practice green, waiting for me to finish my afternoon eighteen. I was too young to fully appreciate the beauty, the brilliance of my summer routine, every evening telling my dad the same story: *I wanted to get out, I tried to caddy, but there weren't any loops. So I decided to play, instead.*

I would win my club's junior championship on three occasions, playing off a semi-legitimate five-handicap as I toyed with the idea of playing college golf. This was back when a five-handicap might get you a scholarship to a respectable program. As worthless as a 79-shooter might seem to a college coach today, my childhood golf wasn't being played all that long ago. I am twenty-eight years old and played my last junior tournament in 1993. And yet, those golfing years feel like they belong to another age, a distinct golfing universe. The game looked different, smelled different, the clubs felt different in your fingers. Everything was different about the game in those years B.T. (Before Tiger).

Nine years old is a late start by today's standards, but it was near unheard of in the 1980s, a twenty-year head start on the average hacker who took up the game after making partner at the bank. The junior golf scene comprised a handful of members' sons slapping it around on a Saturday afternoon. We heard mumblings about some junior golfing tour, but it sounded sort of silly, like some rich kid's summer vacation, flying around the country playing tournaments against the thin strata of sixteen-year-olds who could afford to do the same. Most high school golfers I knew played a handful of local tournaments a year, then spent the rest of the time playing basketball, lifting weights for football season. As a junior golfer back in ol' '89, you didn't brag to your friends about your handicap, didn't mention that tomorrow you had a tee time at Merion and you were just so psyched. Golf wasn't cool. Not until we started hearing about some skinny kid from California named after a cat. After Tiger, the sport we all loved in secret, that we shared with just a handful of other kids, as if junior golf were our own private tree house—after the 1997 Masters, it was everybody's game. Our little clubhouse came crashing out of the tree.

Born just a year apart, Tiger Woods and I stepped into the same golfing milieu, a world where they didn't teach golf in PE, where the First Tee was where you picked up your purple golf ball and your putter, where the golf section in the sporting goods store consisted of one dusty pair of tasseled shoes and a sleeve of Dunlops—it wasn't a game for kids, you played only if Daddy did. This happened to be the case for both Tiger and me, and while my dad didn't put me in a high chair to watch him hit balls (for the best probably, or I might have inherited his grooved slice), we were both led into golf at a time when we had few contemporaries. You see pictures of Tiger as a very young man in those outfits, when golf fashion was still content in its own goofiness—and I see my junior golfing friends, hard-brimmed hats and stiff polyester collars, leather bags with angry straps, before Ping and its soft velour shoulders. I see myself, over six feet tall at the age of fourteen, built like a five-iron, golf shirts falling off my nowhere shoulders. But I could hit it. Stringy arms and bony legs, but I could whip it out there.

There might have been a time, when Tiger and I were boys, when I would have noticed the other lanky kid at the range, Dad watching him hit balls, and I might have nodded at him, mumbled a hello, as if to say, *me too*. There might have been a moment where we were both standing at the same crossroad in our young lives. Two roads diverged in a wood, and I took the road *more* traveled by. And that has made all the difference.

Ten years ago, I left for college with my five-handicap and a full head of red hair, neither of which, I soon learned, made me very special at the University of Notre Dame. I planned on cruising out to Indiana and showing the farmers and the fullbacks how we played the game back east. It took five minutes on the putting green at tryouts for me to know—there was so much good golf out there, and it found its way all over.

There were players from Texas and California, the warm weather, four-season players, kids with equipment I had never heard of, shirts from places I had absolutely heard of, and I knew that look on their faces from all the practice tees growing up in junior golf, a look that said they were going to be as rich as their fathers and even better at golf, so stuffed with that knowledge they could barely open their eyes to look at you. And I don't know if it was my being a stupid freshman, or being too nervous to know any better, but I wasn't quite interested in being intimidated. Halfway through my first round of tryouts, I found myself two strokes better than par.

The head coach started following my group as we made the turn, and my playing partner, a fourth-year golfer on a full-ride, started wondering out loud why I wasn't on scholarship. I cruised along through my second nine, imagining my name stitched down the side of those Notre Dame golf bags you can't buy in the bookstore. The shots were happening without me thinking about them. It was real golf, not in drips and drabs but in a deluge, and I knew what those kids knew, those self-satisfied faces who understood the effortlessness of the game.

Of course, this was before that one shot, the one that reached down deep into my throat, squeezed my heart until it stopped.

It was a two-and-a-half-footer on the fifteenth green. A no-brainer, could have sneezed it in, *should have* sneezed it in. It spun around the lip, wiped the bowl clean, and as easily as I had found golf, I had lost it. The curtain flew back, the visage crumbled, and what I had taken for a simple game was now all cogs and wheels and complication. My terror level jumped two levels to severe, and my next drive went hunting for Knute Rockne's grave in the cemetery along sixteen. It wasn't a moment before the coach conspicuously slipped off to watch the group behind us. I finished the day triple, triple, triple, wonderful if I was trying out for the baseball team, but as far as my golf career was concerned, it had vanished as thoroughly as my last tee ball.

Legendary determination, superhuman focus, a messianic dollop of talent was all that separated Tiger and me in the end, my golf dreams left hanging on the lip in freshman tryouts. Around the same time the world was discovering golf and Tiger Woods, my golf clubs were being stolen out of my car in South Bend. I took the insurance money and bought an electric guitar. The clubs weren't replaced for years.

By twenty-six I had no home course and a girlfriend of many years, who, while amused by the prospect of golf and pleased to be in possession of her own proper collection of golfing utensils (my law school graduation gift that would eventually go the way of the tennis racket, the Rollerblades, the yoga mat, all permanently exiled to the car trunk), was more interested in new restaurants and weekend sales than in joining me for an early-morning eighteen. Allyson enjoyed that Sunday when the Masters was on, and lunch on the patio of my dad's golf club was a stolen treat from some life we might be living twenty years down the road. But twenty-six years were telling me that there were more things to do with your day than find an empty first tee, and more people to do them with than those dozen names on your mind's phone tree of available golfers.

The game became a distant friend, the high school buddy whose life had not changed at the same pace as my own, and what was once my life's passion devolved into an excuse to drink beer outdoors. And that was plenty good for me. Even though I was playing off a bloated fourteen-handicap, I was recruited to play bar and charity golf outings the way better players were recruited for Division I programs. On any given Monday, I would have two or three not-for-profit golf scrambles to choose from. I blossomed into a golf-outing connoisseur, versed in each particular tournament's prize history, catering quality, course conditions. I was an in-demand free agent because, firstly, I could still play a little bit (there weren't too many ex–junior club champions playing the Stinky McCormick Memorial at the Dirt Patch Golf Club with kegs on alternating tee boxes and dancing girls in the clubhouse basement). And as an author of discarded novels and unfinished screenplays, my availability was outstanding. Born of the country club golf team, my fellow linksmen were now bartenders and contractors and the gainfully unemployed, guys who could take off on a Monday to play a beige golf course for the chance to win an inflatable chair. Guys like Jack and Gavin and Damon, who could hardly believe I once ever called myself a golfer.

I'm watching a tournament replay on the television when more Irish wit walks into my afternoon. I give a half-nod to Padraig Mahoon, our friend from Galway whose accent seems to get twice as thick when he's giving out, which he almost always is.

"Would you look at this foursome. Some greenskeeper's working overtime tonight, trying to salvage whatever course it was you all were playing," Paddy says. "And, Coyne, by the way, your gym called. Wanted to know where they could send the refund," he adds, pointing to my ever-ripening belly, choosing to overlook the fact that he himself is built like a football (and that's his kind of football, not ours).

Padraig has been in this country more years than he hasn't, but he's still Irish first, and like most Irish, he can tell you you're a useless piece of shit in a way that would make you say thanks and offer to pay for his dinner. He was the assistant pro at my golf course, we worked together in the pro shop when I was in college, back when "work" entailed figuring ways out to get caddies to do your job. Padraig was a good teacher, substituting wit and charisma for what he didn't know about the golf swing. Considering his Woosnam-like stature and the fact that he only started playing golf in his twenties, he was quite a good player, always a few putts away from making that big check at the local PGA events. He would give me lessons from time to time, when our commitment to getting better at golf would actually find its way out of the pub and into real life.

Paddy knows there was a time when I could hit it, and I know he's not impressed with my new stature as MVP of the Monday scramble.

"It might be good craic, but playing scrambles on shite courses, looking at shite golf swings all afternoon," Paddy says, "how are you going to get any better doing that?"

"I play twice a month. I don't have a handicap, I don't have the time, I don't have the money," I explain. "Why would I care about getting better at golf?"

Paddy smiles, trying not to laugh at this last load of bullshit that is far below Irish bullshitting standards. This is why Paddy and I are better friends than most of our buddies from the pub or the driving range—we share a secret: Once upon a time, we both could play. We both brushed up against our possibility but never quite grabbed it, and every time we pick up a golf club, we aren't just thinking about the things we're about to do; we're wondering about the things we didn't. We've never discussed it, but on the golf course I know that Paddy is one of those who can hear that everywhere, all the time: *What if?*

On most evenings, Paddy answers that question by retelling a favorite story, the one about the sports psychologist who once asked Greg Norman how he became the greatest golfer in the world. The Australian's answer was: "Because I wanted to be." When asked to explain, Norman said that as a young man, he arrived at his local course every morning before sunrise. He would do his stretching in the parking lot while it was still dark out so that he could be on the driving range as the sun came up, not wasting a single minute of daylight. He practiced all day, until it was too dark to follow the golf ball, when he would head off to the gym to lift weights and swim laps until close. Then finally to home and to bed, and up the next morning before sunrise.

"And that's why a sports psychologist never had to bother asking us that question," Paddy says, sticking a finger in my chest. "Greg Norman didn't talk it. He lived it. If you would have had that attitude, who knows. You might have even been a better player than myself."

"I am a better player than you."

"Not if you're losing money to that lot, you're not," he says, looking over to the Golden Tee, where Jack is now playing Gavin for twenty bucks a hole. "You could hit it, Coinage. There was a time. When I was working with you, I had you striping it good as anybody I'd ever seen, that high and lovely ball-flight. That was as good as you needed to be hitting a golf ball. Christ, I'd hate to see the ruins of your golf swing now."

"Once in a while. I can still hit it. If I played as much as you do . . ."

But Paddy isn't listening. Maybe he doesn't want to hear my excuses—not that I have any to offer. His eyes drift off to the leader board on TV.

"Look at these guys. Johnny No-names. Ten millionaires there nobody ever heard of. Look at that name"—Paddy points to the screen—"now who the hell is Donald Hill? You know that guy can't hit it like Tiger. You put him on the range with the top ten in the world, he'd look like he should be shining their shoes. But look there, third place, Donald Hill, he's going to cash a check big as your belly. Because he's hitting fairways and hitting greens. Getting 'round the golf course, simple as that."

Paddy's fingers push around an empty bottle as he watches the screen, looking for his own name, it seems, convinced that the difference between D. Hill and P. Mahoon is a little bit of time and a little bit of money and a little bit of luck.

"It's a simple game," Paddy explains. In his brogue, it sounds more like a question.

———

The next morning, I find a blank pad of paper sitting on my desk. Scribbled across the top of the first page:

One year. One shot. No excuses.

I've missed sunrise, but I head directly to the public driving range, and I beat balls off the mats until I can't feel my fingers, until I can't stand up straight, limping back to my car a few hours shy of sunset. I am sore in an adult sort of way, my body having grown reluctant to being posed and twisted, protesting this unexpected full day of exercise. Yet with each swing, with each six-iron inching closer to my target line, with each thin metal click, I feel younger. The driving range is quiet, no more questions to consider, no potential to ponder, just the sound of golf ball after golf ball that sounds like sixteen years old to me, young and obsessed and free to be so. No more *What if?*—only *What now?* And *What now?* is work, Greg Norman style, not a minute of sunshine to spare. I have checked the Web site, and my PGA Tour Qualifying School is only eighteen months away.

After a week of my buying up the range balls as fast as they can pick them, the guy in the pro shop can't help asking me what I'm up to.

"You getting ready for the tour or something?" He laughs, unlit cigarette stuck in his teeth.

When I tell him, "Actually, yeah," I see the confusion, then the pity, this man looking at me like I'm too old to still believe in Santa Claus.

He's quiet for a moment, waiting for the punch line, I suppose. Then he reaches into the register and throws me an extra token for the ball machine.

"Here you go," the man says. "You're gonna need a lot more of these."

The last summer flew by in a blurry mix of joy and terror, fantastical expectations, and breath-robbing realities. I spent the days building up my calluses at the driving range, spent the evenings mapping out my upcoming months, researching golfing intelligentsia and looking for a home to rent in Florida, my launching pad for the countdown to Q-school. While I had been giddy about my plan to do nothing but golf for the next twelve months under the tutelage of the world's finest coaches and shrinks and trainers, a part of me felt like the kid who begs to go to the circus for years, then sits there in the front row, mouth open and eyes covered, scared to death. There is safety in sitting around and wondering, imagining your successes and blaming cruel circumstance— I always win that game, with nothing put to risk. But the idea that I had committed every penny and minute of my life to one goal— such a clear focus felt slightly unnatural. When you take away all your excuses, funny how lonely your ego can become.

I embarked on this golf journey from the blankest of slates. In Philadelphia, I had no home course, no golf membership, no inside deal at the local driving range. I had $35,000 in the bank and $30,000 more in empty credit cards, a mixed set of golf clubs bought off the rack, and golf shoes with about as much spike left to them as a pair of flip-flops.

One of my first steps toward golf greatness was to go put a camcorder and tripod on my MasterCard. I had never before mixed technology into my golf game. When I was learning the golf swing, VHS and VCRs were state-of-the-art, precious, and pricey science. It seemed inconceivable that such technology could be taken outdoors, let alone applied to a golf lesson. A golfer could play the game for fifty years without ever knowing what his swing actually looked like (a blessing for most of my old loops). Players guessed, teachers surmised, but it was theory and fundamentals—what happened between takeaway and follow-through was mostly left to mystery. But now it is impossible to think of a golf lesson without considering that most important eye of all, the one made of glass. My purchase of the latest in digital technology not only was a monetary commitment to my regimen, but it pushed me closer to that club of golfheads who got tingly over swing-planes and wrist-hinges and launch-angles, a clique in which I knew I needed to soon gain acceptance.

With each passing summer day, I told myself that I had to produce tangible evidence that I was a more complete golfer in the evening than I had been that morning. It might entail spending two hours in the bunkers, hitting one more fairway than yesterday, or playing an entire round of golf sans three-putt. But it almost always involved beating balls in front of my new camera, replaying each day's progress against the day before's and scribbling wipe-erase marker all over my TV screen, comparing and figuring my angles, not entirely sure what I was looking for but understanding enough to discern my good from my bad from my ugly.

If I couldn't make myself better on the practice range that day, I went to the mall and improved myself through shopping. I embarked on dysfunctional buying sprees through the golf mega-warehouses, collecting golf gadgets and swing-aids like some country club pack rat. I bought a Medicus (the club that breaks), a Momentus (the club that's heavy), a swing-fan and a swing-vest and a putting track and an indoor green. If I had a three-putt during that afternoon's round, I might purchase a new putter that evening, or return the one I had bought the evening before. And if I couldn't get to the mall, I went to the computer—my first trip to Amazon saw me order nineteen new titles, everything from *Golfer's Diet* to *Yoga for Golf, Zen Golf, Golf for Enlightenment*. I read them all, to the point where I didn't know if I was preparing for Qualifying School or Nirvana.

We call it a thinking man's game, but with so many golf problems and golf solutions to consider, might we have turned golf into an over-thinking man's game? It is a question I must confront as I learn and prepare: How much information is too much? What is the balance between knowing and doing? How far should I head down that rabbit—rather, that gopher—hole of golf knowledge?

The mind-set of the writer and the tournament golfer could not be more opposed. The writer overthinks by necessity, collecting and complicating small details, while the tournament golfer needs to be simple, myopic, fixated on one detail at a time. I received some good advice on this dilemma this summer. I was playing in August as a guest at Aronimink Country Club, explaining to my host how I was planning on spending my upcoming year. And his advice to me: "If you're going to get really good at this game, you're going to have to get a little dumber."

There is a real genius in being able to play a mindless round of golf. In golf's pacing and in its rules and in its endless minutia, the game tempts you to outthink it. I suspect that the player who can play dumb, who can know just one simple thing—*get this ball in that hole as quick as I damn well can*—is going to be better off than the one who just took an entire page trying to explain why that is.

With the help of all the books and the tapes and the swing-aids, my game took huge leaps toward respectability between May and October. Like a fat man who's found Atkins, those early pounds slid off the quickest. By swinging a golf club each and every day, I was able to figure out my misses and my mistakes, plan for my worst cases, and get myself around a golf course in a few less strokes every week. While my first official handicap in years clocked in at 14.2, by September, I had worked my way down to a 9.6 with no instructor and no idea what I was really doing, just doing it all the time.

I had made a new home of the Golf Course at Glen Mills, a nearby public-friendly track that is owned and operated by the Glen Mills Schools, the longest-operating school for troubled youth in the United States. The new Bobby Tweed design has been ranked tops in Pennsylvania (a *Golf Digest* Must Play), and the practice facilities are as good as any in the area. But the greatest thing about Glen Mills is the view from the practice tee, where you overlook three sloping green fairways, up to the spires of the school buildings that sit atop hills of high yellow grass, like some elite New England college. The kids at the bag drop, the young men working on the golf course, the golf team hitting balls beside you on the driving range—they have been sent there by a judge, from cities across the United States. While I can't call Glen Mills my home course (memberships are for school instructors only—the greatest perk in all secondary education), it seems the ideal spot for my journey to begin. The summer has been full of lectures from superior golfers as to why my quest for Q-school is absurd, an insult to their great game, a total waste of an opportunity (that they all seem to covet for themselves). Maybe they're right. Golf doesn't give second chances or do-overs, but everywhere you look at Glen Mills, you see second chances walking around with their heads up, succeeding, inspiring their peers and maybe a few of the passing golfers to ask, *Why not?*

When it rained this summer, I didn't take a day off (unlike Greg Norman, I didn't go to the gym, either). I would leave Glen Mills and find a spot at the old rubber-mat driving range. It had a sad little putt-putt layout and a nine-hole golf course whose upkeep was left to a team of Canadian geese. The range balls had a Ping-Pong texture, and the battered targets looked like they had been brought up from Guantánamo Beach, but the hitting bays were dry and covered, and the golf was beautifully honest.

In the non–private club world, there is an almost exact inverse relationship between golf aesthetics and golf passion. It is in these aspiring-for-average surroundings—in these lounges with yesterday's coffee and fluorescent lighting and prehistoric hot dogs turning on blackened metal rollers, in these clubhouses that can be split in two and thrown on the back of a trailer—it is here that you find the great men of this game. Take, for instance, the gentleman whom very few of the other entrants in this year's PGA Tour Qualifying School will know much about—some call him the rubber-mat maharishi, the boss of the moss, the god of the golden tokens. But I call him Larry.

I could always find Larry spending his lunch hour in the same hitting bay, dressed in suit pants and an Izod shirt from the trunk of his Buick, a shirt faded from purple to pink that I suspected him of wearing three afternoons in a row. His hair wasn't what it may have once been, but he couldn't be bothered. He would stride up and down the line of swinging golfers, videotaping his friends' moves with a camera big enough for a dolly track—*Is that Betamax?*—then rewind the tape and call his pals over for a look at their swings through the viewfinder. Larry would toss out bits of wisdom more befuddling than anything I ever found in the pages of *Digest*:

"You need to get more three-dimensional" seemed to be one of his favorites, right up there with "Your swing is too round." "You have to get your right side moving through to left field" was not an uncommon diagnosis, but it felt less imaginative than his axiom "Your hands have to stay on the Hula-Hoop."

Larry worked with a regular cache of students. There was gray-faced Bob, a Marlboro devotee built like a puff of smoke. He would hit a small bucket of three-woods every day, between the hours of one and two o'clock, as regular as if his doctor had written him a prescription for fifty worm-burners every afternoon. Most of Bob's golf balls ended up sprinkled around the front of his hitting bay within a ball scooper's reach. Larry had been known to stretch his lunch hour to give Bob a few pointers that I never actually heard Bob ask for. Larry thought Bob needed to get wider in his swing, and make an earlier set.

Then there was Randy the Roofer, who pounded drivers at the back fence for twenty minutes, three times a week. I once watched Randy leave his truck running in the parking lot as he jogged to one of the rubber tees in his steel-toe boots and grease-smeared jeans, smashing a dozen golf balls with a $600 driver, then back to his truck, tossing his golf club in the back like it was a two-by-four and speeding off before his last drive had landed. Larry believed that Randy needed to get more vertical, and spend more time working on his wedge game.

And then there was the Picker, a sixteen-year-old with unfortunate skin who drove the ball-picker three hours a day for the right to unlimited range balls. He looked up to Larry as if Larry had taken a break from coaching Vijay to come take a look at his swing.

"You've been working on your lag. I like it," Larry would say, watching the Picker drop five-irons on the crooked 200-yard sign. The kid could hit it, and if he ever found himself a whole golf course made of Astro Turf, he'd probably be deadly. Larry looked on through the viewfinder, nodding at his protégé, lips turned up like a placated Bela Karolyi.

And then there was me, trying not to listen to the symphony of hosel rockets and toe-hits all around me, trying to block out whatever unsolicited wisdom Larry might have to offer. He wouldn't tape my swing or comment on my own sleek camera; we didn't really talk. Until one afternoon when I was back at my swankier Glen Mills digs, and there was Mr. Larry coming off eighteen.

It was the shirt that gave him away. His forehead soft with sweat, his body folded from the heat, he had the stature of an accountant on April 16. We recognized each other, and while we didn't trade hellos around the old 'hood, we decide we could chat at Glen Mills like we'd bumped into each other on vacation.

"Had enough of the mats, huh?" Larry said. "Beautiful range they have up there. It's nice to hit off grass for a change. Really makes you go after it with an entirely different angle. . . ."

I suspected that so many days on the rubber had cost him that day. Hitting off a surface that bounces back, one can groove a scoopy swing. While he might have strolled his range like he was king of the hill, this is a *real* golf course, there's a *real* player at work here. I didn't even know if his name is actually Larry, but I couldn't resist asking him what he shot.

"Let me see here," he says, flipping over his scorecard. "I guess that's 70."

"70?" I said, waiting for him to say he forgot to add up the back nine. "70—that's one under."

"Yeah. I made three birdies on the front. That eleventh hole killed me. I'll tell you, they can bulldoze that hole, as far as I'm concerned."

"70?"

"I'll be kicking myself all night. I put that three-iron in the fairway, I shoot 68. Oh, well," he says, looking up from his card. "It'll bring me back next week. Did you play today?"

Yes. Actually, I played this course this morning, in easier conditions, and I shot a beefy 81.

"Me? Nah, not today. Just working on my game. Nice bunkers up there, good place to work on the short game."

Talk about your wake-up calls. I was ready to deal with the college kids and the club pros, I was preparing myself for the Texas kids and the fearless teenagers and the nine-foot-tall Floridians. But Larry? Larry can play, too?

On my next rainy day, a Wednesday in early September, I headed back to the rubber range and found the regular crowd on station. I was on nod-and-howareya status with most of the bunch, except with my new friend Larry, who came over with his camera to watch me make a few passes. He didn't press record, just watched for a little while, and I could hear him thinking of a dozen insights he wanted to toss out at me, but he didn't. He smiled and he nod-ded. "Great swing," he said, then kept moving down the line, ready to help Bob get that three-wood airborne again.

I knew I needed to be hitting balls amid palm trees, in front of accomplished eyes, working beside other tour hopefuls. But right then, at least for a little while, I needed to be hitting balls with Larry in the rain, I needed to be bouncing seven-irons off the mats with guys in Timberland boots and cutoff jeans, men who were spending money they couldn't spare on a game they would never master. This was where they understood what it was to give some-thing to the game, to love it when golf wasn't pretty, or easy, or nice. So even though he might have taken me for creepy, seeing as I wasn't supposed to actually know his name, I took the short walk down to the other end of the range.

"Hey, Larry, can you tell me," I asked, "what exactly do you mean when you say 'more *three-dimensional*'?"

I didn't tell Larry about my plans. I didn't tell any of my new friends from the practice tee that I was leaving to go live their fantasy for a little while.

Tomorrow morning I leave for Florida for six months on my own, a self-imposed golfing exile. Yet Allyson has somehow roped me into her boss's husband's fortieth birthday party on my last night at home. Okay, the guy went to Notre Dame, and the insurance crowd has always proven to be a surprising bit of fun, but I don't feel overly selfish by suggesting that this is a bit of a stretch for my final Friday evening, my last chance to masquerade as a well-adjusted young man among the non-golf-infected population.

I should start the complaining early—*Am I even going to know anyone? How long are we actually expected to hang around?*—laying a solid groundwork of disapproval so as to make our extraction from the party all the simpler later this evening. Best to make my displeasure clear in the cab en route, I surmise, rather than allow us to get settled into the affair when, God forbid, we may have actually begun to enjoy ourselves. But, instead, I get in the taxi and I hold my tongue and I do not complain, because if there's a person in the world I should not be bitching to this evening, this month, this year, she's sitting next to me right now.

Allyson and I step out of the cab and hustle into a pub called Fadó, where we're supposed to be meeting up with the rest of the half-enthused partygoers from Allyson's office. On our way in, I get a nod from Damon, the golf-deficient bartender, and I head through the crowd along the dark oak bar to our regular spot, where we can always find a stool. But tonight, our usual nook is jam-packed with people. Taking my favorite seat is Allyson's sister, and she's standing next to my best friend from high school. There are my caddy friends, and my buddies from the suburbs, and there's Paddy smiling with a pint of Guinness, shaking his head at me like my fly is down. A giant banner is plastered across the back of the room, and it reads GOOD LUCK TOM!

Allyson is right behind me, a beautiful red smile across her face.

Surprise parties might feel silly, a little bit second-grade, but I have never felt quite so special as I did that night. I spent most of the evening being told I was the craziest, luckiest bastard on the planet, fielding question after question regarding my suitcase and if there happened to be any space left within it. Some of my newly married and newly fathered friends, they looked at me with such hope, such envy glazed over their eyes, jealous that someone was allowed to reject the ordinary plans and try to go play golf for a living, yet pleased to know this was still a world where that might happen, where they might wake up one morning, ready to take some nonsensical shot of their own.

Some girlfriends would have sent your sticks through the window when you told them that you were going to go play golf for the next 365 days. Some women, had you dated them for eight years before deciding it was time to leave town so that you might live up to your golfing potential, they very well might have sued. But Allyson, she looked at the plate I was handing her—*Okay, for the next twelve months you are less important than a little white piece of plastic, you won't hear from me while the sun is shining, when it's dark, you are still less interesting than the Golf Channel, and I promise to spend more time looking for a lost drive than I will thinking about your birthday present*—and she threw me a party. It can be easy to resent a loved one's dreams or good fortune (this seems to particularly be the case in Irish families, where my experience has shown that the only accomplishment you won't be resented for is dying). But not Allyson. No matter that she wishes things were otherwise, that she is nervous about traveling down this detour so far along in our relationship—it's just too exciting not to be happy about something so uncommon falling into one of our lives.

There are only a few faces left picking over a small clump of chicken wings when I finally get the chance to speak to her. I kiss her and thank her for one of the most enjoyable evenings of my life, silently congratulating myself for deciding not to start complaining early about the phony fortieth birthday party.

"Did you see your sign?" she asks me.

"I love the sign."

"But did you look at it up close? Cristin worked on it all week."

We walk over to where the sign is plastered across the wall. Allyson's sister is quite an artist, and below the giant GOOD LUCK TOM she had painted a little cartoon of two tropical islands. On one island, a redhead with a Howdy Doody grin is sitting in a beach chair, an upturned book lying in the sand at his feet, a golf club propped against his chair as he reclines with a tall pint of stout. And across from the smiling figure, at the other end of the banner, separated by an expanse of blue ocean, is a small island green, red flagstick planted in a tiny black golf hole.

"See where your shots ended up?" Allyson says, pointing to the cartoon.

I had not noticed it before, but surrounding the empty island green, there were dozens and dozens of tiny white dots floating in the pretty blue water.

USGA Handicap Index: 9.4
Weight: 226.4 pounds

I know nothing about Bonita Springs aside from an address and the fine print on a rental agreement that states with my six months' rent I am entitled to a golf club membership and un-limited balls at the community driving range. Not a month after my twenty-ninth birthday, Allyson and I fit ourselves into a stuffed and sagging Honda, and we join the scattered parade of white-hair and Cadillacs rolling down I-95, pulling into the first stop of the two-stop Auto Train.

It's not Florida yet, but it might as well be, this train station a Fort Lauderdale embassy smack in the middle of Virginia. The waiting room is bright and crowded, everyone is smiling, but every-where there is the whiff of those anxieties that have brought us all to this place. Fear of the cold. Fear of flying. Fear of not making it back here to see another October. We're all escaping from some town up north where the weather has already gone from sweaters to coats. I knew I was going to be young for my new surroundings, but with all the oxygen tanks and breathing tubes spread throughout the Amtrak waiting room, you'd think the train was taking us all to the moon.

The Auto Train was a handy way to get my wheels to Florida, but what I was most eager to avoid on our itinerary was a walk down a Jetway. Of all the exciting aspects of a golf tour grinder's life, the one I am least looking forward to is the constant, unpredictable, last-minute travel, most of which involves an airport terminal and too many suspicious overhead dings. Should you find yourself airborne at this particular moment, apologies, and rest assured that in the extensive research I have done to grapple with my issues as an airline passenger, the mode of transport you have chosen is by far your safest travel option. I've been told that my fear of flying is a control issue, but I think it's firstly an issue of vanity. I can't envision a plane ride without reminding myself that, of course, I am the one who's going to be wiped out in some plot of international import. No matter that the airplane is the safest conveyance man ever designed—that's only if I'm not on it. If I am, then you're in deep shit, because I'm the one God wants, and I'm pretty sure he wants to make a spectacle of it.

Florida and Los Angeles are the two places I have spent time where you can begin any conversation by asking a stranger where they are from. That's not necessarily a blot for either locale—it means you have arrived at a destination, some place desirable, magnetic even. I've been to Bismarck, I lived in South Bend, and while they are both fine towns in their own honest way, they are not places where you would assume to find people who have migrated from afar. But south Florida is like a sprawling bright colony, wild expanses of buggy swamp giving way to new roads and new golf courses and new patches of discount-outlet pricing. This whole bottom half of the state feels like it wasn't even invented until Reagan, and it all seems to be populated by pioneers who have somewhere in the world abandoned something, whether it be a snowy winter, a changing neighborhood, an ex-husband. It is a land of people who are not afraid to pick up and start anew—rootless, maybe, or perhaps just braver than the rest of us who are still telling ourselves that we like the change of seasons. Florida feels like a new chance, for the rich and for the bankrupt, for the crazies and the crooks, the hopeful and the hopeless. And that's just the golfers.

As we draw closer to my new home in southwestern Florida, you can see the construction frenzy revving up with each mile south along I-75, everywhere a race to get your backhoe tracks in the mud. The buildings all look the same, casualties of the real estate rush, everything low and square and stuccoed, a few awnings for an authentic feel. It's tough to tell a home from a doctor's office from a SUBWAY sandwich shop.

This is the anti–Philadelphia suburb of my youth. There is no stigma here about the nouveau riche. Everything looks nouveau, and it all feels riche. Driving up and down the megastore promenade of Highway 41, where there's a Staples for every Office Depot, a Borders for every Barnes & Noble, a Wal-Mart for every Target, you can't help but get the sense that if you found a building that had been here twenty years ago, you would find a historical society plaque stuck on it. I didn't expect Ponce de León's paradise to be so young. Or to have a P.F. Chang's.

You can't blame anyone for packing up and following the birds. Planet Florida might be random and overdone, but such whining is all background noise when you see those lazy-leaning palm trees in October, the breeze blowing through your screened-in patio, sun on your pillow waking you up all winter long. Check your taste at the border, and soak up all the comfort. And the best part of it—you could have never heard of the game before, but spend five minutes in southwest Florida and you would have the unavoidable urge to say, "Now, this would be a great place for a golf course." That is, if you could find a vantage where you weren't already overlooking one. On our five minutes from the highway to my condo, we pass one gas station, one Arby's, and four golf courses.

I had a stroke of good fortune with my Realtor—Coyne Realty, no relation, what are the chances—and I got a good deal on six months for a condo that was up for sale. As long as I didn't mind the place being shown to prospective buyers from time to time, I could live in far better digs then I deserved. It was a great deal for me, not so great deal for my long-lost cousin Realtor. My penchant for piling up the dishes like I was playing Jenga, for turning a blind eye to the state of the bathroom, for enjoying a noontime snack in my underwear—*Don't mind me, come on in, have a look-see*—needless to say, it was the one piece of Florida property that did not flip in the six months I was in town.

We open the door to my new second-floor condominium with two bedrooms and two baths, and ceilings that were high enough to swing a driver inside. Allyson isn't crazy about the blue carpets, or the wall that's covered entirely in mirrors, but I couldn't have asked for a grander decor for this extended golf retreat. Carpet that won't show dirt, and a reflective wall that turns the living area into a swing studio, allowing me to watch every angle in my swing long after the sun has set.

"How awesome is this? They didn't say anything about all the mirrors," I tell her. "I can do all my mirror work right here."

"Pretty awesome," she says, not even trying to be convincing.

None of it is quite as awesome as the view off our back patio. We slide open a wall of glass doors, and there it is. The reason we took this ride in the first place. If I fell asleep and fell off the living room sofa, there was a soft green fairway to catch me.

"They said it was on a golf course, but this is ridiculous." I open my arms to my new home. "Are you kidding me? Look at all this."

She looks, then asks where the bathroom is. On her way to look for it, she tells me, "Must be nice to be retired at twenty-nine."

We find some cheese and a bottle of Chardonnay in the refrigerator—welcoming gifts from the Realtor. We sit on the patio and watch a few smiling groups roll by on their golf carts. In forty-five minutes, we don't see one player hit a shot worth leaving the cart for—my suspicions about Florida condo golf seem to be coming true: No one seems to be able to play, but nobody seems to mind. Allyson is even inspired enough to note, "Is it me, or do these golfers all stink?"

"It's not you."

"This doesn't look like a very hard golf course. Seems kind of flat. I could play this course."

I laugh, which is predictably unappreciated, particularly when "I want to golf" is now code for "I want to see you at least once in the next twelve months." Allyson's budding golf career has historically been a bit of a joke. I surprised her with that set of clubs for her graduation, and she has the athleticism to play well—five feet ten, ex–softball player, when she gets a hold of one during her infrequent trips to the range, she can hit it like a dude. But the good intentions to take lessons have taken a backseat to the things she's already quite accomplished at that don't require lessons at all (her new love of cooking, her monthly recommitments to the Philadelphia Marathon, her never-ending quest to explore the boundaries of her credit cards). We brought her clubs to Florida, anyway. If she wasn't going to play this year, it was never going to happen.

"I want you to play," I tell her. "You should play down here. It's either play golf with me, or sit by the pool by yourself until dark."

She thinks about it for a little while. The old couple out on the fairway, they're wearing matching red shorts and white tops, and the woman whiffs her three-wood like she's trying to keep the flies off her golf ball.

Allyson shrugs. "We'll see."

We walk over to the community clubhouse to register as the newest members of Spring Run at the Brooks. Our street is called

Streamside—and while we don't see any streams, or springs, or brooks, for that matter, it is a peaceful enough place full of eight-condo stacks like mine, interspersed with rows of short, careful houses cut from four or five architectural selections. The colors are all off-white, off-pink, off-beige, and the backside of every home has an elaborate fenced-in porch, mosquito cages encasing all the in-ground pools. It makes me think of the cat house at the zoo—*Okay, everybody, at four o'clock the tigers are coming out from inside to sun themselves.* In any other part of the world, all the civic mimicry would be spirit-crushing. All this hasty, safe planning could easily come off as a parody of suburban sameness. But not here. Add some sunshine, a few funky-looking plants and a putting green, and it's not cookie-cutter. It's perfection, repeated.

The sun is setting as we walk around the back of the clubhouse, past where the golf carts are being put to bed, out to where the driving range is closing down for the evening. A young man is collecting empty plastic baskets that are spread across a long plateau of tight Bermuda grass. A practice tee the size of a football field, not an inch of Pennsylvania Astro Turf anywhere, and I want to do a cheer. I can see the next six months of my life, and they are starting to make sense. So much time, now so much space to improve. I can't help but tell myself, *This is going to happen.*

At the front edge of the giant tee, a pond of dark water stretches deep into the distance. Three wooden islands are floating in the water, their tops painted green like huge lily pads, golf flags planted where the flower would have been.

"This is it," I tell Allyson. "All the balls I want. No more paying by the bucket. If you're ever wondering where I am, it will probably be here."

We look at the water for a little while, brave little birds with necks like boomerangs poking up from beneath the surface.

"Where do you hit to? You have to hit over this pond?"

"You hit them into the pond. It's a water range. The balls float. They're floaters."

"Then how do you get them back?"

I guess by the rubber waders the young man is wearing. "They scoop them out, probably fish them out with a net. The balls float over to the bank, and somebody goes down there and picks them out."

"Who does?"

"The guys that work here."

"Sounds like fun," she says, looking out at the water and the thousands of little eggs bobbing just below the surface. "They're going to love you."

There was something wonderful about the possibility of six months solo. It felt like a stolen chance at youth, a new dawn that most men approaching thirty had long stopped hoping for. But on the morning Allyson leaves to return to Philadelphia, I feel physically ill. I did not think this could possibly suck, and yet it does. Where I had planned on being tough and cool and embracing every minute of my new bachelorhood with Teen Wolf abandon, in reality, I am a baby. A thumb-swallowing infant. I am needy, sentimental, more attached than I imagined possible. She's returning to a world she knows, a place inhabited by friendly faces, while I'm here in a world where I can't pick out my own condo from the street. I don't know my area code, let alone a good place to get takeout, and my only friend in the world is my Realtor, who calls only to see if I found the key to the mailbox—*Yeah, but where the heck is the mailbox? And what's my address?*

This was supposed to be a kick in the ass, and yet I wonder, What will happen if I slip and crack my head in the shower? Will it be months before anyone finds me? What if I have a heart attack, or my hip goes goofy on me? Maybe I need one of those alarm necklaces, in case of emergency. Or maybe it's the Florida that's getting to me. I'm worried. I've been here a week, and I'm aging a decade every day.

As a means of coping with my new surroundings, I book Allyson's return trip before her plane home has even landed. I found her a handy price on the Internet. As nervous a flyer as I was, I wasn't nervous at all about putting her on $69 one-way specials on airlines with names like Fly This.

My first week in Florida, we spent the time unpacking and running to Publix and introducing myself around the pro shop. The shop staff seem amused to have someone their age hanging around the practice tee, but they already seem confused by the amount of time I am spending at the range. I can tell that some of the assistants want to explain to me that they're not running out of balls, there's plenty for everyone, I don't have to try to hit them all in one week. But they don't say anything, they just give me sideway smiles and save it for the back office in the pro shop.

I grew up working behind the scenes at a golf club. First as an underachieving caddy, then as an absentee range picker, and finally as a bag-room hustler. There are few environments where more shit is dished than at a private country club, behind the backs of the membership. Poker games, knitting circles, Republican Party fund-raisers—all temples of civility compared to the vicious back-room gossip that makes country club employment tolerable. No matter how cool a member you consider yourself, at some point or another, your club staff has killed you. Perhaps it involved imagining new ways to describe your wife's waistline, keeping tabs on your gray then black then gray again hair, coming up with nicknames for the spoiled little shit you call Junior—don't take it personal, it's part of the circle of country club life. When you have to smile for three hundred bosses who all want to feel like they're the only golfer in that particular zip code, you've got to have an outlet. And I can only imagine the fun they are having with me.

Before leaving her at the airport, Allyson and I had successfully rearranged the condo's pastel Florida showroom look, reimagining the space in a design motif that a decorator might describe as Golf Brothel. The dining room was turned into an obsessed golfer's bunker, three dozen golf books and golf tapes and golf journals piled high around the laptop, cords running from the computer to the printer to the camera that was perched atop a tripod and plugged into the front of my twenty-eight-inch television. Out on the patio, we piled the furniture into the corner and spread out an eight-foot synthetic putting green, replete with a dozen different putters and a new Putting Arc to help coach a proper swing-the-gate stroke. The stools were stuffed into the spare bedroom, and the breakfast bar was turned into a display rack for a spare set of irons, my Medicus, Momentus, my newly acquired driver that I was afraid to take out of the plastic until I figured out how to stop skying pop-ups off the tee. The walk-in bedroom closet looked like a pro-shop clearance sale: three dozen faded golf shirts on hangers, five pairs of shorts, three khaki pants, a dozen golf caps neatly displayed on the dresser. It was a beautifully inefficient wardrobe, and I loved looking at it knowing that, for the next year, there was no reason to even consider long sleeves.

All around the mirrors (that have indeed been a handy swing aid—in five days, my evening practice had already worn a powder-blue patch in the navy blue carpet), we plastered the walls with inspirational quotes and clippings and snapshots of my swing downloaded from the videos, stuck there beside pages from golf magazines that showed swing positions I would like to imitate. And above it all, a giant banner stretched halfway across the living room, GOOD LUCK TOM, there for every condo buyer to see and wonder who the hell this Tom was, and if he was seeing someone about his golf problem.

The sign hangs behind my dining-room-table-turned-desk, above where the largest wipe-erase calendar we could find is pasted to the wall. October is pretty empty at this point, but tomorrow is circled in red marker. Today reads **Allyson leaves** in small black letters, but there are red and green stars drawn where tomorrow's appointment reads DAY ONE.

Tomorrow is the first day of the 2003 PGA Qualifying School. Tomorrow, I am a fan with ringside seats. One year from tomorrow, I am the fighter.

PART TWO

Alligator Alley lived up to the billing—more rewarding than the whale-watching trip, not quite as good as the safari at Six Flags. There are abundant gators up and down the edges of the highway, eyes poking out of the run-off swamps, a few slabs of green trouble sunning themselves next to the breakdown lane. I make it across from Bonita Springs in a little less than two hours, a straight shot across the state to the nearest host site of Qualifying School, Stage I.

Now, the PGA Qualifying School is not a school, unless your particular school was curiously expensive for a four-day curriculum, and a spirit-crushing failure for 97 percent of your classmates. There are no desks or blackboards, no pens or rulers—pencils, maybe, but no erasers. Yet it is a school insofar as there is certainly a test and plenty of hopeful students, some of whom will graduate to greatness, many more who will return to retake their exams next year.

Stage I of Q-school takes place at twelve different locations across the country, at courses in Florida, Georgia, the Carolinas, Texas, and California, usually during the last two weeks of October. More than one thousand golfers will fill out their applications, sign over a $4,500 entrance fee, and begin their PGA Tour journey at one of these four-day competitions, hoping to be one of the top twenty-five players at week's end who will graduate from this preliminary tournament and move along to the next event.

Stage II takes place the following month at one of a half dozen different locales around the country, and the tournament field is comprised not only of qualifiers from the first stage, but also a host of "exempt" players whose pro track records have given them a free pass into the second round of qualifying. If a player should survive the second four-day tournament, once again finishing in their site's top thirty, they advance to what most golfers think of as simply *the* Q-school, the final six-day December tournament they watch on the Golf Channel, where lives are changed by a dropped putt or wayward drive on the 252nd hole of competition.

The competition at Stage III is obviously among the toughest in the world of golf—not just because of the size of the field, the unusual length of the event, or the desperation of the competition, but because requalifying players from the PGA tour, along with studs from the Nationwide and foreign pro tours, are often entering the final stage fresh, hopping into Stage III via their PGA exemptions. Not that a player coming off the PGA Tour hasn't earned such treatment, but it's got to be tough for the twenty-two-year-old who's been grinding since October to see guys come out to the track to run the last lap when they've done the whole mile. Let's just say that for the new blood, they're not making it easy.

Stage III and the Q-school are almost more famous for the lives they crush than for the careers they start. Thirty guys who play well for six days and avoid the train wrecks will get their card—and in doing so will avoid becoming one of the Q-school legends that lurk amid country club grill rooms across the country. Q-school lore is rife with tragedies of Buckner-esque proportions. Consider the trial of Jaxon Brigman, who shot the exact qualifying score at the final round of the 2003 Qualifying School only to sign the wrong score. He signed for one stroke higher than he shot, and a matter of simple addition sent him from millions of PGA dollars back to another year on the mini-tour.

There are books' worth of Q-school horror stories, tales of final hole shanks and water hazards and triple bogeys, few of which can rival the legend of Joe Daley. Coming to the seventeenth hole on Saturday in 2000, Joe Daley found himself well within the cut-line of earning his tour card. He hit his ball into the water, but recovered to where he was left with a two-foot tap-in for double bogey and would *still* finish inside the cut. But as it turned out, the seventeenth cup had been improperly installed—the metal lining was a fraction too high inside the hole, high enough that a ball struck on exactly the right line, at exactly the right speed, could drop into the center of the cup, *then hop right back out*. Which is precisely what Joe Daley's tap-in did—in, and out, like a back-rimmed foul shot, as if the angels had stopped dancing on pins to put money down against him. It wouldn't be the Q-school if Joe Daley hadn't missed by one shot that year. As PGA Tour winner Jim Gallagher Jr. once noted, "The Q in Q-school is for quit. It just makes me want to quit."

Just by virtue of making it to Stage III, a player receives "conditional" status (code for very little) on the Nationwide Tour, and the top eighty finishers are granted full Nationwide playing status, which today can make for a very comfortable lifestyle. But it is not the minor leagues for which these guys are playing. Those who can slide under the radar and avoid the notorious crap-luck of the Qualifying School will receive a year's worth of tour playing privileges (along with six, possibly seven, figures in clothing and equipment endorsements), and whether they ever win another golf tournament, it is unlikely that they will have to do anything for the rest of their lives but chase around a little white ball. All told, it's three stages, 1,000-plus entrants, fourteen rounds of golf, approximately $5 million in entry fees, all whittled down by the PGA Tour to $1.1 million in prize money and thirty smiling faces.

You could take one hundred of the wealthiest, most successful men on this planet, list the treasures they might covet but could never own, and that little plastic PGA card with their picture on it would have to rank up there near the top. Peace, love, happiness— they can all be priced and purchased with enough capital and imagination. But that card is a dream all their fortunes cannot realize, not if they don't put in the work, not unless they want it like Greg Norman wanted it.

And maybe not even then.

I pull into the parking lot of Heron Bay, a Tournament Players Club (TPC), a label in the golf world that has become synonymous with overworked layouts, triple-digit greens fees, and rumors of golf courses for sale (would the PGA Tour ever consider investing in OPCs, Ordinary Players Clubs, where one could find a good old ordinary golf course at an ordinary price, with decent practice facilities and competent teachers to help grow the game? Golf needs more average courses where you can get a game on Saturday afternoon, and fewer millionaire getaways). I'm nervous just setting foot on the property as a spectator, the parking lot crowded with cars but library quiet. I feel like I showed up for the SAT two hours late. I have a feeling I might be removed from the property—*You shot 80 yesterday, you fraud, beat it!* I wonder how I'll feel next year when I'm reaching into my trunk not for my steno pad, but for my spikes and sticks.

I walk into the clubhouse, and the place feels deserted. There are no banners, no sponsors' vans, no TV trailers. Except for the photocopied pairings sheet on the front door, you wouldn't know if the course was closed for maintenance instead or hosting one of the legendary tournaments in golf. In the shop I find an assistant flipping through the morning talk shows, wondering what he'll have for lunch. I buy a khaki hat. I wanted a Q-school souvenir, but at Stage I, the best thing I can find is one of those pairings sheets.

"The Q-school started today, right?" I ask the pro.

"Yup. They started at seven," he says, as if he were talking about a sleepy shotgun scramble.

I look at my watch: quarter after ten. "Is it okay if I go watch?"

"Go for it," he says, picking up my TPC souvenir. "You want a bag, or you want to wear this now?"

Out through the back door of the clubhouse, the course feels empty. Here and there you spot threesomes wandering the Bermuda fairways, slow and quiet, like packs out on safari. I hustle to catch up to the nearest group, three players with three caddies about to bang drives off what I guess is tee number one. I'm conspicuous with my pad of paper, waving it like the press badge that it isn't, hoping to come off as more of a golf journalist and less of a golf stalker. Golf is the one game—aside from bowling, perhaps—where having an anonymous spectator is such a rare occurrence that it's a sort of milestone, a career moment to play the game in front of an otherwise uninvolved party. Some players would take it as motivation, some might take it as an annoyance, so I am careful to try to blend in to my surroundings (of which there are none, just a bunch of grass and a lot of blue sky), tracking this threesome like a biologist hoping to observe a Q-school golfer in his natural habitat.

The players are young and deadly serious, with clothes that fit better than any of my golf outfits, ensembles tailored to their wide shoulders and nothing waists. I knew this wasn't going to be a giggle-fest, but the faces on these young men—you'd think this was TPC Falluja. Their drives off number one are long and high and straight, each one a more pure-center hit than I could have found with a bucket full of range balls.

I lurk behind at an awkward distance. Two of the group find the green with their second shots, while the one kid who looks fresh from high school PE—but with a turn like Ernie Els—dumps his flip-wedge into the bunker. Easiest approach shot of the group, and he doesn't hit the green. And worse, from a pretty simple bunker shot, he doesn't get up and down. Bogey, on the first hole of his first Q-school.

I am ecstatic! Not to wish anyone bad luck, I'm sure he'll recover fine, but I adore the fact that he just made a sloppy bogey. Because I have made a sloppy bogey. He didn't get up and down. I don't get up and down—it happens all the time. He missed an eight-footer on the low side, same way I probably would have missed it. For all the silence and the grave faces and the caddies who look even more wound up than their players—for all this being a Tournament Players course, it's still a golf course. And they're playing golf. They aren't walking on air, they aren't eight feet tall, they don't have circuit boards planted in the back of their heads. They are trying to get the ball into the hole in as few strokes as possible. Granted, they're a lot more businesslike about it than I am, but they're just playing golf. And with regard to the bogey this young man just made, it looks very familiar.

Then I come across the driving range. The long stretch of grass is empty, but the remains of the morning's work has yet to be cleaned up. It feels like the remnants of a once great golfing civilization. Each spot is still scattered with balls, the expensive kind, real Titleists that, if they did not have PRACTICE stamped on the side, I would be stuffing into my pockets.

It's the divots that get me. Take a trip to your average club driving range, and examine the turf where a regular player was warming up. It probably looks like someone was playing pogo stick with a garden spade, random chunks of earth torn out of the smooth surface. But here, where the Q-schoolers have warmed up, each practice space looks like the grass has been surgically removed in pristine patches, like Martha Stewart had come along and carved out spots for a dozen little gardens.

It's one of the golf detective's clues: You can tell a player by his divots. Normal golfers, we treat the practice tee like it owes us money, while the real players, their swings repeat, flawlessly efficient, and each pass of their irons takes the same little slice of bacon as the last. It's tidy, it gives off the air of knowing what the hell you're doing on the golf course. Your greenskeeper would love it if you learned to do the same.

The fact that I am intimidated by driving range divots, I take it as a sign that I am really doing this, that I am going to someday play in this very tournament. But even more impressive or, in my case, terrifying, is the state of the targets. There are six or seven practice greens cut into the driving range at all different distances, considerably superior to the plastic blue barrel where we aimed our wedges at the rubber range back home. But it's not the quality of the targets that gets me, it's the way they are absolutely smothered with little white pearls. It's like the holes themselves had spewed forth golf balls. Even the green at 250 yards—if you walked out there to drop one, you would have a hard time finding room for one more Titleist. The pins are sagging as if beaten by that morning's assault. I can't help thinking that this was just Stage I, and only twenty-five of these perfect divot patches were going to make it through, and that if I had arrived a few hours earlier, any single one of them would have probably been the best player I had ever watched hit golf balls.

The ladder I am attempting to climb this year is surely a long one, with rungs separated by almost impossible distances, the bottom of which is much more crowded than the spots at the top. It's really more like a pyramid—a slippery-sided pyramid of golf greatness—that I feel like I'm trying to climb in tube socks.

Consider the golf-greatness pyramid's base, a wide mass of good players, great players, best ball strikers you have ever witnessed firsthand, the only ace you have ever been accidentally, terrifyingly, matched up with—we'll call him or her The Best Player You Know. Maybe he's your club champion, maybe your neighbor's sixteen-year-old, perhaps it's your boss who has the scorecard from Pebble on the wall and tells all the clients, "Shot 73, couldn't make a damn putt." The real sticks, guys who talk about what they might have done in golf if they steered their life a little differently, if they only took their shot. A two-, three-handicap—maybe even a scratch player. If you watched them hit balls, you would weep inside.

And here's the news about The Best Players You Know: They're shit. Scratch is shit. The Best Players You Know simply cannot play. They are the mere masses, golf's faceless proletariat, utterly forgettable. They are little more than the wide sprawling base of wannabes on which the pyramid is planted.

Slightly higher up the talent chain, but still miles from the pinnacle, are your Club Pros, the teachers who disseminate their golf wisdom for a living, the caretakers of the game who taught you how to hold a golf club and whose insights you take as gospel. When they hit balls on the range, the members all stand back, whispering and nodding, cheeks pink with envy. But in terms of golf ability, these Club Pros, they give hopeless a bad name. Just because somebody wears pants on the golf course and took classes in how to run a successful caddy program doesn't mean they can play. Not to say they couldn't once go low, not to say they weren't on the cusp of being household names, but the nature of the golf business is such that, if you really want to get good at golf, go into real estate. Cash registers and equipment reps and golf committees have laid waste to more golf potential than alcohol and expecting wives combined. Spend sixty hours a week kissing ass in the shop and curing shanks on the range, and the last thing you want to do is go work on your swing path. You would be shocked how many head pros and assistants can't break 80 from the tips at their own golf club. I'd almost have to rank this group below The Best Player You Know, as they surely play a helluva lot less golf than a good club player. Yet I have to give them the nod, on account of the genuine golf potential that suckered them into the business many years ago.

Next in the rankings comes the Stud Amateur. This is the college scholarship type, the soon-to-be-pro player, or the dedicated amateur who loves golf but never wanted to make it his living. They are often consultants or salesmen, half-employed with flexible schedules and memberships at coffee-table courses all over the country. It's not uncommon for the Stud Amateur, should he make a run at the U.S. Amateur or the Mid-Amateur, to be invited to join the country's most elite clubs. You want to get into Pine Valley? Win the U.S. Mid-Am Championship, because at the most coveted clubs, nobody is impressed by your portfolio.

There is a quiet dignity to the Stud Amateur, good enough to pop up in the US Open every once in a while, but still hold a day job (or the semblance of one). They are not the scratch player you know from your club—they are plus fours and plus fives, giving strokes back to the course, guys who you're not really sure how low they could go if they decided to play for a living. It's sort of like the sidelines, but with honor and esteem.

Closely related but just outranking the Stud Amateur on the pyramid is the Attached Club Pro. The Attached Pro is a professional at a country club, not a Country Club Professional. They are set up with cushy jobs where they spend minimal time answering phones or selling putters. When they're at the club, they're mostly on the driving range. Maybe they stoop to do a little teaching, but their own games come first. They compete, and usually collect, at all the local PGA section events. These pros are trophy pieces, sometimes merely "affiliated" with their country clubs, kept around by a membership who likes to see its club's name in the paper, backed by members who enjoy following their guy through US Open or PGA qualifying. Attached Club Pros don't necessarily make their living playing tournaments, but their winnings make them wealthy by Club Pro standards.

The next cross section of golf greatness is a large and crowded slice of the pyramid—it's the spot for the Mini-Tour Philanthropist. There is really nothing mini about the mini-tours: The players aren't shrunken, the courses aren't shorter, the schedules can go year-round, and the competition isn't any less intense. The only thing that is mini is the crowds, the dollars, the lifestyle. Mini-tours can cost players anywhere from $10,000 to $20,000 in fees for a season, and without gate receipts or TV money to bolster the purses, these tour pros go out and play for a prize pool made up largely of their entry fees (it's sort of like buying into a giant Nassau—don't think about asking for strokes). Go any place in America with grass and year-round warm weather, you will find them congregating at driving ranges, bunking up five guys to an apartment, living off dollar-menus, and beating up their parents' Sunoco cards. The vast majority of these players are burning through sponsorship money (sponsors being their parents, grandparents, or a syndicate at their club), winning a couple grand every couple months on the Grey Goose or the Hooters or the Golden Bear, trying to extend their golf careers past college and dodge the working world for as long as possible. They are touring pros, and they are maybe just a few big wins away, but the reality on the mini-tours is a lot of golfers fill up the pot, and a handful of players empty it. If it was a poker tournament (which in some ways it is), the Mini-Tour Philanthropist would be considered dead money.

Which brings us to a thinner slice of the talent, where the pyramid moves out of the red and into the black with the Mini-Tour Grinder. These are golf's great journeymen—think of them as old cowboys, the last remaining heroes of a grand traveling tradition. You have never heard of any of them (until Todd Hamilton won the British Open, thus forfeiting his journeyman status); they travel the world hunting purses on the Australasian, South African, South American tours. They don't have personas, they just have game. They earn modest, often comfortable lifestyles playing in golf's shadows. For one reason or another, they haven't broken through into the elite, but that's not as important in the life of the true Grinder, who's too busy playing events you've never heard of, winning on tours that sound made up, traveling to far-off places where you didn't know they even had grass, let alone golf courses. It isn't glamorous, but it's noble, a throwback to touring pros who were more sole proprietors than superstars, getting by in golf when the margins were so much stiffer than they are today.

Go from the Grinder to the Nationwide Earner. The Nationwide, formerly Buy.com, formerly Nike, formerly something else tour, might be considered a mini-tour were it not for the considerable bump in talent, venues, and purses of the Tiger Era. The PGA Tour's minor league has its own television contract, and its purses have ballooned to where Nationwide players can make the same money they would have made on the PGA Tour not fifteen years ago. You can now become a millionaire playing this "secondary" tour, and any player on the tour is just one good week away from the big dance. The tour's top-twenty-five money winners get their tour-cards (winning an event near guarantees you'll end the year in that company), and any three-time tour winner is automatically promoted from the Nationwide to the PGA Tour—it's called a Battlefield Promotion, and while the military jargon fits, it's really more like an honorable discharge, from suffering anonymity. This is where serious, soon-to-be-superstar, top 1 percent of 1 percent golf is being played, and it's perhaps the cruelest part of the pyramid for that reason. This is where the talent bottleneck gets tightest. Nationwide exempt players are all good enough to be household names. They can taste their childhood dream, just a handful of putts away, but few will ultimately break through to the big time. Most will watch their lucky friends and colleagues tuck into the fame and the fortune, while they have to settle for another year playing in front of a few dozen people who aren't quite certain who they're watching.

Up at this height, the pyramid's capstone really starts to sparkle. This is the rarified air of the PGA Tour professional, where even the lowliest earner is blessed, anointed, touched by divine golfing fingers. The sponsorship money can be absurd, and just making a few cuts bumps you into upper-class America (again, thank you, Tiger). The most ordinary of this extraordinary bunch are the Six-Figure Survivors, pros who get by on pro-am money and a half-dozen paychecks, usually made at the lesser-known tour stops. They might be tour rookies or one-hit wonders or ex-tour greats getting by on sponsor's exemptions. By tour standards, they are below-average talents, many of them will be sent back through the Q-school at year's end to justify their spot on the pyramid, teeing it up against the younger, stronger, hungrier masses. Still, if you were ever paired up with the lowest man on the PGA Tour money list in a pro-am, you wouldn't be able to discern the difference between Tiger on TV and the golf you were witnessing right there.

After a few good weeks on tour, a Survivor might make the leap to become one of the Players, the names you know on tour who win from time to time, make the majority of their cuts, who have carved out for themselves a big worry-free golf life. They might get discussed when it comes to dark horses for the Majors, might have their name bandied about as a captain's pick for the Ryder Cup, but for the most part they are happy to take a lot of top-twenty finishes, get invited to a few funny-money off-season events, take home their million bucks, and sign autographs—though the eBay value of their initials is not nearly as valuable as those of the golfers residing at the game's apogee.

At the top of the pyramid, there is only enough room for a

few names to balance at any one time. This is home of the Super-stars. The Tigers, Phils, Ernies, Vijays—even the Sergios and the Furyks. They might be only a few shots lower than the rest of the field, but there is something otherworldly about their game, magical almost, to the point that it seems a PGA Tour could not exist with-out such iconic abilities.

When most people think of a great golfer, these are the few dozen names they think of—Tiger, Jack, Arnie, and the like. Most people don't consider the bulging pyramid of golf talent. They know nothing of how much good golf is really out there. The scratch play-ers at your club—*they* are, by any statistical analysis, great golfers, top-tier, 1 percent players. And yet, the Club Pro and the Stud Ama-teur and the Attached Pro, they could dispatch The Best Player You Know using persimmon woods and a guttie. And none of them are quiet as battle-hardened as the Mini-Tour Philanthropists who are already making hefty donations to the Grinders, and the Grinders don't even dream about the steady life of the Nationwide Earner, who would still ask a PGA Tour Survivor for their autograph. All of them would stand in line to shake hands with a PGA Tour Player. And as for the Superstars up in the stratosphere looking down on all of it? They should amend those ads on TV—*These guys are good. How good? You've got no fucking idea.*

As impenetrable and unscalable as the pyramid might seem, the reality is that the difference between the apex and the bottom masses is about six, maybe seven, golf shots a round. As vast as the talent gulf may seem, a scorecard doesn't know anything about the talent pyramid. A golf course doesn't know if you're a Dreamer or a Grinder or a Superstar. And therein lies the hope.

Take the case of young Sean O'Hair. In the Byron Nelson Championship, in 2005, a tournament where Tiger Woods missed the cut, O'Hair finished in second place. Just a few weeks later, he won his first PGA Tour event. He made top twenty on the PGA Tour money list in his rookie season, and at twenty-two years old is worth millions more in endorsements. And Sean O'Hair was one putt away from a season on the Hooters Tour.

In Stage II of the 2004 Qualifying School, O'Hair finished birdie, birdie, birdie to make the cut by a single shot. He very nearly did not advance to the final step of qualifying. One lipped putt, one tugged eight-iron, one heavy wedge, and this tour phenom is started down the road to selling you shirts. This is a kid who, a few months later, is besting the likes of Mickelson and Tiger and Vijay while he was mere inches away from being one of the 900 nameless Q-school non-qualifiers. Some guys finish with the three birdies, but thousands more aren't ever able to quite slide through the traffic jam of golf ability.

The gap between the haves and have-nots can go from a yawning gulf to a little pothole if you have the noggin capable of finding those three birdies when you have to have them. Hall of Famers and anonymous range pickers can be separated by a three-putt here, a ball in the Evian there. If I walked out onto TPC Heron Bay this afternoon and shot 72, there would still be a wide difference between the likes of them and the likes of me that wouldn't show on the scorecard. You can see it in the divots on the driving range, you can feel it in the parking lot, and you understand it when you shake hands on the first tee. There's a difference, and it's bigger than six strokes. I'm not sure what that difference is, if it can be earned, bought, or faked.

I have 364 days to find out.

I've come to the right place to start looking for an answer. Stage I is made up of the broadest range of golf talent in the world. From college studs to club pros to club champions to ex-tour greats, they're all here. The largest contingent is definitely that of the mini-tour philanthropist, young players hardened from a season playing for one another's entry fees, ponying up the $4,500 to try to leapfrog to the top of the food chain. When I meet Jimbo Fuller, that's about where I'd put him, loaded with strength and talent, a good break away from never having to worry about anything for the rest of his life. Just like everybody else here today.

I choose to latch onto his group because his is the only three-some with a gallery following them. It is a modest gallery—two people, to be exact—but it still helps me feel slightly less ostentatious, and makes the golf feel a little more exciting than the group I had been following: Boring McSerious and his buddies, about whom the most interesting note I had made about thus far was that the young guy in J. Lindeberg slacks had taken two bogeys and three pisses through only four holes.

I sidle up to the two onlookers I assume are somebody's parents. Mom is a pretty red-haired lady in her forties (always nice to chat up a fellow carrottop), and Dad shakes my hand with just the right amount of pressure to tell me that his boy is playing well.

"That's our son, Jimbo," Mom explains, pointing to his name on my pairings sheet: JIMBO FULLER, OKLAHOMA (honestly, what chance does a Tom have against the Jimbos, the Bos, the Heaths of the golf world?). He's two-under through eight, and currently taking his time behind a fifteen-foot birdie try. He's got thick shoulders, six feet of strong, good looks befitting his tight haircut—he's got the sort of all-American looks that makes one miss their college days, and he seems the perfect specimen for observation. Charming Southern parents, interested, but not pushing, fans instead of the taskmaster cliché—Dad is closely watching every stroke, but Mom seems happy enough to see that her boy's just getting some sunshine.

Jimbo is the young man you see making old men jealous at thousands of driving ranges across the country—handsome, driven, genuinely gifted, comfortable in khakis, probably didn't have to take the bus to school. It's easy to resent the privilege of most young golfers, but you have to admire the discipline. Plenty of kids have money and opportunity today; most of them just get C's in marketing and wear out their PlayStation. In a way, you have to respect it a little bit more, for kids who otherwise have it made, still wanting to make more of themselves. Jimbo is certainly more sports-built than most of the wispy kids who had to pick between golf and cross-country. (I'd peg him for a good 174-pound class wrestler.) He's very much like the thousands of AJGA and NCAA golf talents around the country, aside from the fact that he's at the PGA Q-school, two-under through eight, and he's stupidly, ridiculously long.

I consider myself a player of above-average distance. At just about six feet three, I have physics on my side. There is an advantage to my big arch and my dollop of belly fat that engineers a wrecking ball effect going through the golf ball. Jimbo isn't overly tall, and he takes about as quick a cut as the other two players in his group, but on a 600-yard par-five, while I watch his playing partners bomb their drives close to 300 yards, Jimbo's golf ball proceeds to just fly on past them, an express train to their locals. I step off a bunker at 345, and he has carried the sand by a good ten yards. A bunker that was originally put there to trouble the players' second shots is Jimbo's target off the tee.

It's not that Jimbo's partners can't hit it—count them among the average long-ball hitters where I count myself: capable of popping one 300-plus from time to time (usually downhill, downwind), still among the longest players at the home club, always the longest in the foursome, which legitimately puts one's average drive at around 275 yards. Driving distance is the most oft-exaggerated calculation since boys started bringing rulers into the bathroom. If you tell me you hit it 250 on average, I know you hit it 235 on a good day. You think your regular drive carries 230? After five chances, you'll be owing me five bucks. But Jimbo's partners, yes, they can hit it, they can certainly play, and even though they can't quite keep up with his cannon blasts, they are making numbers of their own. What's great about this threesome that seems about as chummy as Phil and Tiger playing for a green sport coat is that, not only are they all under par and indifferent to me and my notepad, they are three entirely distinct species of golfer.

Next to Jimbo, there's Johnny White Hair, who is sporting a bleach-blond mullet, permanent sunburn, sparkling white golf shoes, and a Swedish-looking girlfriend dangling from his golf bag. His style is part surfer-celebrity, part Daddy had a gator farm. He sparks a Marlboro on nearly every tee box, three hard drags and then cashes it out.

It is shocking how many players at this level have a taste for the tobacco—not that they seem to enjoy it, more like they need the beta-blocking effect of the nicotine to settle them after a bending four-footer (some golfers claim cigarettes help handle the onslaught of adrenaline). The only thing more surprising than the number of smokers is the mass of dipping devotees—rare to find the young mini-tour player who doesn't look like he got punched in the lip last night, walking around the range making little squirting sounds. But Johnny White Shoes, he's a Marlboro Light man. He smokes fast and plays faster. Jimbo plays at the pace of a Florida rush hour, achingly deliberate, unwilling to pull the trigger until he is good and ready. I applaud the mental discipline, but to Johnny Blond, it's got to be driving him nutty. Johnny hardly stops walking to hit his next shot, one fluid motion between pulling a club, stepping into the ball (never a practice swing), and sweeping the ball off the turf, knocking it on down the fairway or up to the green. It's reactive, athletic, more like trying to throw out a runner at second base than trying to hit the perfect golf shot.

The third member of the group is the shortest of the three. Skinny Tony, who's built like a flagstick and who always seems to be chipping when the rest of the group is lining up their birdies. It feels like he's making too many clutch six-footers, like he's hogging all the great saves for himself. He looks like he could be shooting 78, but at the end of the day, after an afternoon of getting to know Jimbo's parents, who are a joy to talk with (Mom wants to know if I have a girlfriend, and she soon talks about Allyson as if she knows her, understanding what it's like to be involved with someone who's trying to do all the things her boy has had to do)—at the end of the moaning and grinding and the awkward applause of a three-man gallery, the group came back with the three same numbers, each one of them carding a three-under, 69.

The fact that the numeral 69 only exists for me in dim memories of grade school graffiti, that it's a score well beyond my present golfing fingertips, I nonetheless take their results as more encouragement. I watched three very different ways to get to three-under: You can overpower the golf course while, at the same time, remaining intensely focused over each and every golf shot; you can grind it out, get up and down from everywhere, chip and putt your ass off; or you can act like you don't give a shit, just step up and hit it, find it, and then hit it again. And just in case 69 doesn't sound impressive enough (granted, some show-off fired a 64 on day one), note that the course rating from the 7,000-yard back tees was 75.2. That makes them all +6 handicaps, in the most pressure-filled round of golf in their young lives. Imagine what they would shoot if they were out with their buddies on a Saturday afternoon—now do you get what I was saying about those great scratch players at your club?

We head into the clubhouse for lunch with Mom, Dad, and son

Jimbo deflating in his chair, his eyes dizzy from the last five hours during which he would not allow himself to give a shot away. His face is burnt and sweaty; his shirt looks like he's been out throwing bricks around the yard.

"What was the first tee like? How nervous were you?" It's a question that plants me firmly at the bottom of the pyramid just in the asking of it, but it's what I really wanted to know.

"Nervous?" he says, like it's a band he's never heard of. "I don't know if I was nervous. Anxious, I was anxious to get going. I've been out here a couple days. I was ready to get it on."

Not scared? Is that possible? Next year, the question won't be if I'm nervous. The big question will be if I throw up before, after, or upon the first tee.

"There's nothing to be afraid about. If anything, I was excited. I've played enough tournaments. I felt confident going in. I made it through at the Tour de las Americas Q-school last week, and that helped. That was a pretty good warm-up for this."

Jimbo tells me about the Tour de las Americas, a pro golf tour through Central and South America and the Caribbean, a good backup for next season if he doesn't make it through to Stage III on this, his first try. He's already spent a season on the Gateway Tour (now the Grey Goose Gateway) in Myrtle Beach, and he has found a pad with other buddies from the mini-tours, along with a swanky home club in West Palm where tour players pay reduced dues.

I begin to envision this players' world of which I am not a part but need to be: the cool kids from cool schools, hungry young men battling one another on the same pro circuits, sharing apartments and hotel rooms—when they're not playing it, they're talking it, watching it, gambling on it. It's a lifestyle I need to find, but I can't help but wonder how so many twenty-two-year-old men find themselves living it. At twenty-two, I had four hundred dollars and a laptop. Jimbo's country club membership, his buy-in on the Gateway, his entry fee into Q-school—it was my entire season's budget. He doesn't really get into it, and I don't want to press him about the unseemly side of dollars, not at a lunch that his parents are treating us to.

"I have some sponsors," he tells me. He's the first kid I've heard say that and I thought, *Good for you, you should have sponsors, you deserve them.* I just watched Jimbo play some of the most gorgeous golf I've ever seen, and with the help of people who can keep him afloat, this talent might just get there. Sure, it's a life that can be lived only by those who know enough people with enough expendable cash, but better they spend it on a kid with true ability who works his ass off than go buy another boat.

Four months out of college, he's got a card on an international golf tour, he's top twenty at the Stage I after day one, and he's picking through his chicken Caesar salad, dressing on the side, sipping iced tea at a lunch that was certainly worthy of an adult beverage (if I just shot 69 in my first round, tough to say if there would have been a round two). 69. Three under par. It's all very normal for these guys who can play, who know how to go low, who come out of college golf ready to tear it up. They have one thing that I do not possess, that I must find somewhere in the next twelve months:

A total disrespect for par.

In my golfing lifetime, par was always perfect. I grew up respecting par, appreciating par, praying for par. Jimbo and this new breed of big-shouldered Titleist-beaters, they are going low—*way* low. At TPC Heron Bay, there was a young man who would shoot such absurd numbers the first three days (65, 64, 63) that he could have shot 85 on his final round and *still* made it through. These studs are like the munchkins you see flying down the black-diamond ski run. No one told them this was the expert slope. They don't see the danger, they see only the possibility. I see the broken neck, I see the out-of-bounds. Courses are getting longer, softer, and more narrow, and some of these young kids are treating them like they're playing a video game. The Tiger effect has brought more true athletes into the game, more Jimbo Fullers, guys with muscles and guts and killer sports instincts. At Stage I Q-school, I see eighty-eight guys who would tell everyone else to get the hell out of their way, guys who would tell you that par is for pussies if they were inclined to think about making pars at all.

I interrupt Jimbo's salad to pry for some more hints, hoping to find a few shortcuts to fearless.

"I do yoga. A lot of stretching," Jimbo explains when I ask him his secrets to hitting it so deep—*Do you have any anger issues? Ever had access to a baseball player's medicine cabinet?* "I do some weight training, and a lot of core work, too."

Core?

"Abs and back. The muscles in your trunk. That's mostly what I try to focus on—a strong core gives you a lot of strength and stability."

Core. *Hmm,* I think as I retract my belly from where it was peeking over my belt buckle. *I'll have to get me one of those.* We go over his daily routine: stretching, weights, yoga, beating balls until the sun goes down. The tour hopeful routine I would come to know well: If you're not asleep, you're in the gym or you're wearing spikes.

"Do you work with a coach?"

"Not a swing coach," he answers, and this divergence from the tour player blueprint catches me off guard. "I think you have to be careful when you start working with a coach. I don't know—I think they can sometimes do more damage than good. One of my good friends, he had his swing all broken down by one of these big-name coaches, and the coach convinced him that his swing was horrible. Now, the kid can't hardly play. He has no idea where it's going anymore. You have to be careful about that—some guys will change things that they don't need to, just to do what their coach tells them."

"The coaches need to justify their rates."

"I guess so. What I try to do," Jimbo continues, "is I try to work on my visualization. I don't think too much about mechanics. You can't let yourself get wrapped up in mechanics, not when you're trying to make a number. I try to see my target, I think about the shot I want to hit. If I can be clear about my target and commit to what I'm trying to do, if I can get to yes before I go, and not pull the trigger till I do—then more often than not, it's a pretty solid result."

I'll say. My current concept of target is anyplace where I have better than a 50 percent chance of finding my ball.

"I don't have a swing coach, but I work real closely with a psychologist. You thinking about talking to a psychologist?" Jimbo asks.

"Absolutely. My head gives me more problems than any of my clubs." I tell Jimbo a few of the names I've read up on: Dr. Richard Coop, Dr. Bob Rotella.

"My guy's better than Rotella," Jimbo says, half-whispering like he doesn't want to clue in the rest of the field. "I've been working with a guy for years. He used to work with Rotella, but as far as I'm concerned, my guy is the man. I've got his tapes up in my room right now, I listen to them every morning. It's just ten simple things I need to remember. It gets me in the right mind-set. I'm telling you, just the sound of his voice, it settles me right down."

Jimbo tells me how he got to the point where he almost quit golf. "It was getting so frustrating—I mean, I could hit the shots, but I couldn't score. I was working harder, and getting worse. I went to my parents and I said, 'I need to talk to somebody about this, or I need to find something else to do.' And that's when we found Dr. Bob. I've probably talked to him at least once a week since. Dr. Robert Winters. You should give him a call."

I tell him that I certainly will. If he can get Jimbo from almost quitting golf to three under par at tour school—that's the type of switch I need flipped in my own noggin. Perhaps it's some cosmic good fortune that I chose this site out of all the qualifiers around the country, that I found Jimbo's group on that tee box, the one kid out of a hundred who would give me a testimonial about the exact sort of mental caretaker I have been searching for. Maybe it is supposed to happen for me, I think. And happen precisely this way.

Jimbo heads out for an afternoon of work in the bunkers (shoots 69, and he didn't get up and down once). I get in the car and head back across Alligator Alley, a little wiser, a lot more worried.

This quest isn't a concept or a benign proposal anymore. I've seen what the Q-school looks like, smells like. I've felt the nerves cracking in the air. I know what I have to do, and I can't write myself around it. I have to go outwork a Jimbo Fuller, the hardest-working player I've ever met face-to-face.

Back in Bonita Springs, I follow Jimbo's score on the Internet for the rest of the week. He goes 69, 71, 67, 71, shooting four consecutive rounds better than par. I would later hear that Jimbo three-putted the final hole of the tournament, but still finished at a mighty minus ten. Jimbo, Johnny, and Tony all played their very different games, and all three finished with the same four-day total: 278, ten under par.

At the 1999 PGA Tour's Honda Classic at TPC Heron Bay, a score of 278 would have been good enough for second place and $280,000, one stroke behind winner Vijay Singh, and one stroke better than that year's runner-up, Payne Stewart. At the 2003 Qualifying School at TPC Heron Bay, 278 isn't even good enough to make the top twenty. All the young men at ten-under—including that show-off who had opened up with a 64—they all miss advancing to Stage II by a single shot.

USGA Handicap Index: 9.4
Weight : 219.2 pounds

I feel like a slut.

How else am I supposed to describe the last three days, each of which began with my feeling cold and indifferent, then somehow gradually warming to the whims of a new swing instructor, abandoning all the sweet compliments that just yesterday had me tingling with hope? By noontime I'm swearing allegiance to my new coach and his method, but by the following morning, I have already moved on, bored and unfulfilled.

For the last three mornings I have visited with three of the top golf instructors in south Florida, names you would recognize from television who are supposedly worth a $150 per hour to their players. We're not talking everyday instructors or common club pros, we're talking coaches, gurus, franchises. The difference between these "swing coaches" and the assistant pro who fixed your slice? Aside from a couple hundred bucks? I have no idea yet, but I'm going to ante up a chunk of my savings to find out.

While some teaching pros talk about Hall of Famer Bob Toski changing the concept of coaching golf for hire (I've heard other pros credit the seventy-six-year-old for being the first teacher to earn $1 million in career lessons), you have to look to David Leadbetter as the pacesetter and pioneer of branding in golf instruction. A whole new market in golf has emerged over the last fifteen years, thanks largely in part to Leadbetter's global profile, a profile that has grown hand in hand with golf's expanding image. With increased instruction on TV (the Golf Channel recently turned ten years old), with the magazines making celebrities out of their "staff" instructors, with more new players needing more golf lessons, and the tour players needing to return to an instructor in order to stay competitive in the new talent climate A.T. (After Tiger), swing coaches, performance consultants, short-game specialists—they have been celebrated and promoted in a manner that has born a whole new industry in golf.

Thirty years ago, ask a touring pro "Who are you working with?" and they might have thought you were accusing them of espionage. Now it's idle tour-chitchat. There's hardly a pro on tour who is not part of a particular coach's stable, a member of Harmon's or Smith's or Haney's camp. Tiger tried to become the famous exception to that rule, but you heard how that story turned out.

The rise of the role of the swing coach has not taken place without its detractors. There are still great players who refuse to work with any steady instructor, and many more players who must resent the credit given to coaches for their successes. It is easy to balk at the seemingly artificial importance that is placed upon a particular name or logo. Look at Mickelson's resurgence in 2003 and 2004—every time he sank a putt, a broadcaster was mumbling about Dave Pelz, a camera cutting to a shot of Rick Smith as if the coaches were the masters pulling Phil's strings. Everyone wanted to explain why he was winning, so they talked about his coaches, his new equipment, the ball he switched to that week. Why did he win? Because he's awesome at golf. Absolutely fucking awesome. A couple good breaks, a few more putts, he could win every single week. God made him that way, not his coaches, and if he wasn't such a class act, he might tell his coaches to beat it back to *Golf Academy Live*.

So I am skeptical about the mega-teachers, the ones I imagine as something of a cross between the department store Santa Claus and the tenured university professor. If you've got twenty-two academies, the real David Leadbetter can't be teaching at *all* the David Leadbetter schools. And if you know so much about the game, why aren't you playing it? Is it a classic case of those who can, do; those who can't, teach? Why have I never heard about the golf careers of Rick Smith, Dave Pelz, Jim McLean? It's an easy and unfair argument, but it's a concern: Are these big names the best teachers, or the best salesman? Is there any link between cost and quality?

The track records, the résumés, the results are splashed all over their Web sites, but what about the students who didn't improve, the people who ponied up and got worse? Could coaches be like Allyson's handbags: two bags identical in all ways, but the one that costs $300 more is far superior, for no other reason than its cost? At the end of the day, egos and reputations aside, if the clubface is meeting the ball square with enough power to knock it forward, isn't that the real genius? But just in case there's something the tour players are hearing that I can't read in a magazine or find out from Paddy for $40 an hour, I decide to sign up for lessons with four of the best names in the business.

I approach each appointment with a diagnosis already blaring in my head. I know my primary swing-fault: I play golf with a dead shut clubface. By "shut," I mean that, at the top of my swing, the angle of my clubface is near parallel with the ground. A neutral clubface would be more "on plane," meaning the angle of the face would be right in line with the plane along which the club swings. A good clubface at the top points back at your golf ball. A shut face points at the guy hitting balls next to you.

A shut face is a manageable condition, and I have grown up with a swing designed to recover from it. Though we never had the same teacher, my brother plays with a clubface even more shut than mine—it must be in our blood, and while it leads to inconsistency, it is a very powerful way to approach the golf ball. Players from

Azinger to Anika to Duval have all played with closed clubfaces, most of them using an active lower body to get the club square at impact. I swing the golf ball like I'm wading through cement, no hip action at all, so I square up the clubface by dropping my hands behind me and manipulating the club through impact. In golfhead speak, I open the face by "getting stuck" inside, then I flip my hands at impact to square the clubface. It is a troubled, yet athletic move— you need to start playing early to groove a flaw that requires that kind of timing and coordination. It's considered a good player's problem, which is very small solace. When you block a drive so far right that you think your best chance of finding it is to start walking left, good players' problems start looking like plain old ordinary problems in a hurry.

In my quest to exterminate my swing bugs, I schedule my four lessons on four consecutive days. Four tryouts, really, though none of the instructors know this is a competition, that I am running off to one of their competitors the following morning, comparing notes each afternoon.

The undercover interviews begin at a Naples golf franchise, an academy named for one of golf's preeminent teachers. The head of instruction (let's call him Robert), is schooled in the teaching ways of the franchise's iconic founder (let's call him the Colonel), whose artfully rendered silhouette is stamped everywhere you turn, sort of like the original franchising Colonel. And much like KFC, the actual Colonel is not on premises, but his minions are there in full force, enthusiastic understudies who are guaranteed to know everything the name on the marquee knows.

My instructor is tops at this particular location, and he is a fantastic guy—bright, laid back enough to tolerate the state of my game, quick to spot a problem with my posture and balance that gets my clubface out of whack. Aside from his constant referencing of the Colonel (it's a little like listening to a born-again trying to work Jesus into the conversation at every possible turn—*Actually, I was just talking to the Colonel on the phone . . . the Colonel was hitting balls the other day . . . the Colonel likes ice cream. . . .*), his Aussie accent makes me stand up a little taller, listen a little closer; makes the criticism feel sort of cozy. I find myself feeling rather comfortable, thinking that this could be the guy.

I hit a couple deep six-irons for him, each pass inching toward the target clubhouse in the distance. When he turns on the camera, I decide it's the perfect time to throw to first base.

"I do that sometimes, too," I explain, not wanting to foul the driving range air with that filthy word.

"Do what? That go right? I was looking through the lens."

"Very right. That was your basic shank."

And he laughs. Good. I've had a history with the shanks. There is nothing more emasculating, more soul-stealing, more breath-robbing than the sensation of stepping up to a perfect lie, hopeful and prepared, making your steady, careful take-away, big turn and finish, and the golf ball spits right at a ninety-degree angle, flying away from you with flair. You feel that hosel click in your fingers, and despite all your work and time, you are reduced to someone who not only can't advance the ball, you have done worse, performed some golf anti-miracle, sending the ball in a violent trajectory for which your equipment was never intended.

Robert takes me inside to watch some video, and though it's pretty much a trailer classroom, the kind you see outside Catholic schools with too many kids and not enough tithing (my grade school was full of temporary trailers—the parking lot looked like a movie set), the academy is clean and packed with bright flat-panel monitors, TVs, and laptops and cameras everywhere, as if they weren't teaching but assembling golf Frankensteins.

We watch the swing. If Robert has one thing down, he's got the computer skills, nimbly zipping through menus and photos on a computer program designed for golf teachers. It's called V1 Golf, and after watching Robert break down my swing with it, I can't imagine ever looking at a golf swing again without the aid of a computer program like this. It's like jumping from a quill pen to Microsoft Word in one afternoon.

It would be the first of many afternoons watching my swing on the screen of a laptop computer. Aside from verifying that, yes, I still absolutely need to drop a few stones, the digital camera plugged into a laptop with the V1 training system seems to me as elemental to modern instruction as a chalkboard had previously been. The big ticket cost of such lessons isn't just about the name—much of its price goes into the TVs, launch monitors, projectors, and laptops that go into today's top-flight teaching studios (by "studio," I mean a room with monitors and bunch of wires, sometimes with a garage door that retracts so you can hit out into a driving range, sometimes with just enough space for two chairs and laptop). On Robert's little PC, which is connected and broadcast on a poster-sized flat-panel TV, I watch him freeze my swing from the front, and from the side, then pop up footage of Charles Howell III in the window next to me. The most space that myself and Charles Howell III and I will ever share are these few thousand pixels, but somehow it feels as if I've arrived at the real deal. This is where I need to be: a laboratory out ahead of the cutting edge.

Robert has plenty of good things to say as we watch my swing move, inch by inch, comparing every angle to that of the tour swing next to mine. My clubface is still shut at the top, and he finds that my knees are angling too close, my arms too tight and restricted, my hands too low and my grip too angular—which makes my hands cup at take-away and help to shut the clubface. None of this is helped by a shoulder-turn that he finds too extreme, that helps get the club back closed and inside. I'm surprised he wants me to make less of a shoulder move (what about Els, Couples, Goosen?), but his diagnosis makes sense, and I like that he has come at my closed-face problem from the angle of my setup and my body positions rather than trying to mess with my hands. My hands do what they want, and in my preparation for coming to Florida, I had come to accept my athletic limitations, that any changes would have to be made with the bigger muscles.

At the end of the hour, I run $125 on my Visa (still working, praise God), and head back outside to the range. The next hour's lesson was ready and waiting.

"So at the end of your year, this project you're working on," Robert says, and I feel an awkward explanation in my future. "The goal is to see how good you can get? Are you going to play any tournaments?"

"Actually, it's sort of tough to admit, after looking at my swing for half an hour," I say. "But at the end of the year, I'm going to go—"

"You're going to try to get your card?"

"I'm going to try," I say, thrilled that he brought up the idea without my having to break out the easel and make my pitch. "It's a long shot, but you never know."

"I think that's brilliant. That'd be great, why not?"

If it's bullshit, I don't care—the Aussie accent passes it off for sincerity. Robert is optimistic about my prospects, though I'm not sure if this is about a return visit to the Colonel's academy, or my actual chances.

There is something a tad commercial about the place. I was hoping to find a learning home that felt a little more organic, a little more gladiator sweatitorium, a little less Bob and Kathy came down from Ohio for the two-day clinic. Nonetheless, I leave invigorated, a tape of my work at the Colonel's academy, a few simple drills to work on—his first point was to get my weight off my heels, accomplished by standing with my heels on a board. He also encouraged me to suck the slouch out of my posture and take the club away on a proper path, all to keep me from pushing my hands out, which, by the time I get to the top of my swing, has led me down a road to shut-face city. It all made sense and though he'd just given me the first pieces of the puzzle to work on, I am ready to go back and learn more, maybe someday even get a few minutes with the great Colonel himself.

My next instructor is advertised as the best teacher in the area, no franchise, a one-man show at his own golf school.

And by school, I mean room 121 on the bottom floor of a one-and-a-half-star hotel, one of those places with "Comfort" or "Clean" in the title, almost daring you to pull into this place and try to find either. I walk into the pro shop of the hotel/golf resort and a young man with egg on his face (literally, he has dried egg on his face) swallows down his breakfast and points me toward the driving range. On my way there, the kid at the bag drop asks me if I'm with the pipe fitters.

"Sorry?"

"The outing. Are you with the pipe fitter outing?"

Six months ago, that would have been a big affirmative. I would usually covet a spot in the field at the pipe fitters' classic—*nice prizes, beer girls on golf carts, endless supply of naughty innuendo*—but I have turned over a new leaf and, for better or worse, I have to be a snob. Today I have to snicker a little and tell the kid no, I am here for a lesson. And whether that makes me an ass, there's one thing I've figured about this year: To fit in and make it as a player, you need to be a good deal selfish, and a little bit snotty.

Teacher try-out number two at the twelve-pack-in-the-cooler academy is with the most affordable, as well as the best-dressed golf pro of the four. Nobody told him this was an interview, but he came decked for the part, tan and visored, in flowing linen pants. He had his script in hand and was reading for Golf Pro #1, straight from central casting. I am unsure where the boasts on his Web site came from, if he really was *the* PGA teacher of the year, or *a* PGA teacher of the year. (Google returned a different PGA teacher of the year for the year his site mentioned.) While the surroundings are modest—a good course for a bar outing, a spotty range with balls reminiscent of the mats back home—this pro seems to know what he's talking about, or if not, at least he has the act down pat. He's genuinely concerned about my swing, like a doctor looking over a suspicious lump. He films my move, then takes me inside to watch the tape in his studio. It's a little different from yesterday—no flat screens or laptops. Instead, it's a TV bolted to a dresser, a bathroom with cigarette burns on the sink. I almost don't want to go inside, like I've been asked by a stranger to come look at some merchandise. Something unseemly was in the air as we stepped into a dark and empty first-floor hotel room.

Look past the surroundings, I tell myself. *Find the substance.* If I hadn't started out in the swanky suite yesterday, I probably wouldn't even have minded doing swing work in a mirror that I surmise was once attached to a set of drawers, guessing from the pale outline of a set of drawers on the wall. I do my best not to skeev the lesson—he's a good guy, obviously an accomplished teacher, the teaching business isn't easy and it probably takes a little pride-swallowing to unlock the motel room door and invite his students inside. He points out that my alignment is all catawampus, something Robert referred to but didn't really work on. We weren't being too specific with the targets yesterday, but today's coach makes me pick out a specific palm tree, a specific palm branch to aim at.

"Before we're going anywhere," he tells me, "we've got to start with some real fundamental changes."

This frightens me, because it is a long road back to square one. I'm willing to scrap this swing and start over, but would much rather start at square two or three if at all possible. Rebuilding a golf swing is like figuring out all the ways you lied to yourself, then uncovering the lies you told to cover those lies. It takes a little bit of soul-searching, I suppose, to be honest about your shortcomings and let go of your quick fixes in order to invent a swing that does more than recover for itself.

Two coaches looking for two different things—Robert focused on my lower body and my big muscles yesterday; Golf Pro #1 sees that my shoulders are open, my stance is open, my clubface at address is dead wide open. We didn't discuss any of this at the Colonel's, but Golf Pro #1 looks at the way I set up as the root of my inconsistency—body going left, clubface going right, each flaw fighting the other.

We watch my tape in slow-motion on the television. He steps into frame to correct my setup, posing me in a proper, square position at address.

"That's what we're looking for, great setup. Looks good, yeah," then, "ooooh," he grimaces, like I just vomited on the rug (judging from the amoeba-shaped stains all over the carpet, I doubt I'd have been the first). "That's trouble. After you do that," referring to my less-than-pure inside-snatching of the club, "then it's all recover, recover, recover."

Sometimes I make it, sometimes I don't, he explains. And I nod, a severe look on my face.

I don't tell him at all about Q-school or get into the specifics of the deal. He seems mildly surprised that I'm a seven handicap. (Full disclosure: In my weaker moments with teachers and professionals, I'm prone to shave a stroke or two.) My goal of getting to scratch seems like something he wants me to let go of, as if I'd told him I wanted to grow up to be president. "We've got fundamentals to nail down first," he says.

Not that he's wrong. He's most certainly right, there's major work to be done here. I'd just like to be fooled into thinking it's going to come easy. Maybe if he could tell me with an Australian accent that my alignment was shit, maybe then he'd be back in the running.

His diagnosis after twenty minutes of tape: It ain't going to be easy. I can't tell if this is part of the spiel to get me back for more lessons, the *We've got a long way to go, baby* sales pitch, or a disclaimer should he not be able to fix me, that I was hopeless from the start. He addresses the shut-face issue from the bottom of my swing, where my hands are flipping at the ball through impact. We work on leading the club through the hitting area, trying to feel my clubhead lagging behind my hands. We end the lesson by spending fifteen minutes on designing a solid pre-shot routine, which I appreciate. I know I need one of those, but never took the time to really dream one up.

He calls his suggested routine GASP: grip, alignment, stance, posture. I don't quite understand the difference between stance and posture, but I can see how GAS would be a less swing-affirming acronym. Stand behind your ball and set your grip, align yourself to your target, check your stance, get happy with your posture, one last look, and go. A sloppy swing would still yield messy results, but GASP essentially guarantees that each swing starts from a good place, that each shot has as equal a chance as the last. Of all the lessons I would take, this was probably the most instantly useful tip of the week. It wouldn't take me fifty hours on the range to incorporate it into my game, and just pausing to breathe and rehearse a routine before every shot would bring a focus to my play that was instantly worth a handful of strokes.

I leave with a videotape of our work complete with instructor's commentary. For $90, it's actually worth the bread, a good solid golf lesson, low on frills, high on information. I give him a copy of my novel, but I don't tell him anything about my overall goals. I would send Damon and Gavin down here for a long weekend of morning lessons and afternoon slap-it-around, but I'm not ready to commit.

I want the bells and whistles, the flat-screens and the wires going everywhere, the anecdotes about the Colonel and his opinion on inerlock versus overlap. This is a county hospital, a bare bones infirmary. I want the Hollywood twenty-eight-day rehab, fix me up Charlie Sheen–style.

As I leave Golf Pro #1, we shake hands, and there's a half-suggestion I would be back to follow up, a sort of, *Had a great time, thanks for dinner, you're number's in the phone book, right?* The Help Wanted sign is still hanging over my swing for now.

Date number three is a little more dressed up—bring a tie, khakis at least. We're off to another academy, this one at one of the most decadent resorts in southwest Florida, one of those places when pulling into the parking lot, if you're in my tax bracket, you try to avoid the valet stand and end up driving the wrong way in a one-way parking lot, or leaving your car in a lot that requires a monorail to get back to where you're going. Anyplace the valet gives you your keys back with a look in his eyes that says, *Sorry, dude,* I find it better to opt for the long walk.

The place is gorgeous, wonderfully overdone in that distinctive conquistador-Floridian-architecture-on-growth-hormone style—everywhere balconies and avenue-wide staircases, and their own brand of bottled water. It is the Florida M.O., the game plan for riches in the leisure-world sweepstakes, the land of choice and competition—drop their jaws with the acreage of the clubhouse/golf course/spa and the lots around it will rent/lease/sell overnight.

In the last two days I feel like I have jumped in and gotten dirty. There is something humiliating about taking a lesson, admitting your shortcomings, then sitting there in front of a judge and his camera and showing him your best effort, trying to pretend it really isn't your best at all. It's freshman PE, drop your boxers, into the Hungarian bath you go, and try not to not peek at everybody's prairie-dogging penises. And like PE, by the end of the first week you can waggle your shlong down the hall to history class without thinking about it. There's a comfort level there that one earns, the same comfort one needs to hit golf balls in front of a pair of eyes you're trying to inspire and convince, a witness who, by his job description, is going to elaborate and expound on all that you do poorly.

It might not occur to some people to even care. Some players don't have that sensitive bone in their bodies, and I know I need to get to that point, unafraid to put all my shortcomings out there in the wind. But when you're giving so much to golf, when it's all you do and all you can think about doing, the game becomes your own private story, this secret puzzle you're afraid to show to anyone else. And here I am, trying to play a game that is staged in front of galleries, judged by scorekeepers and marshals and tournament committees, their eyes all wide open—and part of me wants to just stand at the range all day, alone and safe and as good as I need to be, because when the pro isn't around, when nobody is there to see it, there are moments when I can really play. *Now if everyone would just turn around, look the other way . . .*

But I'm warming up to the showing. And today is the day—while I've made strides, today I'm going for my first lesson with a face and name I already know. Among those of you who, like me, watch the Golf Channel in the afternoon, you'd pick him out of a crowd easy. He's a regular infomercial celebrity.

This is a real Florida factory—a golf-learning, spa treatment-having, greens fee-gouging, name-branding Mecca. Before I even get out to the practice tee, I am run through the office, a veritable golf pro check-out line where I pay my $150 up front (a first for me) and collect a folder's worth of info on packages and stay 'n' plays. I head to the back of the regular range, where there is about a soccer field's worth of training space for this academy, with practice greens and tee boxes, and a handful of teaching pros hanging out on golf carts like lazy cowboys, sunglasses and feet propped on the dash, suntans and visors—all that's missing is a straw dangling from their teeth. Everyone is in white shirts and khaki pants, all looking suitably cocky for the price I just paid.

My guy is in the middle of them. He's more expensive than his less impressive peers because he's on TV. Which makes him better, of course, or at least seated closer to the über-pro whose name and smile are emblazoned all over the clubhouse, on their shirts, throughout my folder's worth of January non-bargains dressed up as steals (one full day with the man, only $2,500!).

The infomercial guru introduces himself. We shake hands and I tell him he looks taller in real life. He fakes a little laugh.

"So how's your game? Where do you think your problems are?" he begins, and I warn him about the shut face. He suggest that I learn how to play shut the way plenty of pros have learned to play, but when he tapes my swing and we watch it on tape, he decides it's not good shut, but bad shut—a strong grip closing the face is one thing, but if you're getting the club off-plane and out of whack and shutting it down, it's tough to get the golf ball around very consistently.

The breakdown begins with the first eight inches of my golf swing—the guru sees my hands are pushing away from my body, and the clubface is shooting in—hands out, clubhead in. It's a recipe for shutting down the clubface. He also gets busy on my posture, trying to get me to lengthen my back. While it sounds like a torture device might be involved, all it means is sucking in my gut and sticking out my ass, keeping my back and head in one long line. I have a tendency to stand up at impact, which he blames on my trying to reopen the clubface, as well as a lack of core strength, a diagnosis I concur with—*Yes*, I inform him, *I have the abdominal fortitude of a six-year-old girl.* My butt comes forward too much at impact, and he alludes to a few problems that we don't even get time to talk about—my shaft angle at address, the position of my right thumb. I leave with my swing suspicions confirmed, that there is indeed plenty to worry about.

One suggestion I do take with me is to put masking tape on a large mirror (got plenty of those) at an angle that matches my swing plane (a stretch of tape at roughly forty-five degrees). To keep my club from jumping inside, or pushing too far out, I should try to make my takeaway while keeping the clubhead on the tape—basically, if I can see the clubhead in the mirror, it has moved off-plane. He also suggests I put a piece of tape where my butt sits at address, and try to swing through without my butt moving forward, thus forcing me to lose my angles. In Tiger's swing, his butt moves outward, his back actually gets longer as he goes down after the ball. Me, not so much—two golf swings literally going in two different directions.

He sees the same problems as the first two coaches, and a few more, and he seems a little more worried than I wanted him to be. There is too much information, I am overwhelmed with opinions and drills and ideas—I appreciate that he wants to give me my buck-fifty worth, but I get the suspicion that the guru is more of a one-shot celebrity coach. You can tell by the vacationing couples puttering about the putting green, the tubby husbands and wives waiting in golf carts for their hour's worth of therapy—the business here feels mostly like guests from the attached five-star resort popping in for the three-day stay-'n'-play package. I get the feeling that the guru assumes I won't come back to him and pay the $150 again, judging by the way I get the A to Z of my golf swing in one afternoon.

Still, I am interested in being attached to this recognizable face, and intrigued by the chance to meet and perhaps pick the brain of his boss, one of the coolest names in coaches. So at the end of the lesson, I tell him all about this little project I've embarked upon, all the cost and the commitment and the destination Q-school. I pitch him hard, with every drop of enthusiasm my overcoached ego can muster. And he nods and smiles like I just told him I was going to have tuna for lunch.

"That sounds super, alrighty, that will be great. I'll have to look for that," he says, already looking over my shoulder for the next lesson that's now running three minutes behind schedule and is going to really throw off his crowded schedule of $150 ducks all lined up in a row.

The guru was a knowledgeable teacher and a nice young man, well suited to a teaching factory like this—gives plenty of smiles and lots of information. The day's money feels well spent. But in the end, I need a guy to bond with, I guy I can call and whine to after a bad round, pull a pop-in when I'm in the neighborhood.

I return home, ready to cancel tomorrow's final lesson. Three lessons in three days was plenty. I was so crossed up on the practice tee, hearing ninety-seven swing thoughts in three different voices. I could hardly decide if I was supposed to swing the club right- or left-handed. After three days, I'm pretty sure that my friend from down under is the man. I was in a good place with Robert, might even someday get a chance to get a nod from the Colonel himself.

I call to nix my Saturday appointment, but I get the answering machine, and I can't remember if I left a credit card or not. Then I remember that the woman went out of her way to make space for me, squeezing me in after a Boston Red Sock, apparently. So the guy knows some baseball players, so what? I couldn't possibly tolerate a fourth lesson. My swing is scrambled, I need to stop listening and start beating balls, and the fact that this final coach is the priciest of the bunch at $250 an hour. Kee-rist, for 250 I better get lunch and a new pair of shoes. This would be an especially good appointment to have a nasty head cold for.

But I can't weasel myself into weaseling out. What if this is the guy? Four lessons was too much, but this year, nothing is supposed to be too much. $250? Who cares? Why go just a little bit broke?

The drive out to TwinEagles was a trip deep into the Immokalee goo. The golf course is easy enough to find, down the road about ten minutes past civilization. Someday Florida is bound to push its way inland to here, but for now, this feels like real estate a few years ahead of its time.

My name is waiting for me at the guard gate, where the guard seemed half-surprised to have a visitor. TwinEagles is not so much a development as it is a kingdom, dozens of nook-and-cranny castles perched on an empty Nicklaus-designed golf course. Everywhere is the whiff of abandoned wealth, like I had stumbled upon a grand lost colony of millionaires.

The clubhouse is massive—new, gorgeous, overdone—reminiscent of a Bible-belt mega-church. I tell a bored-looking cart runner that I have a lesson, and he straps my bag to a TwinEagles buggy replete with TwinEagles water, moist towel, ice bucket, Global Positioning System, even a spike-scrubber on the floorboard. The driving range is massive, appointed with Hollywood director's chairs, laser yardage guides, and, again, completely void of humanity. Larry and the gang from home would weep to see these perfect pyramids of Titleists twinkling in the sun, just waiting to be clipped off this sprawling carpet of flawless green. The target greens look nicer than the real greens at my backyard course at Spring Run, the putting green is the size of a hockey rink, and I see three different practice greens with bunkers and a chipping area large enough for the entire PGA Tour. And I've got it all to myself. It's a little bit eerie.

I drive along a path that leads to the far opposite end of the range, winding through weeds and palm trees and coming upon a quiet little cottage. Dark windows and a metal garage door. I walk around to the side of the house and knock on what I assume is the entrance way.

"Yeah, come on in."

The voice is that of an older man with a bit of an edge, like I was late bringing him his lunch.

I open the door, and in the middle of a yet-to-be-unpacked office, I find a man seated in an office chair, bent over a box of cables. He's digging through tapes and plugs and more cables—"Be with you in a second"—and I take a moment to soak in the surroundings.

The drywall is freshly painted, and everywhere there are boxes and cameras and televisions and computers—a laptop computer on top of a desktop computer on top of a television set. As far as circuitry goes, it makes the Colonel's academy look like a kindergarten. There are three sets of Mizunos in the corner, twice as many brown Mizuno boxes waiting to be opened. Everywhere there are frames waiting to be hung on the walls. I see articles from *Golf* and from *Golf Digest*, piles of awards I had no idea about when I nearly called to cancel—best teacher in the state a dozen times over, top fifty in the country, *Digest*'s number-twelve teacher in the nation, the 2000 PGA national teacher of the year—and there are just as many snapshots of famous players: Loren Roberts, Chip Beck, Fred Funk, standing with a tall man in a wide-brimmed hat, the same guy who is sitting here in front of me, apparently unable to find whatever it is he's looking for.

"You Tom?" He looks up at me, a big Midwestern face, mostly bald with thin, reddish hair still holding on around the edges. He's got the spotty skin of an old-time pro, white sunscreen gooped around his ear.

"Yeah, I have the ten o'clock lesson. . . ."

"Jim Suttie." He extends a hand for me to shake.

He's got big paws and big glasses, and when he puts on his wide-brim hat, he looks like a bigger Bob Murphy (now, there's evidence of my advanced golf monomania, assuming that an on-course commentator's face is a readily accessible reference).

"We just moved in," he explains. "It's going to be a while before we have it all together. Right now I can't seem to find anything, so you'll have to bear with me."

"Of course, take your time."

"Go on and loosen up. I'll be out there in a minute," he tells me in a voice more straightforward than anything I'd heard in the previous three days.

I warm up with a couple dozen confused six-irons (is my ass sticking out enough? what are my hands supposed to do?), and in a few minutes Dr. Jim Suttie emerges with a camera and tripod in tow. He's at least my height, if not a touch taller, and he's got a limp in his hip that suggests his big frame has taken its toll. He videotapes a few of my swings.

"So what kind of player are you, Tom? What's your handicap?"

Right to the point. I don't even get a few throw-away compliments.

"I'm about a seven-handicap," I explain as I hit one big block after another.

"Really? A seven?" he says, not sugarcoating his surprise.

"Well, I was a twelve a few months ago, but I've been playing a lot lately. I'm hoping to get to scratch within a year, actually."

"Scratch? Huh. That would be something," he says. I stop and look at him. He's smiling—at himself, maybe, or maybe at me. "Come on, let's go inside and have a look."

He takes me inside into the room next to his office. "It's not all together yet, but when it is, it will be worth the trip out here," he says as he slides up the garage door, revealing a perfect view into the driving range. In its unfinished state, the Dr. Jim Suttie Golf Academy (as the sign on the floor reads) is already as cool as Q's laboratory. Paddy's head would explode at all these goodies, I think, as I take in the four cameras and the movie lights hanging from the ceiling, the televisions planted in the floor around a hitting mat that faces out into the range. There are balance plates hooked up to a monitor to judge a player's weight distribution, there's a laser launch monitor from Avenger tied into a table's worth of laptops. There are bins upon bins of plastic and metal gadgets, a lifetime stash of swing-aids for the improvement-obsessed. He clears off a spot for me in the corner, hooks into the V1 system I enjoyed at Robert's, and from here, the lesson goes on Dr. Suttie overdrive.

I studied under a prized professor in college named Seamus Deane, who is considered by some to be the world's authority on Irish literature. His lectures could make you weep at your own intellectual shortcomings, a deluge of unrehearsed brilliance spilling forth to the point where you couldn't even take notes, all you could do was listen, mouth open, trying to soak in as much knowledge as possible. My first lesson with Dr. Suttie was the golf equivalent of a Seamus Deane lecture. Amid a landscape of self-promoters and next-big-things, I found an academic, a genuine article, a grumpy old genius. After informing me, "I'm surprised you can break 80 with this swing," Dr. Suttie goes on to discuss my golf swing like someone who has a PhD in biomechanics. Which, I'm interested to find out, he actually does.

Dr. Suttie notices that my weight at address is too far over on my left side. Years of breaking down the tapes of hundreds of tour swings has shown him that an optimal weight distribution for someone of my frame is 60 percent weight on the right foot for irons, 75 percent for woods (for his doctorate, Dr. Suttie taped and studied the top-twenty-five tour players, formulating his theories on the golf swing—this was before they were putting video cameras in cell phones, mind you, and Suttie is considered the first golf instructor to incorporate video technology into his teaching).

Instead of simply telling me, *Get your weight over on your right side,* Doc points to my left knee on the screen. "Your knee is bowed at address. With a left knee pointing inward, you drop your left shoulder, putting too much weight on your left side." When he looks at my position at impact, which he finds to be too upright with not near enough turn, he doesn't talk about turning my hips, but the position of my head.

"You keep your head down too long," he tells me, which no doubt comes as a shocking news flash to the millions of self-hating golfers who have a single swing tip in their vocabulary: KEEP YOUR GODDAMN HEAD DOWN. But for me, Dr. Suttie explains, by keeping my head down too long and not letting it go, I'm keeping my spine from rotating. "You can't make a full turn without releasing your head. It's all connected, your head and your neck and your spine. You do know that, don't you?"

He points to my hips, which, in each take, look as they're made of stone. "Do you have any flexibility issues?" Not that I know of, I tell him. He's the only coach to ask about any physical limitations—tightness, pain, old injuries—because to Dr. Suttie, the golf swing should be tailored to the player and the body type, rather than having a player fit himself to a particular swing.

Listening to Dr. Suttie talk about a player of my frame needing to get wide and tall, needing to enlarge my swing, give it breadth—it sounds like he's talking about a musical composition, about the swing God gave me. "You're slapping the ball here, you're wiping it," he explains as we watch the tape. "A player your size, you should be compressing the golf ball. You should be hitting it forty yards farther."

Forty yards? I never thought distance was an issue I needed to address. Forty more yards, and I wouldn't be able to keep it on the range. But I am quietly thrilled to have found a guy who understands tour distance, who expects his players to be able to beat it over the back fence. While he seems blunt to the point of bleak, I love how he talks about the swing I *need* to have, as if he already understands the lofty competition I'll be coming across, the par-fives I will have to reach and the ball flight I will have to master if I am going to make as many birdies as the young studs make today.

We head back outside and Doc starts me with a few simple drills for building width and subtracting the slap from my swing, one which I would use nearly every day on the range going forward. Take a ball or a headcover or a VHS tape (anything you can slide) and put it directly behind your clubhead at address. As you take the club away, try to push the ball straight back. If you push the ball away straight, you'll find you've got full extension and good width and the clubhead will be in perfect takeaway position.

As he continues to tape my swing, two fancy-looking wannabes show up in slacks and visors, pulling Doc away and interrupting my lesson. I'm annoyed: Who do these guys think they are, a couple of pros? And then I see their bags, tour bags the size of oil drums, their names stitched across the front, two names that I happen to recognize. They are both longtime Nationwide Earners who had both done some time on the big tour, and they had stopped over from the Miami tour stop, popping in on their buddy Doc Suttie.

This, I like. No couples from Minnesota come down for some sunshine to get their grips checked. Real sticks pulling a pop-in on their coach. Come out to hit some balls, maybe sneak out for eighteen if Doc could hook it up with the pro shop, which he does. I'm so nervous to be hitting balls in their company, I feel I'm three feet tall and my clubs are made by Fisher-Price. And they nearly are— I'm still banging around one of Paddy's old sets of irons. Getting an equipment sponsor has proven a trickier task than I had envisioned, plenty of letters and e-mails and phone calls waiting to be returned to the player who would like to be outfitted just like these young men on Dr. Suttie's range, without really being like them at all. I feel like such an absolute outsider in this place that I already can hardly wait to come back. It feels like a new high school. I got to sit at the popular kids' table for one day, and even though nobody really talked to me, I still want to come back and try to sit there tomorrow.

We eventually head back inside to the office, and Doc takes an extra half hour going over my tape with me. It's like I've given him a really good puzzle that he can't quite put down until he unravels it. He reminds me of a teacher who can't hear the bell ring—the schedule doesn't matter, the schedule is boring—what's interesting is the golf swing.

"I'm glad you found me out here. We'll be busier come December, but right now, feel free to come back whenever you want. Schedule's wide open," he tells me at the end of my lesson, handing over the full video of that morning's session. "I think I can help you out, if that's something you're interested in."

I tell him about my quest. I don't try to sell it, and he gets it right away.

"One year. In one year, a regular golfer's going to try to play at the next level," he says. "How good could you get in a year? I like that. That's a book I would like to read."

"And I need somebody to help get me there," I say. "I need a coach for the year. If you would be interested . . ."

"Sounds fun."

It was that simple, done. *Sounds fun.* When I ask him about how he would like me to pay for that day's lesson, he tells me, "Don't worry about paying for today. If you're going to be coming back here, we'll work something out for you."

Yes, Dr. Suttie, that is a tear. The best news I've heard in four days.

We shake hands and I tell him I'll work on all my drills and be back next week. He looks at me sideways and smiles. "You know, I've worked with writers before," he says, pointing to a pile of books on the shelf. "They always screw up everything I tell them."

Florida Handicap (non-USGA) Index: 7.1
Weight: 215.2 pounds

"You looked like you were going to puke. Were you going to puke? I thought you were going to hurl."

"Almost," is all I can get out. I have seen people consume $1 nitrous balloons at the concerts of my youth, and while I never actually indulged, I think I'm getting the idea of it now, the sensation they were paying for. My brain feels like it's a ball bearing, spinning around inside my skull.

"Too bad." My trainer Mike smiles. "I'll get you one of these days."

Sometimes, I think my trainer looks at me and sees the guy who stole his first girlfriend. Sometimes—as I hold my feet in my hands, the tops of my thighs dead with pain, listening to my gut whimper for mercy—it feels personal.

It was the lunges that put me over the top today. Two minutes on my workout-nemesis, a squat machine with Leadbetter's trademark on it that I've dubbed the Life Sucker, and my ass is kicked again. All it takes is one glance at that little torture device and the energy spills out of my shoes. After thirty quick reps (it's like standing backward in front of an overloaded wheelbarrow, then pumping it up and down with your thighs), we move right on to lunges across the room with twenty-pound dumbbells in each hand. On leg day, it's a little tougher to get out of bed in the morning. Mike knows my walking sticks need the extra work, so he pushes me for five more, always another five more. As I sit here recovering with a cup of water, curious if the breakfast in my throat is going to keep working its way north, maybe pop out onto the carpet and make Mike's day, I wonder—*What the hell does any of this have to do with making more birdies? How does this undo all the doubles?*

Golf and exercise always seemed like awkward bedfellows to me. If I was going to go through the trouble of conditioning myself, it should be for the Broad Street Run, for the basketball league on Tuesday nights, not the game I was able to play without burning an afternoon nap's worth of calories. In the brand of golf I had become accustomed to, the golf cart was a more integral part of the experience than the golf course itself, a player was far more likely to leave behind a putter than the beer he had bought at the turn, and the day's most impressive display of athleticism would be to make a full swing with a lit cigarette still stuck in your teeth. But someone, somewhere couldn't leave well enough alone. They had to take a game and turn it into a sport, joining "golf" and "fitness" into the buzzwords of the moment.

The jury is still out in the case of more hours on the range versus more hours in the gym. Can sit-ups really save you strokes? The silhouettes of Craig Stadler, John Daley, Tim Herron don't bolster the case that you need to love the salad bar to make low numbers. Yet I fear that their breed may be endangered. These days, we see less of the soft-bellied, sleeve-off-the-shoulder golf pro and more of the tailored, stick-waisted, broad-back specimens, sneaky muscles popping all around their bony physiques. The way Tiger looks and dresses, the way the young Euro thoroughbreds wear outfits that seem to be painted on—it is all meticulous, and to be a winner in golf's future, there might be little room to be anything but.

Talent is tidy, now more than ever. Tidy outfits, tidy bodies, tidy workouts, tidy practice sessions as prescribed by a bevy of tidy handlers. As golf ability has swelled and the margin for mis-hits has shrunk, golf seems to have become careful, clinical, automatic, in a way it may not have been before. Search the ranks of the junior tours and the teenage golf academies, and then try to tell me that the game is not going to be conquered by blank-faced, muscle-bound technicians groomed to process the golf course like a computer. It seems to have already happened in women's golf, where scores have dropped and records are being busted, but much of the charm has been replaced by so many grave and quiet faces.

I cheer for the Jason Gores of the world. I would love to cheer for a basher who's built like a baseball umpire, who makes golf look a little bit more like ourselves. But at these ever-heightening levels of ability, expect to see more automatons dispatching golf courses like equations to be solved, maybe not so many Golden Bears willing their way around Augusta anymore. We will witness the greatest scores in history in our lifetime. The numbers will go impossibly low—there is a 54 out there, lurking in the not-too-distant future. The only question is, how much heart will the game give up to get there?

So in this New Golf Order of pure golf athletes, the slimmest advantages—a half stroke here, two extra yards there—can be the difference between tour millions, and asking Mrs. Malone if she would like a cart or a caddy today. No matter if it's on the psychologist's chair or laid out on the bench press; players are hunting for advantages in places far from the golf course. Not to mention the need to build a body able to withstand golf's intensified focus on practice and repetition—intensified by, again, broadened competition, as well as an improvement in facilities. Advancements in coaching technology and playing conditions have made practice infinitely more efficient—endless supplies of blemish-free golf balls, targets measured with laser precision, launch monitors that provide a month's worth of feedback in seconds. And as with most things American, a spike in productivity doesn't mean we have more time to recoup; it just means we have more time to work harder. With the billion balls I expect to hit this year, I have to take any step I can to sneak past an injury. If I make it through the year without snapping something, it will be its own sort of victory.

I am not sure how the workouts will improve my ball flight or my course management, but not a month into this regimen and I already know it's adding confidence by the (lost) pound. Not just because my once bloated face is looking less like it was attacked by bees, but because this extra effort is amping my competitive drive, giving me the confidence that by working myself to muscle failure before nine A.M., I am outworking the other guy.

As a testament to my former physique, every one of the four teaching pros thought to ask if I was going to be working with a trainer. When I told them yes, they all recommended the exact same one.

I had never heard of Body Balance for Performance. Not that it's any reflection on the company—until recently, I had never heard of a StairMaster or circuit training or the produce section, either. Body Balance is the original golf fitness franchise, founded in the 1980s by then–PGA Tour Director of Physical Therapy Paul Callaway. Callaway was one of the first trainers to work in the PGA Tour fitness trailer, and he designed what many consider the first golf fitness programs to evaluate, treat, and rehabilitate tour players. With thirty training centers around the country, Body Balance teaches a system of golf-specific strength, flexibility, and balance training. I was lucky to find a center about fifteen minutes from my condo, just down Highway 41, and per the four recommendations, I scheduled an evaluation with the Naples center head man, Mike Willett.

Mike has a stocky trainer's build—thick-chested, with dark hair, he looks like the guy in the gym you'd ask for a spot. Polite but intense, Mike assures me that I am not signing up for a New Year's promotion at Bally's—this is going to be a yearlong, life-changing commitment where I will have a golf-trained physical therapist's undivided attention for three hours a week, as well as unlimited access to their entire golf-fitness facility. I have never had a boss in the gym, and I am beginning to understand why my solo efforts at physique reform have fallen short. I need a partner, a fitness conscience, a voice who won't entertain my arguments about the importance of self-acceptance, the benefits of rest and sleep. Mike is precisely what I need, a young man with a real stake in this business and, thus, a stake in his players' successes. Mike is co-owner of the business, with the NUMBER 1 NATIONAL FRANCHISE plaques proudly displayed by the entranceway. On that first day, as we shook hands on what I was about to do, I got the feeling that as long as I could keep Mike happy, my body was going to take care of itself.

In my physical evaluation, during which Mike had pulled and pushed my limbs around like I was Gumby, he made the same diagnosis Dr. Suttie had noted in my first lesson (which was confirmed by Mike calling Doc to check in on his thesis—as part of my program, Mike was going to work with my coach, even sit in on lessons to make sure my therapy complemented my swing objectives). I had poor hip flexibility, below-average trunk rotation (a previous test at my doctor's office had rated my flexibility range as "caution"), and shockingly deficient abdominal fortitude. He seemed surprised I could breathe at all with the state of my abs. Mike also came to the thesis that I was a sloucher, in life and in golf (bingo, but what do you expect, I've been splitting my life between a keyboard and a couch since graduate school). He pinned my crap posture on my tight hamstrings, as well as a tight back and a tight chest that stuck me with pronating, slouching man's shoulders. My swing coach was focused on body type and biomechanics, and my physical therapist wanted to free up my golf swing by freeing up my muscles—in putting together my little team, I think I've stumbled upon a nice combination.

At the start of my relationship with Mike, it was all flowers and chocolates, long walks at sunset—I looked forward to my daily pop-in at Body Balance like it was a trip to the spa. The first phase of the BBFP system is called the "Release" portion of my exercise training. If I was ever going to build a consistent, balanced golf swing atop a solid golf base, I was going to need to break it all down, squeeze all the knots and tightness and badness out of my body, then start building back up from there.

We started off slow, a little time loosening up on the bike, a half hour's worth of morning stretches and light exercise, and three hours a week facedown on the massage table. The toughest part is all the water I'm instructed to to drink: BBFP recommends one half your body weight per day in ounces. That's 105 ounces of water for me, which means I start sleeping like an eighty-year-old man, wearing tracks in the carpet to and from the bathroom (is it the water, or the Florida?). With my muscles properly hydrated and warmed up, Mike can knead me like a two-dollar brisket. As he forces the tightness from my back and chest, I can feel my posture improving daily, my shoulders sitting back like a proud debutante. Bad walking-around posture equals bad golf posture, so on Mike's orders I walk around town like I am the prince of Naples, shoulders back, chin up. In three weeks we've got the torso turning, and Mike has pried my hamstrings free, giving my legs a full range of motion.

It's the hip-work that reminds me that these are not massages and Mike is certainly not a masseur.

"If your butt is black and blue tomorrow, don't freak out. It happens," he informs me as his elbow digs into my side. Perhaps it's my lack of hip meat, or my lanky frame, but God apparently located my Achilles heel a few inches deep in the side of my ass. The slightest elbow nudge—it brings on the sort of pain where I cannot breathe, where my eyes actually begin to juice up with tears. It sucks, and it's exactly what I deserve—I know the karma of fitness: The more fun you have letting yourself go, the more you will suffer as you fight your way back.

By our second week together, my ass looks like I sleepwalked through the shower at Sing Sing. Eyeing my bruised buttocks in the bathroom mirror is not an experience I would have imagined being a part of my golf odyssey, but the time and the tears do pay off. At the end of the Release phase, I have near-perfect posture and full flexibility. The meat has been seasoned and tenderized. Now it is time to throw it on the fire.

In fairness to my good buddy Mike—and he really did become quite a good friend whom I would recommend to a golfer of any shape or handicap—he is an exceedingly gentle and concerned young man who does not give any of his patients any more than their bodies can handle, and takes tender care of his mostly elderly clientele. He spends much of his day rehabbing old ladies' turned ankles, so when I walked through the door, I could almost hear him licking his chops. Time to party, time for my trainer to break a little sweat of his own pounding on the redheaded project. I gave him carte blanche to whoop my ass: *I need you to make it as tough for me as you can. I have to be in the best shape of my life one year from now. I don't want to do what everybody else does. I want to do double.*

He was too happy to oblige.

Let's go, Coyne, my little one-year-old doesn't whine as much as you. . . . This is supposed to be fun, you should be doing twice that many. . . . Is that all you got? . . . Abs tight, come on, you can't give me five more?

We still spend an hour a week on the table to keep my hips and hammies loose, but we are soon into the Re-educate portion of the training, which quickly advances to the last stage of the training, the Rebuilding phase. In the Re-education phase, we work on integrating ideal posture and movements into my swing, now that I have a body that has been properly Released. It involves a half hour's worth of core work—sit-ups and flutter kicks and pelvic tilts—as well as balance work on a foam roll or balance beam. Mike is impressed with my progress—my age helped (twenty-nine is still young on the flexibility scale), making the Release and Re-educate portions go rather quickly, and within a month we have combined all my stretches and core exercises and balance work, and elevated it all in the final Rebuilding phase. This is what I'm really paying for: golf-specific strength and cardiovascular training.

Mike designs an exercise circuit for my core, legs, and shoulders, the three main areas of the swing and the three areas where my physique happens to be most wanting. The strength training isn't necessarily about getting stronger or bigger or longer, though they are all welcome side effects. I can't muscle strokes off my scorecard. But look at Tiger, and look past the power to the stability and the balance. If you don't have a strong core, it's pretty hard to maintain balance and control when the clubhead is moving around your body at 120 miles per hour. The technology has gotten better—shafts move faster and balls move farther—but if we don't complement some of the advances in equipment with advances in our own makeup, faster means wilder, longer means wronger.

Each session begins with five–ten minutes on the bike to warm up the muscles. Even if all you're doing is stretching, get the heart rate up. Sounds redundant, but Mike is big on getting loose before getting loose. Stretching cold, you're asking for something to pop. Even on the range, swing the club around for a few minutes, get yourself a little winded before you get your full swing on.

During my circuit, I try to maintain a heart rate as close as possible to my training heart rate, or THR, which is 60 to 80 percent of my maximum heart rate. Figure your target cardiovascular rate by:

$$(220 - \text{your age}) \times .60 = \text{low-range THR}$$
$$(220 - \text{your age}) \times .80 = \text{high-range THR}$$

For me, that was training heart rate of 115 to 154 beats per minute (bpm), with a maximum heart rate of 192 bpm. You can take your pulse for ten seconds, multiple by six to get a quick workout estimate.

With hydrated, warm, loose muscles, and a heart rate pumped up to THR after ten minutes on the bike, my four-times-per-week routine alternated between a back-shoulder-chest circuit, and a legs-core circuit. Each routine had its own perks and minuses—I liked working my chest and back. It reminded me of clanking weights around in the football weight room, working big vanity muscles that respond and swell quickly. Everything but the shoulders—I was born with the build of a distance runner (who despises running, unlucky for me): tall with feeble shoulders. Trying to put any meat on my corners had always ended up driving me from the weight room and back to the stationary bike. But Mike won't let me get away. He spends twice as much time torturing my shoulders from all sides—the progress is plodding, moving from no weights to two pounds to five-pound bells. Lo and behold, soon there it is in the mirror, a golf shirt with two rounded-out sleeves, no more Ashworth shirts hanging on two pins.

As ego-sapping as the shoulder routine could be, none of it quite rivaled those sneaky-vicious lunges. How hard could it be to kneel down and stand back up? We walk, sit, get up all the time—what could be so hard about a little lunging around the office? With or without the twenty-pound dumbbells in each hand, it was all horrible. I felt like a daddy longleg trying to carry a watermelon. There was no golf score out there that could ruin my day like those lunges. They were workout enemy number one, unless Mike happened to be feeling creative that day, unveiling a new torture du jour. He was not afraid to invent exercises as we went along, concocting spontaneous techniques that usually targeted my abs or my hips, and usually involved my being hooked up to a belt that was hooked up to a band that was hooked up to Mike Willett's biceps. Whether it be doing lateral leaps or hip rotation or turning through impact as Mike yanked me in the other direction, the focus was on building strength and speed in my hips and thighs. I thought it would be difficult to find golf-specific exercises—how many muscles does a golfer actually use? In Willett's dojo, all of them.

On off-days, when I'm recouping from one of the circuits, I do an hour of cardio, followed by thirty minutes of balance work, usually involving my working my way up from balance beam to half foam roll to full foam roll, where I am like a lumberjack swaying over a floating log, except that I am standing in perfect golf address position: head and neck on the same plane, butt out, abs tight (tight abs for everything, at address, over a putt, everything starts with your core—try it next time on the practice green, putting with a tight stomach, and see how steady you feel over the golf ball). I rehearse my take-away with a weighted club, then I pick up the club, slowly set it at the top of my swing, make a slow-motion move through impact, all while teetering on the white foam log. After working up a sweat (you'd be amazed at the muscles you exhaust trying to hold your balance), I start over and do it all again, this time eyes closed. It's months before I can handle this last part safely, but it's amazing how the swing tendencies that Dr. Suttie has identified—my weight going to my toes at take-away, then moving off the ball through impact—are all confirmed beyond a reasonable doubt by the foam roll.

As does Body Balance's Dynamic Balance System, the most over-the-top golf gadget I have ever seen, a very expensive testament to exactly how far golf and technology have come. The DBS computers and balance plates at the heart of Mike's training center traced my weight distribution through my entire swing, providing irrefutable evidence of my body's teetering ways. An instructor might look at repairing a swing as a simple matter of fixing a grip, realigning a take-away, when the real issue can be a matter of physiology, neurology even—how your body decides to compensate while in motion and under pressure.

Seven days a week it's a mix of cardio, flexibility, balance, and strength, all sweated out by nine o'clock in the morning. I don't know where my golf scores or body weight or bench press will be at the end of the year, and a part of me, the part that has become addicted to the exhaustion, to those deepest breaths you can feel only as you walk away from the treadmill, head clear and light—could not care less how the numbers work out. Up at seven, work until you sleep—that's all this player can control. And for getting me interested in working out, for turning me into the guy who shows up every morning with his workout journal, knocking on the door before the gym is open, a guy who starts hanging around GNC and checking out his pecs and calves in the bathroom mirror—for his role in this unlikely metamorphosis, Mike Willett deserves yet another plaque by his door.

A month into our program, Mike recommends me to a nutritionist who might help design a diet that would complement my effort in the gym and maximize my potential on tournament day. I meet with a woman named Bonnie at her home in Naples. She's a certified dietician, and we discuss my goal of losing a good twenty pounds.

After writing out and studying my current eating habits, Bonnie tells me that twenty pounds is an eventuality with the amount of calories I am now burning. I don't sit from seven in the morning to eight o'clock at night—if I'm not working out, I am walking, swinging a golf club, stalking putts on the practice green. I have already started gulping water by the gallon, I have cut out white bread for wheat, oatmeal has become my steady breakfast, and red meat is now an occasional indulgence, taking a backseat to grouper, tuna, or whatever Randy's fish market is selling that morning. I am burning twice the calories I am taking in, Bonnie explains, and she has few recommendations for my diet, confirming my suspicion that the best way to lose weight is the AA diet: be Active, don't eat like an Asshole. Upon crossing the Florida border, I committed to revamping my diet, designing a new food lifestyle with nothing at my fingertips but a dash of common sense: *If you can get it delivered, it's probably not that good for you; if it's cheaper, it will probably make you fatter; the more complicated the packaging, the harder to burn it off in the gym; if you cook it for yourself, no matter what it is, it's bound to be better for you.* Simple to the point of stupid, my guidelines were already making a difference, and not just at my daily weigh-in. I had my vitals checked in September, and I found my body was at a béarnaise-gurgling 24 percent body fat. By my meeting with Bonnie, I am already down to a healthy 16 percent.

Bonnie proceeds to give me a few tips for staying sharp on the golf course—come Q-school, I cannot afford any metabolism mishaps. There are plenty of things I can't control in a round of golf; what I put in my stomach isn't one of them. A spike or dip in blood sugar, wavering energy levels, a touch of dehydration—any of it can lead to poor decision making, double bogeys. When your clubface is moving toward the ball, all your muscles and nerves need to be participating. If one part of your physique is taking a water break or looking for a snack, it's good night, Mr. Titleist. There is another guy out there on the golf course—maybe a few hundred other guys—who are not going to make that mistake.

She recommends a day-before-competition diet rich in carbs and protein. Pasta dinners work, maybe work in some red meat or fish. The morning of a tournament, she's in favor of a breakfast rich in whole grains and proteins that are likely to stay with me for most of the day but won't sap too much energy in digestion—no food co-mas wanted. And during a round, along with keeping a constant flow of water to my muscles, she recommends I snack every thirty minutes to keep my body functions level. Every three holes, a ba-nana, some trail mix, raisins, and while she isn't crazy about pack-aged energy, a PowerBar is better than nothing. Again, more common sense—eat before you feel hungry. When your stomach starts to grumble, on come the impatient bogeys. When the bogeys come, you're less likely to want to stop and eat, you're more eager to rip at the next shot—it's a vicious cycle, hunger and anger feeding off each other on the golf course, until you're left starving and signing for 84.

I make one further addition to my diet that I don't mention to Bonnie or to Mike, one addition that I am just now coming clean about here. In the hopes of making my workouts even more pro-ductive (i.e., easier), in November I start taking a protein supple-ment called Muscle Milk—not on the advice of my physical therapist or my nutritionist, rather, per the suggestion of the neckless gentle-man behind the counter at the nearby vitamin store. I'm told that Muscle Milk is a powder supplement patterned after human breast milk. *Yum, make mine a double.* It actually comes in a delicious range of flavors (banana cream for me), and while I doubt Doc or Mike or Bonnie would recommend I add a creatine enhancer with purified bovine colostrum extract and an amino acid matrix to my practice routine, I make this choice on my own. I'm the one whimpering on the mats, I'm on a tight calendar, I want maximum payback for every minute of my life that I give to that gym. I would cook it in a spoon and shoot it into my veins if it made those goddamn shoulder lifts any easier.

A few weeks on the Milk, I can definitely tell a difference. Granted, I might just be feeling the residuals from my accelerated workouts, but I take some unexpected satisfaction from giving my body fifty bucks' worth of extra help every month. For a gangly red-head to have his girlfriend mention the new shape in his shoulders, I felt like the brace-faced twelve-year-old who finally filled out, ready to head to the beach and kick some sand around myself. I didn't think I was vain that way, but I can see how it's a slippery slope to musclehead. Those pumped-up 'roid ragers we used to snicker at down the shore—now that I have a couple of muscles of my own to look at in the mirror, I can see how those monstrosities might happen.

I don't believe golf is going to ever have to worry about steroids the way other professional sports do. Perhaps the game requires too much touch and mental steadiness to ever reach that point. Imagine a four-footer to win the Masters if your veins were pumping with juice—your ball might rip the back of the hole off, your tomahawk putter toss mowing down a half dozen green jackets. But I can imagine performance-enhancing drugs being a PGA issue down the road, at least in the way that many controlled substances can quicken recoveries, minimize and mask injuries. As practice regimens grow more extreme, as six-year-olds start beating a thousand balls a day, more bodies will break down, and more options will be explored. And if golf courses keep stretching toward 8,000 yards, if golf talent continues to multiply and grow more athletic while the pool of opportunity remains the same size, some guys are going to be muscled right out of contention. They are going to have to look to something to fill that yawning half-stroke gap as the purses grow larger, the talent grows wider, the margins grow tighter. If they can ever find a way to putt long and straight into a needle, trust me, somebody will be taking hits at the turn.

Let's face it—they're not playing US Opens at Merion any-more. Golf is becoming a game of kill it, go find it, kill it again. And while technology is making the game more playable for the average player, for the upper-tier golfer, it is turning golf into a game of driver and five wedges, a game that every year seems to be less about mind, more about muscle. Being long requires no real imagination, and I doubt golf's patriarchs ever meant for length to be rewarded in the way our modern layouts do. As an aspiring tour player, I know that I absolutely must have a 300-plus yard drive in my bag, that every par-five green must be reachable in two in order to remain competitive, just so that I'm not spotting the field four strokes before we even tee off.

And now that I can hit it that deep, I don't know if I have Body Balance or Dr. Suttie or my daily serving of breast formula to thank, but for now, I'll hedge my bets. I'm sticking with all three.

"Just calling to see if you still suck at golf."

It's the sort of encouragement that keeps me going. Padraig checks in every once in a while to make sure I'm not getting lonely.

I am too busy now for lonely. I don't have time to think that there is nothing to my life but the daily temperament of a little white ball. Each morning I wake up to the sound of the eighteenth green being trimmed outside my window at six. By seven, I am doing stretches within view of a snapping white flagstick, the sun just lighting the tops of the palm trees, pouring into my patio. After oatmeal and vitamins and thirty ounces of water, I am sweating over a foam roll, balancing like a circus bear, and by nine I am beating balls toward the Astro Turf islands at the driving range just a few steps from my front door.

The biggest decision I make all day is settling on where I'm going to practice. Should I hang around Spring Run, sneak out for eighteen if the tee times die down? Maybe head down to Twin-Eagles to bother Doc Suttie, or perhaps slip out to Raptor Bay or The Hideout, golf clubs that have been kind enough to allow me to use their facilities while I was living in Naples and training for my run at Q-school, all within ten miles of home.

The Hideout has as select a membership as one might find in southwest Florida, and they opened up their club to me after only one letter and a ten-minute conversation. This is why the players come to Florida, where people aren't afraid to share the golf because there's plenty to go around, and it doesn't make anyone feel important to keep their first tee empty. This strange, bright place, even at its snootiest, is still all about playing the game, and a single-digit handicap is more interesting here, and certainly more unique, than a seven-figure income.

Whichever course my car takes me to (I try to spread the work around, not wanting to burden one range picker with the four, five hundred balls I might hit in a day), each workday ends in the twilight on the Spring Run putting green, a few yards from my front door. I hit three-footers until my back quits, then home for chicken and brown rice, trying to keep my eyes open for *The Big Break* on the Golf Channel—it's *Survivor* for aspiring golf pros, and it's the first time since Bill Cosby stopped being funny that I have been religious about catching a television program. Ten-tour hopefuls perform golf stunts over a two-week trial, trying to win a shot on the Canadian or Nationwide Tour, many of them players who had once tested a road similar to the one I am traveling, and found competing in a game show a much fairer proposition. *Maybe they didn't work as hard, put in the hours and days and months,* I think, watching nine great players fall by the wayside, finishing off one more jug of spring water before I fold into my sofa, half-asleep, listening for the next morning's mowers.

If I could invent a few more hours on that wipe-erase calendar, I might notice that I haven't seen my girlfriend in a month, that I don't have any friends beyond small-talk acquaintances on the driving range, that if I got sick or hurt and couldn't go play, I would have nothing to do but stare at the mirrors that cover my condominium. I might be lonely, I'm not sure. I might answer the phone when it rings, but usually I turn it off first thing in the morning and don't turn it back on until after the sun has set.

There are always a few messages from Allyson—*Just seeing how your day is going . . . just called to say I miss you, I love you. . . . I can't wait to come and visit.* Our evening conversations have suffered a little bit. It's my fault. I admit it—I have become intolerably boring.

"What did you do today?"

"Hit eight hundred golf balls. Same as yesterday. Same as tomorrow."

From time to time, there is a brief heartfelt voice mail from Paddy or Gavin or Damon.

"Still fat?"

"Break ninety yet?"

"I heard your swing coach jumped off a bridge."

But today on Thanksgiving, there are a half-dozen messages from friends who are wondering if I was back home for the holiday. I don't return any of the calls. Not this year, the selfish time in which I have already missed my ten-year high school reunion, skipped one great friend's wedding and made plans to miss two more. And for the first time in twenty-nine years, I am passing on Thanksgiving dinner at home. For this Turkey Day, I hit the clubhouse gym for an hour's worth of stretches and flutter kicks, then an hour on the practice green, an hour in the bunkers before I drive up to the airport in Fort Myers to meet Allyson, after which I will show her the swimming pool with a view of the driving range. There she can warm her bones and watch me work until three, when we have reservations in the clubhouse for the second dinner sitting of the afternoon.

When we meet up in the airport, it's funny, I watch from a distance and I wonder what it would be like if I didn't know her, if I were just a stranger in an airport watching different women file down the terminal. I'm nervous like a little kid, and when I spot her for the first time in a month—this tall blonde in an outfit from up north that makes her look like a celebrity amid all the flip-flops of

Florida—I am flat-out giggly when she finds me playing hide-and-seek around the coffee kiosk, and it feels somehow miraculous to have this beautiful person I love come pop into this strange little world I have created for myself. I want to show her everything, tell her every minute of my new experience, unveil every bit of my life. And when I start to, it takes all of two minutes—*I'm working my ass off, it's starting to happen, I am really getting better, Allyson*—to realize that there isn't that much to tell.

There is plenty about the experience that only I will ever know about, that I cannot re-create for her or even in these pages for you—it's the aspect of the game I care for least. Some consider it golf's greatest mystical asset, but I think it's the part of the game that can leave you emptiest. Every so often, you hit that pure shot—I make the perfect move Doc has been imploring me to make, I pinch a ball off the center of a six-iron, it flies at a controlled, cannon trajectory, effortless and exact, and in that moment I know that I have changed. I have reached a place where I never honestly believed I would touch—a part of me can strike a golf ball as well as I will ever need to, as well as anyone, anywhere playing the game.

It is an amazing place, where I am almost overwhelmed to the point that my cheeks start to tremble at the thought of it. After six hours in the sun and the aching in my arches, my fingers crumpled over one another, I can barely spread my hands wide enough to grab my cup of water, it all goes on auto and it clicks, and for a little while I can flash ahead to tournaments and galleries and hear my name through the bullhorn, *From Philadelphia, Pennsylvania, Tom Coyne.* The path is long, but at least now it is straight, the finish line bright in my imagination. I am going to be good enough, and that realization is almost more exciting than arriving at the accomplishment. It's the idea of success, that sniff of possibility that gets me up a few minutes earlier every morning, wishing for a few more hours of daylight and always a few dozen more balls.

It's all amazing, and sad, because with all of it—it's really only for the hitter to know.

No matter how genuinely interested Allyson is, there's nothing quite as boring or confusing as watching your boyfriend work on his rotation through impact. She can see I'm getting thinner, there's tangible evidence on the scorecards strewn around the condo, a few 73s taped to the mirror. I show her my hands covered with first-aid tape and tell her how they started bleeding the other day. On the driving range, right in the middle of a practice session—I didn't know they were bleeding until I wiped blood down the front of my white shirt, smeared a steak of crimson across my sweaty forehead. It wasn't a popped blister, the skin on my ring finger just split and dripped blood all over another glove that was torn and ready for the trash bin, anyway.

It's rare, the chance to feel tough as a golfer. There are not very many bowling-the-catcher-over, laying-out-the-wide-receiver moments in this game. But bleeding hands, that's a pretty good one. She looks at my fingers like I'm perfectly insane.

"I think you need to take more breaks."

"It didn't hurt. I thought it was kind of cool."

She shakes her head. She must think it strange that I'm grinning at my bandaged fingers like they're covered in diamonds.

It was our first Thanksgiving together in the eight years we had dated. Maybe not a continuous eight years—there were a few relationship segues, one or two negotiated time-outs along the way—but at the age of nineteen, she came into my life, and has been a part of my life ever since. That I can say exactly the same about my credit card debt is mere coincidence.

We met at the very end of my freshman year at Notre Dame. Tired of the stale air and Sega hockey of Fisher Hall, I struck out in search of an extracurricular activity. Every university student I knew, from the engineers to the premeds to the architects, were all haunted by the sneaking suspicion that all these calculus and chemistry and postcolonial lit classes were for naught, that we were all ultimately bound for law school. If this were the case, we were going to need more for our applications than *football season ticket holder*, so my roommate Tyler went hunting, and he found an ad in the newspaper for the Sophomore Literary Festival planning committee. It was an invitation tailored for the two of us: we were both literate, both soon-to-be sophomores, both pro-festival, and a *committee*—it sounded like something we could blow off at a moment's notice. Perfect.

The truth about the Sophomore Literary Festival was that it was a bright spot in the otherwise spirit-crushing South Bend February, a time in my life that would otherwise be remembered only for the iced-over spectacles, the shoulder-high snowdrifts, the campus-wide seasonal affective disorder. Tyler and I both filled out our committee applications—*Dude, who are you putting for favorite author?*—and before long, we were headed to our first meeting, leaping from the world of dorm day-sleepers into the world of Student Activities—a strange and unexplored planet that, to us, was inhabited by a rare and special breed of geek.

But it wasn't all bad.

"Dude, the chairperson is hot," was Tyler's first estimation of our new surroundings. The group consisted of thirty or so liberal arts majors of varying degrees of awkwardness. There were the kids with Causes, their satchels covered with pins and patches, their outfits and facial hair worn to look carefully careless. Some of the young ladies showed off their underarm whiskers, drawing stares from the handful of overstimulated theater majors who were obviously being judged by the half-dozen burgeoning literati, students who looked serious beyond their station, with their dog-eared paperbacks and note-stuffed journals.

But there was that one young lady sitting at the center of this slightly confused crowd. She was wearing overalls, Birkenstocks, a tie-dyed T-shirt. She was tall and she was blond, and my first thought was that there was no way she was a freshman, too. Graceful in a sea of goobers, sexy and curvy in this crowd of crunchiness, she was the kind of girl who made you feel painfully aware of your own underclassman-ness. I remember thinking that Tyler's first contribution to the Sophomore Literary Festival Planning Committee was dead on the nose.

We went around the room, a little wave to no one in particular, and Hot Blond Chairperson gave us the scoop on the sort of year we had all signed on for—there would be meetings and readings and get-togethers, even a few Dead Poets Society affairs where we would read poetry to one another by candlelight in the Notre Dame woods. There was a better chance of finding Tyler and me saying six A.M. Mass in the Basilica than there would be of finding us reciting stanzas in the forest, but we nodded along, waiting to hear the chairperson get to the really important stuff, i.e., did she have a boyfriend? A red-hair fetish? Uncommonly low standards and/or a busted moral compass? But she was all business, totally un-freshmanly. She didn't often look up from her notes, of which she had plenty, and if she was at all anxious about running her first committee meeting, she passed it off with this cool blond intensity.

After an hour of literary festival rah-rah, she looked out to her thirty new right-hand men and women, asking us whom would we like to invite to our festival. She was met with thirty blank daydreaming faces, a bunch of kids sleepy from dining hall dinner, already drifted off to their next appointment across campus. A few names dribbled forth—Tyler got a chuckle when he tossed out William Shakespeare—but our committee's first act as a committee, our first expression of teamwork was to collectively bring our first meeting to a slow yawning death. I wanted to say something, suggest a writer, answer one of her dozen unanswered requests, but instead I just shrugged like a lump, an ordinary pasty face, just as unremarkable as the knucklehead in the baseball cap that I was.

When it came to the ladies, I was sans moves. I was game-impaired. My dearth of skills may have been precisely why, knowing that I had no real opportunity to worry about blowing, that I stopped on my way out the door, turned to where the chairperson was still sitting Indian style on top of her chair, fumbling through our applications and questionnaires, too many papers dropped into her lap by kids on their way to meet with cooler committees. She looked overwhelmed, and very much like a freshman, and I don't remember doing this, but she remembers it well. She says it was when she first started to like me. Apparently she had been nervous as hell all night, so she started to have an instant crush on the redheaded guy on her committee when he stopped by the door on his way out, leaned over, and told her, "Thank you. You did a great job tonight."

Eight words. Eight years later. Funny how things happen.

Funny that, today, Allyson is the one with the law degree and the MBA who traded in her tie-dye for an office with a view. She's a vice president at a major insurance brokerage, and while I do not actually own overalls, I wear Birkenstocks, and have been known to be reckless with my facial hair. And after eight years, it was becoming evident that it was time to make plans for the next stage of our lives. How that next stage took a turn through Florida, how our future got all wrapped up with a golf tournament, how eight years got back-burnered for a sudden strike of inspiration—I'm not sure. I am suspicious that the answer to that question might be what this trip is really all about.

I had first told Allyson about my new life plan on our way home from a friend's wedding. Going to a friend's wedding with your girlfriend of eight years is like walking into the dentist's office with a mouth full of Jolly Ranchers. You are just begging for a serious talking-to.

"Do you ever think about it?" she asked.

Somewhere between the church and the valet at the reception hall, the calm surface of an otherwise harmless car conversation began to bubble.

"Think about what?"

"You know," she said. And of course I knew, but in the hopes that I could play dumb for the next nine minutes until I was safely surrounded by overworked smiles and mini-quiches, I countered with, "Know what?"

I drove, eyes watching the road in front of me, but I could feel—nay, I could *hear*—the look she was giving me. If I didn't offer something better than *Know what?* the big word was going to explode from her lips, shattering the windshield here in front of us.

"Sure," I said. "I think about it."

"And?"

"I think about it."

"How do you think about it?"

"I think about it."

"Okay. Well, in what way do you think about it? Do you think about it like you think about things you would like to do? Or do you think about it like things you never have any intention of doing? Because I—"

"I think about it," I interrupted, "as something nice for someday."

At most of our friends' weddings, *someday* was usually good enough to get us out of the rising temperature of the car and into the party, where, for a short while, all would be warm and wonderful, until there came that one replenished glass of champagne too many, and the delicate balance of carefree-wedding-fun tipped right back over into panicked-wedding-time clock.

"People ask, they ask all the time. Do you know what people say to me? Do you know what they ask me?"

Actually, I did. There is something about the long-dating couple, close cousin to the long-married-yet-baby-free couple, that invites probing questions as if a couple had found themselves seated at an information booth instead of a dining room table. I've had more miserably married people ask me when I was planning on getting married—the "This tastes awful, here, try it," phenomenon. Children, marriage, I had often thought of them as places people find themselves because there was nowhere more interesting to go, as if the movie they really wanted to see was sold out. And in the theater in which they've found themselves, there are plenty of empty seats, and they can't stop waving to you, asking you to come join them, as if inviting you makes their lot seem a little less ordinary.

And then there are those who do seem happy, married, single, indifferent, who feel the need to lob these night-shattering balls of fight-juice into our evening. Straight from the book of things to ask a young couple—uninspired questions requiring no real thought and no real effort in getting to know two people beyond their tax status.

So when are you going to make an honest woman out of her?

She's dishonest? I had no idea, thanks for the heads-up.

When are you going to put a ring on that finger?

When I can afford one that doesn't come in four flavors and grows smaller with each lick.

Taking your time, aren't you?

Actually, time is exactly what you're taking from me, and the sooner you can put a stop to it, the better.

What the hell are you waiting for?

For you to stuff that shrimp in your face and walk away.

You've already taken the best years of her life.

That one hurts. That's just fucking unfair.

So that evening, I explained it when she asked if I know what they say:

"I do know," I told her, "and I think they should mind their own damn business. They can't think of anything better to say—they just want to know why we aren't as miserable as they are."

It might not have always come out so badly, but this was generally the stage in negotiations where I began pissing gasoline on the campfire. I fumbled. "I do think about it, I'm not against it, I'm not saying it's a bad idea."

I fumbled, but I never lied, because the truth was, I did think about it. All the time. I do want to get married. Some Day. My calendar just hasn't shown me my Some Day yet.

Some Day is a moment preordained from the dawn of a single man's life, a day that will announce itself in full and conspicuous glory, trumpets and fireworks and cherubim. Some Day is the day when you stop taking cash from your Visa, when you join the health club, when you buy your parents dinner, when you ask for the non-smoking section. It will all happen—not today. Maybe not tomorrow. Have faith—you'll know Some Day when it gets here. Pathetic, yes, but I am not the only young man I know with a calendar full of Some Days.

Consider my parents—married at twenty-two, still married at seventy. My father has had the same job for forty-three years. Now look at my peers. Most of my friends are rolling happily into their thirties, entirely uninterested in the tax breaks that might come from signing that ultimate contract with their live-in partner. In one of my regular golf foursomes—one separated, one divorced, one unmarried with a child, and me with a nine-year girlfriend, none of us yet reached thirty-eight. My friends have double, triple the education of my parents, yet they have embarked upon an average of 3.4 distinct careers by the third decade of their life. We grew up in a world where next week everything was going to be better and bigger and faster and cooler. It is a tough time to settle into things when all you've known about tomorrow is that it is going to be so much more mind-blowing than yesterday.

It isn't a question for the relationship column, as simple a cliché as a *fear of commitment*. I am thoroughly committed. I love my girlfriend, I am lucky as hell, and I don't have the interest or stomach to fool around. I'm not anxious about merging our two sole proprietorships (on any sort of balance sheet, she's getting the short end of the deal), and I'm not leasing because I want a shot at next year's model. I know it's not the commitment that I am afraid of.

I think it's the dying.

It starts with opting for the blue run instead of the black diamond, when skiing becomes less of a cathartic adventure, more of something I need to protect my bones against. Then I start taking the bus from Chicago instead of the prop plane to South Bend. I start thinking about family history, wondering when I'm old enough to start checking my PSA, wondering if fish oil can really do everything it promises. Remaining a child a little longer, living at home a few extra years, changing a few more jobs, putting the engagement off for another summer—you can't pin it all on one thing, but the one thing you can pin it all on is the hope that you can stop time, deny change, and everyone will stay right here and now. Getting married is closer to being parents and being grandparents and being dead. It's bleak, but there is something about matrimony that feels so entirely mortal, so high up there on the ladder of my life. It's not that I want a few chances to get it right—I want to get married only once. But do I really want to do anything that I want to do only once?

I could explain that I'm the youngest of five, she's the oldest of three, I'm surrounded with an NFL preseason roster's worth of nieces and nephews, while her family waits for a first grandchild. I could deconstruct my milieu and my history, invent more theories, justify it all on paper—I imagine I could defend myself on *Oprah* and still stand a fighting chance.

But that would all be more bullshit. The truth is—and here's the truth: She's brilliant and wonderful, and I'm an ass. It's just easier to spend years dreaming up excuses than to realize that you're as selfish as a toddler, and slightly less intelligent.

So this time, on the way home from that friend's wedding in June, I tell her the truth.

I do think about it. All the time. And I do want to get married. Someday. Someday not far from now. But first . . . I want to take the next sixteen months for me. I want to spend a year of my life being outrageously, precedent-breakingly, history-makingly self-centered. I want to go play golf. I want to make that game you won't let me watch on Saturday afternoon, or talk about at dinner parties—I want to make that game my entire existence. I want to commit to golf the way I have never committed to anything in life. Let me go play, and I'll come back ready for the next step. But I won't be coming back for a year.

That is the version she would get in time. But that evening, on our way home from another summertime reception, she got, "Have you ever heard of a thing called Q-school?"

Allyson has not only grown to accept my new goals, she's resigned herself to the possibility of life with golf, like the magnanimous ex-wife willing to put on a smile and meet the new girlfriend. It didn't happen very often, but she might surprise me by carrying her clubs out to the range at Spring Run and hop into my cart. Allyson would knock the ball around for five, six holes—she has a good swing, athletic, and when she makes contact, her three-wood pops out in the fairway a good 150 yards. But six holes was plenty of fun. The idea of going on for an entire eighteen, it seemed entirely excessive, like an abusive miscalculation. *Eighteen of these? Are you disturbed?*

We played on Black Friday, when she certainly would have rather been beating up one of the outlets. By the back nine, her clubs had been retired to passenger status, and Allyson went looking for gators and water fowl while I tried to impress her, the big hitter with new muscles in his back, blasting moon shots into the aqua. She wouldn't have been able to tell the difference between a pop-up and a 300-yard blast, but she could tell when the ball missed Florida altogether.

"Splashdown," I explain as we watch another Titleist abruptly find the drink. "Parachute didn't open."

"You shouldn't go in there," she suggests. "I think I see an alligator in the weeds. If you need more balls, there's a million in my bag."

This visit, as would Allyson's half-dozen future visits, fell into a routine, the way everything in Florida seems to settle into a comfortable, predictable, important pattern of events. I don't know if it's the lack of change in the weather (sunny, always), but the state seems to exist primarily so that people may travel from afar and adopt a predictable daily schedule that usually revolves around daily Mass, standing weekly tee times, and four P.M. cocktails at the neighbor's, each afternoon's host decided by a carefully balanced, unwavering calendar.

For Allyson and me, Florida wasn't quite so unpredictable. Allyson went to the bookstore, I went to Body Balance. Allyson went to the pool, I went to the driving range. Allyson stayed at the pool, I played eighteen holes, waving as I made the turn at nine. A few days of that, then a ride back to the airport, wondering why I had spent so much time hitting balls, wishing I had taken a day to sit by the pool with her, just to watch her read for a little while. I promise myself, next time, next time she comes, things will be different.

The weekend after she leaves, I play in my first real golf tournament since college. The tournament is named, somewhat appropriately, the Michelob Light Cape Coral Classic. Advertised as "The tour for the rest of us," the Michelob Light Tour is located in dozens of local golf sections, hosting a schedule of events for guys who want to play competitive golf sans the country club membership. It's an overdue idea, a reason for Johnny Hacker to actually learn the rules or go to the range, a new avenue for growing the game. I would like to see the USGA's or PGA's name on this kind of golf idea instead of that of a brewer, but nonetheless, the tour has been successful, expanding into new markets each season. For some guys, the tour is an excuse to get out of the house, but for plenty others, each Saturday event is their US Open. For me, it's a chance to get the nerves going a little bit, a chance to play that different kind of game where you gotta count 'em all.

I didn't exactly break the course record, and admittedly, 78 is not worth much of a parade. But it is a start. No matter that I win on a match of cards, beating a guy who had a persimmon three-wood, knitted wool headcovers, and mismatched socks, not to mention a mustache that tickled his chin and a manner that was somewhere between reticent and totally flipping shell-shocked—all beside the point. It was real golf, no gimmes or mulligans. There was a field of competitors, they were all playing to win, and I came out on top.

There's a long way to go between the Michelob Light Cape Coral Classic, field of twenty, tourney medalist firing a 78, and the PGA Qualifying School. To get to Jimbo Fuller from here, it's going to take about a stroke a month. A quarter of a stroke a week. 1/28th a stroke per day. .036 strokes each day that I need to improve. Now if I had just told that to Doc in the first place, he probably wouldn't look so worried when I show up for my lessons.

By the end of November, I am friendly with the head pro at Spring Run, a young guy named Joe Allinder, who is a regular stick himself. He's a lefty that hits it so straight, you think he's cheating.

Fairway, green, fairway, green, it's goddamn boring. He even makes a putt from time to time and had qualified for a few PGA Tour events and was regularly tops in a lustrous PGA section. We're playing together one afternoon, and after he gets me for ten bucks, I don't think he's just being a gracious winner when he tells me he thinks I have a legitimate shot.

"You sure as hell hit it far enough," he tells me. "There's no reason you can't go play well in a qualifier. You never know. Some guys just figure it out. All of a sudden, they go out and shoot 68 one day and they never look back. Everything's different. Sometimes, for some guys, it's like flipping a switch."

Allyson's not back in Philadelphia ten days before I get a phone call at dinnertime. I hear the phone ringing inside, but I'm out in the parking lot firing up a chicken breast on the grill. The sun has set and I've returned to my good, exhausting routine, ready to eat food that I've prepared myself, that I know won't make me any softer, that I feel like I've earned after grinding out that day's 1/28th of a stroke.

After dinner, I'll call her back and tell her it was just another good day. I'll tell her that I miss her—miss her as much as I possibly could in this place that, when the ball is working straight, is absolute paradise.

But before I sit down, the phone rings again. And again, right as I dig into my dinner. I answer it and it's her, and she's trying not to cry. Back in Philadelphia, it was the first snow of the year. She slipped on the ice outside her office, and she was in the emergency room. She thinks she has broken her arm.

"I'm sorry," I apologize. "I'm sorry, I'm sorry."

I am inarticulate, useless, scared to remember that there might be problems in the world that have nothing to do with golf, and I have no inkling how I might tackle them. I am sorry, feeling that in some way this was my fault. She's up there living a real life, where you come out of your hard, complicated day and you fall on the ice, nothing like this life, where your biggest problem is a sunburn, where deep down you know that a little white ball has become the only thing that can truly break your heart.

"Golf is hard. That should be the first line of your book."

It's not necessarily the advice you're looking for from your swing coach, but it is an undeniable fact, and a point I seem intent on proving, ball after ball after ball.

Golf is not so much difficult as it is absurd. The design of the pursuit—to place a walnut-sized bit of plastic into an imperceptibly tiny hole, contacting said plastic with nothing but the flat end of a bent stick—it sounds like a riddle more than a sport, a bad practical joke played on first-timers, as if some smiling prankster's going to come up to you in the middle of the first fairway, pat you on the back, and tell you, "Just kidding."

Golf *is* hard. A few months ago I was focused on making contact. Now I am worried about trajectory and ball flight and optimizing the spin off my clubface—I have come a long way, but every few steps has led to a new staircase. They say good players think about hitting the ball, great players think about where they're hitting it. I can now sit in Doc Suttie's studio all afternoon cracking fresh Titleists, doing a pretty confident imitation of the latter.

"Takes ten thousand golf balls for a swing change to become permanent," Doc explains as he tapes me trying to feel the club lagging behind my hands.

We've been working on a few recurring themes in most of my

lessons—balance, posture, trying to get my clubface in a more neutral position, and trying to get my club working down the line. (I had a tendency to swing inside out, trying to compensate for the closed face.) A few swing thoughts I have been returning to daily:

1. Keeping the clubhead outside my hands, keeping the club in front of my chest as I make my turn. By keeping the clubhead moving in front of me (as opposed to my grooved move where my hands push out and the clubhead pulls in), I can keep my club on a more neutral plane, keep my clubface from shutting down.

2. Posting on my left leg, turning through the shot instead of sliding into it—this helps me "lag" the clubhead by fighting the early release in my wrists, which was to blame for my flippy hands and inconsistent contact.

Every golfer responds to different cues—some work by feel, some work by images, some need the physics explained to them. For me, if I focus on the sensation of keeping the clubhead in front of my chest on the way back, and again on the way through, I am able to make a connected move where my right elbow works down in front of my body and my right side "covers" the golf ball.

I tend to not cover the ball, meaning my right elbow stops at my right hip, and my hands slap or scoop at contact—handsy play, with good timing, can bang it plenty far, and usually a mile high, but there's the obvious issue of never knowing quite how high or far the golf ball might be going. It's a very un-Tigerly way of getting around the golf course, and by trying to find a more neutral club position on a better swing path, I don't have to scoop as much, and my shots begin to take on that beautiful, boring, piercing trajectory.

At this point, I could hit fifty deep, soaring six-irons for your run-of-the-mill golf pro, and they might tell me not to bother changing a thing. But Doc, he's not impressed by pretty. My high and deep results might seem consistent, repetitive enough, but Doc looks at the way my body is working, and he doesn't even look to see where the ball went.

"You can't play with your hands working that way." Doc slow-motions the tape, showing how my wrists cup through impact like I'm topping off a sugar cone. No matter that every ball on the tape was juicy off the center, raining on the 180-yard flag. "If your hands are working under the ball like that, there is no way you can have a consistent ball flight. Some days you'll hit it fat."

Some days, I do.

"The next day you'll be hitting it skinny. I'd bet that your divots are toe-heavy, and your misses are toe-hits."

It's like he's been following me around the last month, though he's never actually seen me scrape it around the golf course.

"You can even shank it swinging like that. You might be playing great, then all of a sudden, good-bye. Does that ever happen?"

When did this become a golf intervention? It's a moment before I make the slightest nod, eyes cast down at my shoes. "I thought I was standing too close to the ball."

"That's got nothing to do with it," Doc says, rewinding and zeroing in on my hands and my little slappy move. "A shank is caused by an over-rotation of the wrists. Overactive hands. People try to fight the shanks by manipulating their wrists. That only makes it worse. Look at your hands here—you've lost your wrist angle halfway into your downswing. You've lost your lag so early that's going to give you all sorts of problems. You need to know that a six-iron goes 175 yards, or 180 yards, whatever. Not sometimes 192, not 157 if you get it heavy. Throwing it up into the air and hoping, that's not going to get you very far."

Doc pulls up some tape of Sergio, and we watch his insane clubhead lag—his clubhead is so far behind his hands, it's like his shaft is made of rope. "Lag is power. Lag builds control and consistency. That's what you've got to get."

To start building lag and erasing scoop, we begin at an unlikely starting point. He traces the way my hands are working to the way my left side slides through the ball, sort of like a pitcher moving off a rubber. My left knee and hip move laterally, disconnecting my swing, causing my arms and wrists to throw the clubhead at the ball, creating that early release that so often would just wipe the golf ball.

"If you slide, the ball will hide," Doc tells me, one of his many spontaneous Seussian moments. He stakes a metal Dr. Jim Suttie's Training Center sign into the ground, pushed up against my left hip so that I cannot possibly move. "You're either going to stop sliding, or you're going to slice your arm on this sign. So either way, you'll learn."

In Doc's first book, *The LAWs of the Golf Swing,* he threw the teaching establishment for a loop. He and his co-authors identified three body types, the Leverage, Arc, and the Width players, claiming that each body type needs to be taught an entirely different set of swing mechanics. What Doc essentially argued was that no two golfers can be taught exactly the same way—a liberating idea that flew in the face of the magazine gurus and franchise coaches who had patented a singular teaching system, who had made a living off one-size-fits-all methods, marketed to golfers of all different sizes around the world.

In my short time with Doc, it already seemed clear that his one simple rule of teaching the golf swing is that there are no simple rules. Hitting balls on the range, I would watch him help one student fight an over-the-top move, while with his next student, perhaps an older gentleman of a different build, he might ask him to exaggerate an over-the-top swing. In one lesson, Doc might be teaching an exaggerated shoulder turn, while in the next, he wants students to forget their shoulders even exist. It's like going to a real doctor; different patients get different prescriptions, quite refreshing in the age of mail-order golf lessons and teaching via TV. God made us all different, and I'm beginning to think it's okay to swing different, too.

Doc's prescriptions usually involved a heavy dose of drills.

"A lot of players won't do drills," he says. "Some of the guys I've worked with on tour, they won't do them. They get embarrassed, I guess. They don't like looking like they don't know what they're doing. But I don't know any better way to feel a swing change. A good drill can make a change in half the swings it takes trying to feel a swing-change on its own."

So along with being the *real* swing doctor, he's the Willy Wonka of golf drills. I think he dreams them up as the lesson goes along, always a half-dozen new tricks at his fingertips. He goes into his workshop of a million gadgets and returns with a rope, a piece of PVC pipe, and five-feet-long golf club and turns it into a golf lesson (maybe MacGyver more than Wonka). To feel lag, he ties a bath towel around my driver and makes me swing it for ten minutes. To feel a shoulder turn, he wraps a piece of rope around the bottom of an office chair, puts an end in each of my hands, and has me pull on each opposite end like a pulley, helping me feel my back opening, hips turning. I feel a proper swing plane by swinging a double-length club shaft slow-motion. I need the drills, and they help—I am a feel player, I learned to hit golf shots by playing. I need to feel that metal sign digging into my thigh. It's easier for me to re-create the sensation of a proper golf swing rather than imitate lines on a computer screen in my head.

The tapes of my lessons are starting to pile up atop my television, and as I watch them over and over at night, I worry. Not because I am not improving—I am, dramatically—Doc has even complimented me once or twice. Not so much compliments, rather, a lack of nonflattering descriptions. Maybe, *That's gotten better,* or

That looks like a real golf swing. It's not that he's negative, he's just honest. Curmudgeonly in the most charming sense of the word. It's a little bit like my own father, who isn't inclined to blow smoke, and his father who wasn't much for it, either. Honesty goes further and takes up a lot less air.

But as I watch my slow, subtle improvement, I worry that I will not live up to my end of the bargain. I can win as many green jackets as I want on the driving range, but I am still unsure about whether I am going to be able to make that transfer to the real golf course in conditions that count. All this work we do, in front of the cameras and on the computers, mastering drills out on the range, none of it matters in the end. The game is about playing, showing up on a certain day and stepping into a certain moment and performing, like a kid on a basketball court, like a dancer in a ballet. For anyone to suggest that golf isn't athletic—just because you may not sweat or need manufactured muscles, the game nonetheless requires you to perform under great pressure, to maintain perfect control of your body under the greatest strain, to envision what needs to be done, and to go do it without pause for thought. It's jump-shooting. It's as athletic as it gets. Maybe that's my problem. I haven't swished a jump-shot since grade school.

The first time Doc and I head out onto the golf course, it feels wrong, unnatural. For a moment, I wish I could have dreamt of becoming a professional driving range rat instead of an actual player. I've been showing off in his studio, pretending I belong here amid the players from Florida Gulf Coast University (whom Doc coaches, some of whom have come from Europe to work with him, all of whom seem as solid as solid gets) and with Mark Lye, who has been popping in every other week, and the kid who flew in from North Carolina for *one hour* with Doc, then went back to the airport and flew back home, the kid who was thirteen years old and a plus-one handicap, whom Doc told there was almost nothing he needed to change.

"Kid had a much better swing than you have," Doc informs me, not to rub it in, just a clinical observation. "And he's only thirteen."

I nod, not sure what to do with the information. Then he adds, "Grab a cart and grab your clubs. Let's see how you handle yourself on the golf course."

It is that locker room moment again, back to freshman year PE. Stepping out of my golf cart, unpeeling my driver, walking to the first tee at TwinEagles in front of Dr. Suttie's omnipresent camera—trapped. They finally got me. For all my talk about being able to play, for all my progress in the studio, now I actually have to go out and be a golfer, see if this costume I've been wearing on the range has stuck.

Sometimes a modicum of terror can act like a swing-preservative on the golf course, the juices pumping in your stomach blocking your muscles from communicating with your brain. The more anxious you are, the more easily you can go on autopilot. Before I know what has happened—and I wouldn't realize until watching that evening on tape—I have ripped a drive down the right side of the first fairway, dropped a nine-iron fifteen feet short of the pin and, after misreading my first effort and Doc kicking the ball back to me, made a birdie on my first hole with the aid of only one mulligan.

"Hey, look at that," Doc says, pleasantly surprised as my ball rattles into the cup a few inches in front of the camera he's laid on the green. "Right in the heart. Nice birdie. Sort of."

The problem with the pseudo-birdie on number one, it flushes most of the swing-preserving nerves out of my system; and on the 210-yard, number two, with my head adrift in useless swing thoughts—*golf is easy, birdies are fun, yeah, I was right, I am the best*—I make a long, easygoing pass at the ball, blocking a four-iron onto TwinEagles Boulevard that was, thankfully, Rolls-Royce–free for the moment.

"Whoa, where did that go?" Doc says, peering into his camera screen for any evidence of who or what might have kidnapped my golf ball.

"Not too good, Doc. That one went a little right."

"Hit another one."

And for the rest of the afternoon, there would be plenty of *hit another one*s, as if I was determined to transform this golf course into a cozy driving range, hitting three, four balls from each spot until we found one that was worth taping. It wasn't long before Doc stopped getting out of his cart to tape each chip and putt. By the fifth hole, he had figured out that "Your irons are not very good."

And, as if trying to prove him wrong, I flat-out top a three-wood from the middle of the fairway. *Hah, take that,* I say, burning another Titleist into the Florida brush, *my woods aren't very good, either.*

"Oh dear, oh boy," Doc says, and I feel like I'm nine and I've just spilled grape juice all over the carpet.

I head home that evening with another tape. I fast-forward through the decent swings, dwell on all the mis-hits, hoping that the rewind button will somehow figure a way to get my right side through the ball.

My cell phone rings, and I let it go to voice mail. It's not that I don't want to talk to Allyson, I'm just tired of not having much to report. Sometimes—maybe all the time—going to go play golf for a year feels as ridiculous as it sounds, particularly when she's snowed in with a broken arm (I sent her a stuffed animal, by the way) and all I want to do is bitch to somebody about how unfair Bermuda grass can be.

When I finally flip open the phone, I see the message isn't from Allyson. It's from Jim Suttie.

Fuck about sums it up. He's never called me at night before. I hit voice mail, wondering if a teacher can fire a student, or if I was going to be the first.

"Tom, this is Jim Suttie. Give me a call as soon as you get this. I just got off the phone with the head of sales and marketing at Mizuno. They want to fly me and you up to Orlando so they can fit you with new clubs. They're going to put you on their staff and handle all your equipment. Call me back if that sounds okay."

Every once in a while, going to go play golf for a year—it all makes perfect sense.

G olf every day means golf every day.

Sleeping in on Christmas morning is a sad milepost on the road of life. It had been fifteen years since I didn't need someone to shake me out of bed, remind me to come downstairs and root through the pile of presents that had grown smaller by the year. From cardboard boxes you could hide in, to wrapped-up bundles of socks and underwear, to a personal check hiding in the bottom of the same gift-bag you got last year, dollars that are going directly to Visa to pay off the Christmas presents you bought yourself that July.

But this Christmas, for the first time since I was a child, I am awake while it is still dark out. There isn't any tree in the condo, there's only one wrapped gift placed under the TV with care, but I leave it for later and head out for seven A.M. Mass. By 7:45 Christmas morning, I am blessed, eucharized, and loose enough to rip driver down the left side of the first hole of The Hideout Golf Club.

The grass sparkles like a million shards of glass—a million strings of tinsel, if you will. You can see the dew smoking in the morning sun. I have the course entirely to myself, and this is one of the many moments of the past months where I feel truly spoiled. It usually comes late in the afternoon, or early on a morning like this, when I am alone and just tired enough, and I feel as if I'm watching myself from a close distance, this lucky person with the range or the first tee or the final hole all to himself, with nothing lying in front of him but golf today and golf tomorrow, followed by the likely prospect of more golf.

A round at The Hideout is the perfect Christmas gift to myself, a chance to play a course that is everything Florida golf is not: no pool, no spa, no overdone clubhouse, no homes perched along every fairway. Like the clubs up home (two of the owners are from Philadelphia, while the third was famous for breaking Philadelphia hearts), you don't need a tee time, and you don't ever have to wait—there are plenty of caddies, plenty of action, plenty of room on the range, plenty of brand-new Titleists to beat to my heart's content. The club has more single-digit handicaps than any membership I have ever seen. Provided you can find it (the name is no joke—you drive inland until you start hearing *Deliverance* banjo strings plucking in your ears suddenly emerging out of the woods and into a lot full of cars you'd be nervous parking your dusty Civic next to), and provided they need any more members—if you would rather play another eighteen than nap in the spa or fumble around the tennis court, then this is the place for you.

Christmas morning is even less crowded than usual, just myself and a healthy-sized gator sunning himself aside the fourth green. He seems surprised to see me, as if this were his day to have the run of the joint. Playing golf on Christmas doesn't feel as strange as I thought it might. (It's Florida—what else are you going to do?) I make the turn at a few strokes over par, and am surprised to see that the parking lot is still mostly empty, considering that most Floridians probably aren't spending their Christmas putting together a swing set. But I'm glad for this peaceful round of golf. It feels stolen, an extra treat to play alone when the courses were just starting to fill up with the snowbirds who had found 10,000 square feet of paradise that came with a homeowners' association.

I come to the last hole and bang driver on a line that requires a 250-yard carry over the rocks, and I watch the ball bounce safely onto the short grass. I'm swinging carefree from the back tees, the way one would expect to swing before noon on Christmas. I card a legit 73 (two over, but on a slope 74.1), as legit a score as you can make playing solo. There are no witnesses to my number, but I had a witness just the week before, when Gavin was down in Naples sizing up a new building project. He stayed in the guest room a few days, and he was surprised to find me stretching in the living room at seven A.M., surprised to see the food stock was mostly vegetable and whole-grain in nature, nary a Dorito or frozen pizza in sight, and he was downright shocked when we snuck out for eighteen and I birdied the last three holes to shoot even par. My first legitimate round of even par, 72, signed and attested and witnessed by a source from home who I know would be spreading the news: *That ginger-head is beating the hell out of it*, or, at least, *That redheaded bastard ain't a fat bastard anymore.*

I have to attest my Christmas 73 myself, and it's one of the few cards I date and keep. I don't expect to have too many good rounds on 12/25 in my lifetime, but still, Christmas golf feels perfectly natural. It was Christmas Eve that felt all sorts of wrong.

In my family, the night before Christmas was always *the* night. Going back to my parents' Scranton Irish upbringing, Christmas Eve was the night to splurge on lobster and roast beef, the night for midnight Mass and Pollyanna and the patriarch's annual State of the Family toast. No matter whom you married, no matter how thoroughly you had procreated, no matter where you chose to spend Thanksgiving, Easter, or Christmas Day, all persons Coyne are expected to spend Christmas Eve in the perfectly spiced air of their mother's home.

Until this year. And until me. I spent Christmas Eve sitting at the bar in Outback Steakhouse. I splurged on Victoria's filet. I couldn't bring myself to go for the accompanying lobster tail for just $11.99 more. Too many memories.

I have never felt lonely in an Outback. It is the unofficial headquarters of the hungry partner-less male, a beacon calling to the business traveler, the freshly divorced, the roaming golf pro, a place in any city where you can find a spot at a pleasantly crowded bar, eat a full meal by yourself without feeling quite alone. Unless the bar is perfectly bare, unless you are sitting aside thirty empty stools like some drunk past closing, unless you're *That Guy*, the one all the beef-satisfied families try not to look at as they file out of the restaurant, whispering on their way back to the mini-van, *How would you like to be that guy, eating alone at the Outback on Christmas Eve? Makes you thankful, doesn't it?*

A twenty-year-old bartender with a tragic complexion who's been complaining to his busboys about having to be here on Christmas Eve slides me a second bonzer draft, on the house.

"Merry Christmas," he says, as if the idea itself—comping drafts on Christmas Eve—is kind of funny.

If he wants to go further in the drink-slinging business, he's going to have to get a whole lot better at pity. But I thank him for prolonging my stay at the lonely bar. I lip my icy mug, nostalgic, recalling the Christmas classics of my youth . . . *'Twas the night before Christmas and all over my plate, Aussie Cheese Fries, Bloomin Onion, do you needa 'rita, mate?*

Golf has taken me to some unexpected places—mixing up my morning breast milk, scoping out my black-and-blue buttocks in the locker room mirror—but I never imagined the game could be responsible for such a strange holiday. Who'd have thought a few lessons at my father's club in 1983 would end me up here?

———

My father did not take up the game until later in life. Growing up Irish in Scranton, Pennsylvania, afternoons at the country club were not a part of the summer routine. My father isn't a very big guy (my brother and I tower over him), but when he was a young man, he started on every team at Scranton Central—he made varsity basketball as an undersized sophomore, and he played on Penn's lightweight football team back when the Quakers used to suit up against the Fighting Irish. He celebrated his seventieth birthday a couple years back, and he's been made a grandfather thirteen times (that's without me even pitching in yet), so he spends half his weeknights and most of his weekends attending soccer games and school plays and band recitals. He loves it, though it must make him wonder—when did having kids come with season tickets? Do parents ever just drop their kids off anymore? Is the falling price of video cameras to blame? When he was growing up, my father said that his own dad saw him play just a handful of times. He would come home after a contest and give my grandfather all the details, shot for shot, relaying all the action as Pop sat in his big corner chair on Arthur Avenue. My dad once told me that in all his years of football and basketball, my grandmother never saw him play a single game.

After picking up golf in San Diego in the Navy (I wonder what kind of debt golf owes to those military golf courses?), Dad became a solid golfer, a short-hitter who can do more chipping with his trusty nine-iron than I can do with the five wedges in my bag. He's always happy to take a few strokes on the first tee, then sneak up on you with another one-putt par, *snatching the bread from your mouth*, as he likes to call it. I will never be more grateful to golf than for the time it made for my father and me. I spent more time with my dad than any teenage kid I knew, whether it was carrying his bag or playing alongside him. And in all those afternoons and early evenings together at the club—the time I finished with four birdies in a row, that day I eagled eighteen from the wrong fairway, how I almost got to that unreachable ninth green in two, just needing one more bounce—there was never any pressure that I didn't apply myself. He never pushed, even when he probably wanted to. Even when I probably wanted it.

I remember the evening when the game changed for both of us, when we silently said good-bye to our golf dreams, the day I didn't make the team at Notre Dame.

I came home to an empty dorm room, my roommates off in Chicago for the Northwestern game—they had left a dozen noisy messages from the parking lot of Soldier Field, just to let me hear all the fun I was missing. I cleared my voice mails, and I dialed my Dad.

It was the first time I ever spoke to him as if he weren't my father, spoke to him like he was a guy I knew from across the hall.

"I fucked up, Dad," I said. "I was right there. And I fucked it up. I fucked up, I fucked up, I fucked up."

It was the first time I could recall saying *fuck* in front of my father, and I repeated the word as if this was some sort of confession—*yes, I say bad words and I do smoke cigarettes and I do skip Mass, and I am not very fucking good at golf at all.*

He listened, and he didn't ask me to excuse myself or to apologize. He didn't berate me or ask me why I didn't play tougher, why I let that two-footer get under my skin. He just listened for a while, and when I was done painting the phone line blue, he told me to turn it over.

"Everything in life happens for a reason" was what he said, and pretty soon we were talking about the new quarterback, and where I was planning on watching the game.

My grandparents, maybe they were on to something. I don't know how easy a conversation that would have been for the other kids on the team, the ones on scholarship whose dads had helped lift them up to that level. I don't know what that would have been like, to fail for two people. No matter how many times I missed, no matter how far and how hard my siblings and I would stumble along the way, we would never have to apologize. The way I didn't have to apologize that afternoon, didn't need to explain why I was going to be a Notre Dame fan instead of a Notre Dame athlete, a golfer who might someday go low, instead of a golfer who had already been there.

I wish I had made it home for Christmas.

I finish up my Christmas morning eighteen and head to the airport. With their youngest son bound to Florida for the holidays, my parents cleaned up their Christmas Eve feast and hopped onto a plane for Fort Myers.

My mother doesn't seem to recognize me standing in the middle of the terminal. It's been only two months, but in nearly fifty trips to the gym thus far, I've built a little bit of V to a body that was all O. Not quite jacked, but there's no more jiggle. I grab their golf bags off the carousel, and we head back down I-75 to Spring Run. Along the way, I proudly show off my new surroundings as if the palm trees and the sunshine were all my idea, as if I'd special-ordered seventy-six degrees for their arrival. My dad has had a job for the last fifty-four years, and here's his twenty-nine-year-old son, already settled into cozy retirement digs.

I can tell my father is excited to come watch me play, and after the last couple of weeks, keeping it in the low 70s, ready to break through par, I'm anxious, a little cocky, even, to show him the new game. The day after Christmas is ideal weather as always, and we head out to play the course in my backyard. Mom rides in the cart, and Dad plays well on this flat track, a stroll down a moving sidewalk compared to the hike he was used to around his home course in Philadelphia, where the caddies double-duty as Sherpas. At Rolling Green, there wasn't a level lie on the property, a track that boasted one of golf's original unreachable par-fives, a William Flynn 614 yarder.

But here in friendly Bonita Springs, I hit two par-fives in two, then drive three greens on the back nine (317, 309, 306 yards), firing one-under on the back side after a forty on the front. I shoot 75 after looking at five eagle putts—you don't need to be Leadbetter to figure out where my skill-set might be wanting. Still, Dad is impressed, and today that's certainly what matters.

The next morning, my mom is out in the living room, her regular routine: coffee and prayers at sunrise. This might be the first time she's ever seen her boy in the light of six A.M.

"Where are you going?"

"To the putting green. I have to work on something."

She looks outside. Just a few patches of orange poking through the palm trees.

"Is it open?"

"It doesn't really close. I have to go now because I have Body Balance at eight. And we're playing Raptor Bay at ten. And we've got TwinEagles this afternoon—we're going down to see Dr. Suttie."

She sips her coffee and nods. "Maybe you and your father can find some time for more golf."

My father brought the article from *Golf Digest* with him on the plane, the issue where for eight pages Doc Suttie shows off his gadgets and his lasers, demonstrating how technology can help a player break 100, 90, 80. I know he has been showing the magazine to friends, *Here's Tommy's coach—number twelve in the country.* So when we walk into Doc's studio at TwinEagles, it's a little like meeting a celebrity—actually, for a golfhead, it absolutely *is* meeting a celebrity. Sometimes I forget how lucky I am, to think about hanging around Doc as an everyday thing.

He's sitting at the monitor in the corner, going over tape with one of the members, a woman of about fifty who, judging from her video, can put some serious stank on the ball.

It's funny watching him meet my father. Doc is quite a bit taller than my dad, but they have similar faces, all full of sunspots and likeable wrinkles, a few wispy hairs clinging to their scalps for dear life, a frame that's a little tubby, but more bony than it used to be. It's their personalities that have always struck me as most similar—warm and gregarious in public, but plenty happy to be left alone. They would get along very well, I think, if they had time today to do more than shake hands and say hello. They share the same ballbusting sense of humor, both of them from a generation that seemed to know how to do two things far better than my contemporaries: work and laugh. Their work ethic has rewarded them both. Doc and my dad have been very successful over long careers (my father, a stockbroker for forty years), and yet I get the sense that they are both unsure if the world played as fairly with them as they played with it. With all they got out of life, I think of them as two men who gave quite a bit more. The fact that they accept that with wisdom and with dignity—it's a quality otherwise known as class.

"Thanks for all you're doing for Tom boy," my dad says. "You've got him hitting it great."

"We're working on it. He's been working hard, we're trying to get him there. We'll see what happens," Doc says, sounding unconvinced, as expected.

I show Dad around Doc's bunker. To a guy who taught himself the game on a navy golf course, this all looks like pure science fiction—the lights set up like a television studio, cameras popping out of the walls at four different angles, the monitors planted in the floor beneath a player's feet. It looks and smells like golf, but a version of the game being played by a more highly evolved species.

We're poking around the gadgets, my father studying the awards covering the walls—the dozen plaques for best teacher in the state, they're stuck on the wall like they're there to cover nail holes, slightly crooked as if to suggest that Doc isn't terribly impressed with himself. Dad's taking it all in when, suddenly, I spot them.

Those beautiful cardboard boxes.

"Oh, yeah, almost forgot. It's good you came by today. Some of those boxes there are for you," Doc says over his shoulder. "Merry Christmas."

And in a flash I am in pajamas on Christmas morning once again, trembling at the top of the stairs. No matter that it's three days late, that I missed the lobster. Who needs Pollyanna when you have these long, gorgeous cardboard boxes?

Golf, as a pastime of choice, works with so many men for so many reasons. But one of the sources of golf addiction that cuts right across all levels of ability is that it satisfies the male need for stuff. Golf helps to quench our thirst for accumulating crap. Goodies, toys, playthings—we never get over them. You can have your little blue boxes, ladies. We'll take anything that arrives in big, brown, corrugated packages.

Mizuno had flown Doc and me up to Orlando a few weeks before, hosting us at the Faldo Institute, where Mizuno's master fitter, Bill Price, taught Doc and me the ins and outs of the Mizuno product and their club-fitting process. For a kid who didn't know the difference between casting and forging (cast clubheads come from metal poured into a mold, while forged clubs are pressed into shape, creating more consistent, lighter, stronger clubheads—forging is markedly more expensive and labor intensive, and it's Mizuno's calling card: They are the only major manufacturer with their own exclusive forging facility), this golfhead immersion has had me talking about lofts and lies and swing weights, the potential benefits of soft and hard-stepping your shafts (placing a three-iron or five-iron shaft into your four-iron to acquire a softer or harder flex). A few days after returning from Orlando with my club fitter's certificate (I actually became a certified Mizuno club fitter—can't have enough options, should I leave another one on the lip), Mizuno's top fitter in Florida, Dale Welker, comes over from Fort Lauderdale to measure me for my new set. Dale spends an hour on the range at Twin-Eagles fine-tuning my order form. We discovered my "specs" (they're all the rage, every good player's got them), which are two-up, plus a half.

Translation: My new irons would arrive with a two-degree up-right bend in the neck, and they would be one-half inch longer than standard. This would enable my clubhead, with my particular swing, to arrive at the ball flush and square. We decide on these specifications by hitting balls off a plastic board (called a lie board) until I found a club in the Mizuno fitting cart (a bin on wheels that holds three dozen six-irons of varying lengths and lies) that allowed me to scrape the board clean (not digging the toe or heel into the plastic) while making dead-center contact.

Why does any of it matter? Knowing your specs is sort of like knowing your jacket size. I have two suit coats I bought off the rack, size XL. They fit fine, they do the job when the occasion calls for them. But if you wear a suit every day, if you're serious about your business, then you get your duds tailored to your most precise measurements. The long and short of the multitudinous benefits of club-fitting (I could do a whole chapter on it, but I will spare you): more center hits, more sweet spot, more shots hit square off the grooves—it all equals lower golf scores. Standard clubs off the rack never killed anybody, but custom-fit clubs tighten up the golf course, making your mis-hits far more livable. If you're going to spend the money, might as well get a set that swings your way, rather than you trying to swing theirs.

Watching Dale tick off club after club on the order sheet—*You want a five wood? Yeah, we better order one. How many wedges do you need? Three enough? Better put you down for a Fli-Hi, too*—I just about wanted to throw my arms around him, hoist him on my shoulders, proclaim this day Dale Welker day. I'm woozy with the prospect of free golf clubs. Just like the tour pros, noses in the air as they pick over the best their company has to offer—and this isn't just any company. This is Mizuno, the number-one iron on tour for ten years, the Gulf Stream jet of the golf club world. If you're not good enough to know you should be playing them, then you're just not good enough yet. The Mizuno forged blade is the most ballsy club in the game—copied by almost every manufacturer in the game, beloved by Tiger Woods (he grew up playing Mizuno— funny how his current swooshy irons look an awful lot like classic Mizuno blades). Doc has worked with a number of manufacturers, and for a guy who wouldn't blow smoke up anybody's ass, he is un-apologetic in his praise of Mizuno.

"I don't see anyone in the business making equipment of this quality," he explains as he and my dad watch me rip into the boxes.

No time for scissors, my fingers make short work of the tape, and in a moment, I am spinning a gummy new grip in my fingers, a twinkly bauble of forged iron gleaming at the end of the shaft, pre-cisely an extra half-inch away.

"They might not have the muscle to throw a million bucks at every kid coming out of Q-school," Doc explains, "but I don't think any of the billion-dollar companies can touch their product."

I line up my new driver next to my new three-wood and my new MP-30 irons and my three new wedges, all on display around my new stand-bag with the fancy backpack strap. If I could possibly be disappointed, there's a twang of regret that they didn't send a big tour bag with my name stitched down the front. The monster staff bag is the coolest bit of eye-candy any player can possess—it screams, *I'm a pro, I'm part of a staff, I'm sponsored, my name is worth all this leather and all these stitches.*

But that whiff of disappointment passes, and I am giddy about my gorgeous new sack of sticks. The irons look like silver-tinted butter, the metal so clean and bright, you couldn't imagine ever throwing it at the turf. The look of a golf club, it couldn't matter more—golf is a game of appearances, and to saunter up to the tee box with a set of clubs from a company that doesn't sponsor just anybody, clubs your competitors know you can't just go buy at Dick's. Basically, my list of excuses just got a whole lot shorter.

I'm skipping out the door when Doc calls to ask me, "By the way, did you pass your PAT?"

"Didn't take it yet. Next week."

"Okay. Let me know. Got to get him playing tournaments," he says to my father. "Playing the game is a whole other thing than what we've been working on out here."

I f you think America is cranking out too many lawyers, there is a critical dearth of attorneys in comparison to the glut of young assistant professionals trying to find a place for themselves in golf, or, as those on the inside refer to it, the business.

An assistant pro position can be one of golf's great purgatories. In order to survive in the business, an assistant pro needs to someday graduate to a position as a class A head golf professional. A lack of good head pro positions forces a major bottleneck among seven-bucks-an-hour assistants—there are five apprentices for every head job, and that math doesn't change unless a developer plunks down $10 million for a new golf course, making room in the world for just one more head man.

With Florida's links' surplus, assistants have a fighting chance of moving up the ladder, but in the golf business as a whole, we are welcoming more young men into the business every year as the prospect of quality, lifelong golf employment shrinks. The PGA has rapidly expanded the number of PGM programs in the country over the last six years. The Professional Golf Management Program allows undergrads to not only earn a bachelor's degree over four and a half years, but to satisfy nearly all their PGA requirements as well. It's premed for golf pros, and the PGM program is likely coming to a campus near you. From 1975 to 1999, there were four PGM programs in the U.S.—Ferris State in Michigan, Penn State, Mississippi

State, and New Mexico State. Since just 1999, the PGA has added *thirteen new PGM programs* to the landscape of higher education, bringing the total to a bloated seventeen. I fully support the PGA doing more to bring qualified, educated, professional young men into the game—I have friends who have graduated from the PGM at Penn State, and they have gone on to have successful careers in the business. But unless there are thousands of empty pro shops out there yearning for golf pros, what is the purpose of growing the PGM program, aside from creating more business for the PGA?

Consider the fact that the majority of assistant golf pros do not even go through PGM college programs, that they probably graduate from the bag room to the pro shop and enter the PGA program after or in lieu of college (which ain't cheap—the cost of materials and "checkpoints" for the assistant working at your club is over $6,000). So you can understand that there are a lot of qualified young men being tossed into the business with nowhere to swim. If the PGA points to the number of professional job openings, don't buy it—most assistants parachute out of the business after just a few years. If there's enough slack, it's because so much of the industry soon sees the writing on the bag room wall and beats it for a job at the bank.

It might all be different if the available jobs were getting better, but from my rosy perspective, they're getting worse. The glut of qualified candidates has made career golf pros more interchangeable—to find themselves a serviceable head man, clubs can get away with offering less. And the spread of the corporate ownership of golf courses hasn't helped, either. Gone are the days of the 100K golf pro, the sole proprietor who had a piece of the club's range and the carts and the snack shop and the merchandise, who earned that piece by servicing and maintaining all of the above. Long gone are the erstwhile country club days when the golf *pro* actually owned the *pro* shop, and arrived is the era of the hourly wage golf employee, of margin-squeezing management in golf—*We're paying that button-pusher in the pro shop how much? Can't we get someone to run the outings for half that?* They probably can, and in my experience, often do.

Do not get me wrong—to earn your spot as a PGA club professional is a considerable accomplishment. The PGA golf professional is a career to be respected and esteemed. These are educated, professional men and women, dedicated to this game and their association—it ain't easy becoming one, you don't just sign up online. They have given much to the game, but more and more it seems like the life of the club pro has become just that, a life, not so much a living.

And yet, there is one more roadblock holding back the assistant golf pro, yet another boot planted firmly on his or her neck. This final obstacle has frozen thousands of golf careers in an extended club-cleaning limbo, while closing the coffin on thousands more altogether. The name of this not-so-silent killer?

P-A-T.

A seemingly innocuous combination of initials, these three letters placed in the right position strike terror in the hearts of third-assistants across the golfing land. The Playing Ability Test is a one-day, thirty-six-hole event held every few months in every PGA section around the country—and if you ever want to be a head pro, you've got to pass it. Contestants must shoot back-to-back rounds of 77 or better, depending on the host course's rating (difficulty). The *target score* is to finish no more then five strokes over par from the men's tees in consecutive rounds. Simple, no? For a golf pro, it should be like tying his shoes. But when it's your career, the hole gets a little tighter. When every bogey, every lip-out puts you that much closer to another year running carts, 76 seems like a near impossibility. If you can't make the number, you can't move up. Simple as that.

Plenty of players never do quite make the number, which ensures they will have earned their card to be back on next season's PAT Tour. You don't want to be too recognizable a face at a PAT, but some assistant pros have been grinding on the PAT circuit for twenty years. They say hello to all their friends, go out and shoot their 85-85, and head back to their pro shop to check the calendar for the next event on the schedule. If Samuel Beckett had played golf, the PAT Tour would have been his milieu.

You'd swear some guys are signing up for these tournaments as something to do on their day off. And some admittedly are—for the $65, it's not a bad price for thirty-six holes. Most of the players are grinding to fight their way out of the bag room, but there are plenty of players out there for a sixty-dollar suntan, knowing that unless Tiger Woods pops out of their butt and hits it for them, they are the deadest sort of money.

And at my first PAT, held at a barren public track in Fort Lauderdale (the tour is notorious for its mediocre venues), I am fortunate enough to meet a longtime PAT Tour legend. Lucky me, we end up in the same damn golf cart.

His name is Joe. But to be kind and to protect his identity, let's just call him Fucking Joe. FJ for short. In the portrait of our foursome, it's FJ who stands out like the proverbial turd beside the bowl. There's me, Mr. Mizuno, with pressed slacks and a newer, flatter belly. There's Mr. Titleist, twenty-two and sporting every piece of sponsors' gear he could find—I have no doubt he's wearing FootJoy underpants. And there's a Mr. TaylorMade, hat to match the bag to match the driver, fresh from high school, dishpan hands from wiping down clubs at the bag drop. And then there's our FJ. It would be only a slight exaggeration to say he has the build of an Oompa Loompa—he's taller, if only slightly, and his face isn't orange. Instead, he's got a bushy beard, a grinning prospector look about him, and he's dressed like *that guy* at the wedding, the one who shows up in an old Izod shirt and dock-siders. He's within PGA fashion bounds, but if you were ever serious about being a head golf pro, you would have taken FJ's whole outfit and set it ablaze. He's playing Pings—Ping Eye *Ones*, which is awesome if you're a club collector— they are important enough to place in a museum, but have no business still knocking around your golf bag today.

Listen to the everyman golfer playing the elitist—I judge FJ not as a snob, but as a fellow competitor. Looks matter at a tournament, they project care and confidence, preparation and experience. And it isn't like FJ is a mere shopping spree and a few sit-ups away—the man is pushing fifty years old. I originally pegged him for sixty, but all the dignity of old age escaped as soon as he opened his mouth. And not that fifty is elderly, but in PAT years, my twenty-nine years puts me in the senior-senior division. Our foursome looks like our embarrassing grandfather has taken us out for eighteen at his ol' golf club.

I'm as much a sucker for a jolly old man as anybody, but there is a fine line between *Look at that nice old man* and *Get out of my lane before I mow you down, you petrified piece of crap.* And from our first handshakes, FJ starts hop-scotching his way over that line.

The rest of us state our names, firm handshakes and *good lucks* all around with nary a smile between the three of us. While, for FJ, it's, "How the hell are you guys! What a day, huh? This is going to be a good time, man, I needed to get out of the shop. Man, are we going to tear it up today or what! Ha, course record, watch out! Ha, yeah right!" Chuckle chuckle, nudge nudge. And then the questions: "Where do you guys work? How many hours do you do in the shop? Get to teach any? I've been doing sixty hours a week, we do about sixty thousand rounds a year. Any of you guys do that many? Jeez, our place is a factory. Christ, PAT's the only time I get to play anymore!"

We start off the seventh hole (shotgun start so as to fit in a morning and afternoon round), and my first three-wood of the morning is high and deep and just over the palm tree I targeted on this short dog-leg right. I thought I would be more nervous, but your first PAT is probably your easiest, knowing that you are playing your first and potentially last while all around you are guys taking their third, fifth, tenth test—guys who have earned their first tee-jitters.

I take the approach, false as it may be, that I am the player to watch in this group. I don't think any of them would be impressed to hear about another win on the Michelob Light Tour, this time a 78 in the Raptor Bay Classic (it was a good 78, considering I played army golf down eighteen—left, right, left, right—and closed with a nine). It ain't exactly the Masters, but I did win $150 in the pro shop, which was good enough for three sleeves of ProV1s (balls remain my biggest playing expense—if only Mizuno made balls, if only I treated the ones in my possession more preciously!). While my win didn't exactly make it into *Golfweek*, I am nonetheless an unknown PAT quantity today. Working off a good month of rounds around par, I know the numbers are somewhere in my bag. Today's target of 153 (76 plus 77) should not be a problem, not when the pressure will only tighten my focus all the more.

I push a little seven-iron on my second shot, and I end up with a tricky short-sided bunker shot. I open up the blade on my new sixty-degree wedge, and the ball pops straight up like a champagne cork, landing soft and releasing down the slope toward the hole—but for a few more bumps in the Bermuda, I would have started my morning with a hole-out birdie. I take my tap-in, and as I have been given his scorecard to keep, I attempt to do the math of FJ's first hole in my head. I quickly realize there are plenty of ways that today is going to be tougher than anticipated.

It's not just that FJ can't hit it—which he can't. His opening drive plays hovercraft before nose-diving fifty yards in front of the tee box. He blames his knuckleball second shot on a bad lie—which is the truth, though you can't get too pissed at the greens crew for bad lies when you don't make it halfway to the fairway. For his third effort out of the rough, he whips out an old original Cobra Baffler with a clubface like he's been banging nails with it. I almost applaud at the sight of it, it's cool to go retro—but to FJ, the Baffler isn't an heirloom, it's his go-to club. Two more Bafflers and he's in the actual vicinity of the green.

It doesn't matter that he isn't a player. None of us really care that he has no shot of scoring near the target number, or that his golf swing is something an asshole friend would e-mail you a picture of to spoil your day. We try to look away when he swings, because bad golf can move through a foursome like smallpox, particularly when the stakes are heightened and the nerve endings are exposed.

Living in Florida, you build up a tolerance for golf pairings. I have played with more beginners and duffers in the last three months than I ever knew existed, but there is always fun to be had, always something to take from the experience, wisdom, conversation, a new friend. Unless they are behaving like FJ, who has the incurable, terminal golf disease of believing he is far better than he really is.

I know the sickness. I've been a Phillies fan since 1980. We are riding *If we only play up to our potential* to our franchise's 10,000th loss (most of any team in any professional sport, dating back to the inception of scorekeeping). FJ would make a good Phils general manager, but as far as a golfer goes, his is the most unpleasant breed to be around, the player who believes he's twenty shots better than he really is, who is openly convinced that the course, the wind, his clubs are conspiring against him, who cannot understand why they're having such a terrible day—day after day after day. It's the old Scottish story made new by David Owen: *I wish just once I could play my usual game.*

Joe is incredulous that his wild Baffler does not hold the green. "What's this green, goddamn cement? This is like my new patio. Let me tell you about this new patio I put in. . . ." On the next tee, it's, "My wife hits it furtha than that, damn fairways must have been underwater. Did it rain last night? I don't remember it raining." And on the greens—fifty years before, an architect allegedly designed eighteen greens with the sole intent of exposing FJ's outside-in putting stroke. "That ball can't go right." "That ball was in the goddamn heart!" "How does that ball stop?" Then: "How does that ball *not* stop?"

It's about seven holes into the round that FJ's tone changes, from aggressive accuser to a passive blamer.

"It's just not right. This course is not for me. One of these times they'll have a PAT at a course that's not all tricked up like this, somewhere that's a true test of golf, know what I mean?" FJ kicks back in his cart and fires up a long black cigar. "Might as well get a beer at the turn. No way I'm making the target today."

Already fourteen over after six, it's the most salient observation of the day. He flat-out couldn't give a shit by the back nine, lobbing balls into the water, four and five putting, which would all be fine, except that the further he eclipses the target number, the chattier FJ becomes. Not to be a sourpuss, but I am still trying to make a number. Amid all the wisecracks and dangerous swings, somehow I am still in this thing.

"Another triple, just to make sure I'm out of it. You must be doing okay." FJ looks at my scorecard. "Yeah, wow, you're doing great, keep it up. That's cool, man, good for you." He puffs his cigar and nods, satisfied, happy at least to be sitting in a cart with a partner who has a chance.

I grind through a few more stories about life at a Dade County resort course, getting a few bad breaks on the way in—a good drive runs through the fairway into the water on the last, and I come in with a four-over 76. Not bad for my first round of psuedo-professsional golf. I sign my card with a little phony disappointment, as if I really had a 59 in my bag. But inside, I am beaming to be among the vastly shrunken field of players who still have a shot.

I take a look at the five-dollar buffet in the clubhouse—hot dogs adrift in murky waters, a tray of gooey barbecue chicken wings. My nutritionist, Bonnie, would have wept. I suppose one could en-vision a less convenient menu item for a ten-minute break between rounds of tournament golf (Whole coconuts? Crab legs, maybe?), but I end up passing on the whole buffet, opting for the PowerBar in my bag. Bonnie warned me about keeping my blood sugar and energy level balanced, but my body just doesn't want to eat. I am nervous and excited, my swing is getting better on every hole. I sit in my cart and tap my feet, impatient for the next round, itching to go lower.

I am a little surprised when I see FJ return to the cart, less sur-prised to see that his fingernails are full of barbecue sauce. After his 108, I thought his next stop might be the parking lot. I had been sending him the vibe since 15—*'course, isn't that special, afternoon round's going to take forever, be great to be able to leave now, beat all that Miami traffic.* But he plops down next to me in the cart.

"108," he declares, smiling like it's the winning lotto number. "All I need to do is shoot 45 on this eighteen to pass." He laughs. "I'd leave right now, but if you don't post a score, they don't let you play next month," FJ explains, as if it would break his career streak. *Tiger's 142 consecutive made cuts, almost as impressive as FJ's*

174 consecutive PATs played. I suppose the rule about posting a 36-hole score is meant to scare the 108-shooters out of the process, but all it does is guarantee that the three of us get to watch a full afternoon of hit, puff, and giggle.

It is amazing how quietly my afternoon eighteen starts to slip away from me. There are no great blow-ups, no huge numbers, it just starts to fall through my fingers until, on the eighteenth green, I am not holding on at all, just waving the day good-bye. I can't point to one hole that turned the afternoon into 81. I can't pin down that one big mistake, promise myself it will never happen again. I just made too many bogeys. Too many little putts I had taken for granted, too many yardages that I didn't think enough about, too many of the same old mistakes—chunky irons, blocked drives, stubby chips—mistakes I had worked out of my system, eradicating them with practice balls by the thousand, still, in letting my mind wander for just a few holes, they all came rushing back to the party, ready to scribble all over my scorecard.

I am on my way back across Alligator Alley, contemplating stopping for a roadie (the only consolation for shit golf—a twenty-four-ounce can), when the cell phone rings, and *Jim Suttie* pops up on the screen.

"Hello, Tom. Did you pass?"

I don't think I ever actually say no, though that would have been the most sensible approach. Instead, I start talking about how thirty-six holes is a lot for one day, in the heat, in slacks, with a stomach grumbling from half a PowerBar. I should have eaten a lunch, drunk more water, should have kept my chemistry balanced, should have never let my mind stop caring. I talk about lip-outs and patchy fairways, how it wasn't a course for scoring. It wasn't me, I assure Doc. It wasn't my swing. If I had played my game, I could have shot that number in my sleep.

I bitch about my pairing and my cart and my stomach and the

damn superintendent, "How that guy has a job—I wouldn't let him water my lawn."

I go on like that for a while until I realize who I sound like.

I'll see my new friend next month, at the next stop on the PAT tour. I'll know a few more people this time, and I'll be sure to pack a lunch. I wonder if Joe will bring one of those cigars for me.

I was once told a story about a hotshot rookie on the PGA Tour, Johnny all-American. Back in the 80s, Johnny was amateur champion this, college champion that. He came out to his first tour event, and on the driving range he explained to one of the reporters that he wasn't nervous at all. He had won every tournament he'd ever tied his shoes for. He was all-American, for goodness' sakes, why wouldn't he be a smash on the PGA Tour?

As the story was told to me, it was Craig Stadler who wandered over to where the rookie was hitting balls and gave the young man a few quiet words of advice.

"You see the guy next to you? And the guy next to him? Every one of them, all-Americans. There's an NCAA champion, a U.S. Amateur champion, a British Open champion—hell, some of these caddies were all-American. So just so you know, nobody here gives a damn if you're all-American, or if you even went to college at all. All anybody here wants to know is," Stadler reportedly said, "can you play stick?"

I was not all-American. Didn't even make the college team. But week by week I am convincing myself—whether I can play stick, or whether I can play at playing stick—if I keep working, I might have enough time to persuade myself that there's very little difference between the two.

I'm home on the range, at my usual spot on the far end, feeling pretty good about myself as I work my way up through my bag to my driver, which, if I were the Boston Pops, would be the *1812 Overture* of my practice routine. A few of my neighbors from Spring Run stop by to watch me crank floaters out into the deep end of the aqua range. I have made some good friends over the past months—I've joined the Men's Association, I pop in on the Wednesday Happy Hour (free apps, I can't afford not to). I'm not *that young guy renter* anymore, I'm *Tom from building nine, spends more time on the range than Vijay Singh*. It's easy to look at a gated golf community and build a decent stand-up routine about geriatrics, but I have met some tremendous people in Bonita Springs who have cooked me dinners, invited me into their homes, treated me like one of the guys though I was years younger than any of their children. Some would stop by my end of the range to have a look, particularly when the hot face on my Mizuno driver sounds like I'm smooshing the float out of these floaters.

Making the swing changes has been a war of attrition. Each stop Doc and I take forward, a new issue emerges, a new battle begins behind us, on turf we had already crossed. My swinging too far from the inside is soon swinging too far outside the line. Pushing the clubhead away overcorrects into my yanking the club inside. Trying to keep my right elbow connected to my golf swing has developed a shortish, abbreviated backswing. After a big correction, there's a few weeks where I'm striping it perfect, then the swing thought that works becomes the swing thought exaggerated, and I need a new dose of insight, a new drill to fill up the hours on the range.

Not that I mind. Of all the sleepy Florida routines everywhere I look, mine is the lamest of them all—on the big calendar in my condo, there's no drinks at the pool on Thursdays, no Monday morning skins game. Just golf balls and sunblock and blisters.

From dawn to lunch, from lunch to dawn, it's the same satisfying setup on a flat stretch of driving range somewhere: Prop up the bright blue Mizuno bag on its legs, towel wet on one end (only one end, always), hanging off the end of my clubs, carefully, like the flag of my particular golf nation. And not a beach towel, or the souvenir towel from the country club, but the towels the sticks carry, plain white towels too small for a good shower but perfect for a caddy, the sort found in health clubs and one-star motels, which is handy as that is where most sticks have made their reservations. (Confession to Motel 6: I shamelessly pillaged your linen supply this year. I hope someday I can repay the favor.)

I work my way up from sand wedge, minimum fifty balls with each club. I understand training philosophies where you hit balls only until you're loose or confident, or you quit as soon as you've hit a few good ones in a row. While I know the staff at Spring Run wishes that were my particular mind-set, it's not the philosophy I am working with here. I am attempting to integrate major swing changes, I have cracked open the back of the clock and ripped out all the sprockets. To put it back together the right way, to make the alterations automatic, there is no substitute for an overwhelming onslaught of muscle repetition.

Every club in the bag gets its turn, and I pause between irons to wipe down the soft metal faces, scrubbing the grooves until I can see the corners of each channel, then fanning my clubs around my bag to dry, a spread of silver tools gleaming in the Florida sun. Slow, methodical, I work through the buckets, no rush to my work at all. I'll be here all day. All week. And never in any of it (or as little as absolutely possible) am I hitting a golf ball just to be hitting a golf ball. I work my drills, work my routine—pick a real target, as specific as the particular branch on a palm tree, use a board to align myself and envision each shot like it is happening on the golf course. Deliberate. Intent. Again. And again.

In October, my body could hardly stand in good posture for fifteen seconds without the piano strings in my lower back popping. Now, good golf posture—butt out, weight in my arches, chin up, back and neck in perfect line—it's become my fetal position. I sleep in good golf posture. In line at a restaurant, I'm standing in good golf posture. Thanks to Doc's camera and Mike's distaste for whining, I have at least fully mastered one part of the golf swing: the look. It's amazing how tightening your abdomen can pull your body into a balanced, athletic position, that strength in your core can make your hands and arms and shoulders feel effortless, uninvolved almost. The only muscles I think about over the golf ball are in my gut. Considering the role my belly previously played in my golf swing, that of a temporary malt beverage storage facility, it is a whole new way of thinking about the golf swing.

Every once in a while I wander over to the ice machine for another tall cup of water, sauntering back along the range, small-talking with new friends about how they played in the Wednesday better-ball, then back down to my spot where the portrait is waiting— the bag, the towel, the forged blades shining like mirrors, and the divots—a thin, square patch of earth exhumed with surgical precision. A player is at work here, it seems to me. Satisfied, I enjoy a cool drink and check the messages on my cell phone, finding one from Padraig Mahoon.

"Hey, Coinage, your old buddy Paddy here. Listen, I heard you shot a 72 with Garvin—just wanted to check in how many mulligans it was taking you to shoot even par these days. All right, now give us a call, don't go being a stranger."

When I call back, Paddy asks me where I am.

"Where do you think? Wasn't Jesus in the temple? I'm at the driving range."

"And that's where Jesus would have been if he'd had as wicked a golf swing as yourself." Paddy laughs to himself for eleven seconds of my phone time, then continues, "So did you pass the PAT?"

"How did you know I took the PAT?"

"Read about it in *Golf Digest*." More laughter, another eight seconds wasted on my calling plan. "For fuck's sake, did you pass or what?"

"Came close. Made the target score the first round. . . ."

"Someday, Coinage—someday you'll be able to keep it up with the likes of me, the *class-A PGA Professional*," he says, with an extra dollop of Galway brogue. "And you better be getting your act together because I'm looking at flights here, and there's a cheap one this weekend. Think I'll be making a visit to come down and check up on you. You didn't have any plans, did you?"

"*This* weekend?"

"The flight comes in at 8:30 and, like, don't be making me take any taxi."

In the forty-eight hours Padraig Mahoon was in Naples, I developed the shanks, lost two fresh sleeves of Titleists, shot my highest score in three months, and had my first cast of Irish flu since moving to Florida.

The first round of our thirty-six-hole match started early Saturday morning at Spring Run, after a Friday evening of making Padraig sick with envy over my new Mizunos. I had all my sticks tweaked at Shane's Golf in Naples in anticipation of Paddy's arrival. Shane bent the irons a few degrees stronger, compensating for my high ball flight; as my bunker play was getting more precise, we took a little bounce off my wedges; we stuck new shafts in my driver and three-wood according to the numbers Shane's launch monitor was spitting out (I didn't even know there was such thing as frequency in a golf shaft, but when Shane stuck my three-wood in a vise and plucked the shaft like a guitar string, a read-out said my stiff steel shaft was actually suited to my father's swing speed). Now every club in my bag was truly custom, tweaked within fractions of a degree to the particulars of my golf swing.

"So when I still kick your ass," Paddy says, "do you have to write an apology to Mizuno *and* this Shane character, then?"

By the time Paddy left the Spring Run pro shop that Saturday morning, the shy Irishman knew every one of the assistants by first name, had carte blanche for a day of free golf, and was already of the opinion that "Allyson better get down here and give a look at that girl in the pro shop. Jaysus, she was eyeing you up you like you were made of chocolate."

Twenty minutes into the first round and I have gone birdie-birdie-birdie to Paddy's par-par-par. I can tell he's shocked by the fact that he's not talking. Then on the fourth tee, he starts in on his low-murmuring BBC golf analysis: "First time in his life's he's been three under par, Rossie. You've got to wonder if he can keep this up all day."

"Nice. Keep talking to yourself," I tell Paddy, as I embark upon the first of my back-to-back bogeys.

We throw bogeys and birdies at each other for most of the morning, and though it kills Paddy to admit it, he's a little impressed—as well as downright stunned by the fact that my drives aren't stopping to wave as they soar past his. He would never say anything, but Peter Allis isn't afraid to address it: "Looks like a new man out here, Rossie. Don't know where all this new muscle came from all of a sudden. That driver there looks a shade suspicious, I'd say. The R&A might like to have a peek into that bag after the round."

I finish the morning match up two holes, but there is trouble brewing. Paddy is shaking off the winter cobwebs, and while his drives aren't going to keep up with mine, with irons in our hands,

"The advantage seems to have shifted to the able Paddy Mahoon, don't you think, Rossie?"

It's TwinEagles for round two, and thankfully Doc is on the road with the team from the Florida Gulf Coast or I would have never gotten Paddy out of his studio. We both shoot one over on the front nine, and the dogfight continues until I lose a drive in the left weeds on fifteen. Paddy thinks about helping me look for it—he gets up, takes a lap around the cart, then sits back down. "I don't see it. You better play your provisional."

He's one down when we come to fifteen, a bite-off-what-you-want par four with a green surrounded by water. I am standing over the perfect drive, a hundred yards to the pin, sand wedge in my hands. I look at the cart and see Paddy smile, propping his feet up on the dash.

"Wow, Rossie, he's got the wedge out. You know it's not the strongest club in the bag for young Tom Coyne. But he can't hit the driver here, no, he's going to have to show some touch. You can't forget about that water. This would be a tough enough shot for a lot of players. . . ."

"Would you shut the fuck up?"

"Oh, Rossie, he'll be hearing from the tour office for that one, no doubt. You'd have to say the young man is rattled. . . ."

You hear the stories about Tiger's dad lobbing golf balls at him while Tiger was practicing in order to teach his son focus. I think I would have preferred my dad hurl golf baseballs at my nuts than have Paddy lobbing his joke of the week. In terms of how we respond to our focus training—again, no reason to confuse me with Tiger Woods—my sand wedge on fifteen goes after the turf like I am digging for potatoes. I watch my ball leave the earth with all the force of a baby's burp, and all that remains to be decided is which is going farther: the ball, or the divot that looks like a bath mat flipping end over end through the air. It's a tight contest, but the ball out-strecthes the turf, just reaching the water's edge and trickling into the drink, inches from where we saw a lazy brown gator slip into the water a few minutes before.

The entire golf cart is jiggling with laughter. And yet, that first wet Titleist would turn out to be quite the trendsetter for its other friends from the sleeve. As if sending in a search party to hunt for the first ball, I send two more sand wedges chasing after it—one blade-skinny, followed by a chunky monkey—before finally knocking one up to the green, four feet away from the hole. Of course I make the putt for smooth nine—I rarely miss a short one for nine—and we go to the sixteenth, cart still shaking with muffled Irish laughter, our match all square.

We halve sixteen with pars, and on seventeen, Paddy drains a bomb with his new Bobby Grace long putter to make an improbable birdie and go up by one. Eighteen at TwinEagles is perhaps the best hole on the course, a long blind driving hole that bends left, then back right to a green that is goddamn déjà vu, surrounded by water. Once again I'm standing over a perfect drive in the fairway. This time, a seven-iron in my hands. I step up to the ball. Silence. Nothing from Paddy. The quiet is blaring.

I step away, breathe deep, spin the club in my fingers. I step up to the ball again, "Don't even, fucker," I say without looking up, settling my clubface in behind my golf ball.

And it comes, just more than a whisper. "Rossie, you can only imagine what's going through this young lad's head. . . ."

"Jesus, you shoulda seen him. Strangers in the pub were coming up to him, asking if he was all right. He looked like somebody stole all his Christmas presents."

It is unusual to see someone so pleased at telling a story about someone being so depressed. Paddy relays the events of the previous day to his wife as I drive him to the airport, happy for the visitor but not crazy about this morning's headache.

"You've improved, Coinage. No doubt about that," Paddy tells me with a pat on the back as I pull his golf bag out of the trunk. "You're a lot more serious about your game, I can tell. You are on the right track. But just remember, no matter how good you get, you can't beat old Paddy boy."

The weekend was a step back. But maybe it was also a necessary break, perhaps a little bit of a wake-up call. If I can't beat my old golf pro from home who hadn't picked up a club in four months, how was I going to fare come October? But I can't control next October, all I can control is today. All I can do is go out and earn my .036.

Up until our Saturday fun, I had been well outpacing 1/28th of a stroke a day. I keep every stat from every round of golf on my computer. Doc gave me a program called Aviary Golf Software, and may I wholeheartedly recommend it for the golfhead in your life—the program tracks your scores, hole by hole, and spits out your stats like you're a real tour pro. Putts, saves, driving distance—but most valuably, it shows you which holes you score best on, which clubs off the tee yield the most birdies, which clubs are most likely to hit the fairway and, if they don't, what are the percentages that they will miss right or miss left. It takes some time to input your data, but I've gotten pretty slick with it—and as most golfers can recall the four-iron they hit seven years ago on the sixth tee of their home course, recalling club selection and results after a round is easier than it sounds. If a computer can help me get better, if it can help me pick the right club off the tee, if it can help me put the driver back when I don't need it, or tell me which club has the best chance of ending up on the other side of those white stakes—it's nerdy and a little neurotic, but you can't build confidence if you don't trust your numbers.

Judging by Aviary, my fairways, greens, putts/round, birdies/round have all improved, some quite dramatically—my fairways and greens are only one or two below the tour average. And on the course, it has shown. I've gotten it to three-under on more than one occasion, I've made four birdies on one side (capped off with a quadruple bogey eight). My birdies and stats and yardages are all up, but I can't take a spreadsheet to the golf course and ask it to hit the ball. I can't take Doc to Body Balance and impress him by benching fifty-pound dumbbells, by doing twenty dead-bugs (one of Mike's abdomen torture techniques) when in October I could hardly squeeze out five. I can tell my coach that I'm improving, but until I show it to him on the course, I am an albatross lurking around the driving range—and I don't mean a double-eagle, I mean the student who takes the most time but returns the fewest results.

I wasn't scheduled for another checkup until next week, but on Monday night Doc calls me and tells me to come out to the center tomorrow afternoon.

"We've got to make sure you're improving," he says, bluntly. "I want to make sure you're not getting worse."

Jack Nicklaus once told his father that playing in front of him made him nervous. His father's response was, "Get used to it." His son was going to play in front of all sorts of people, and Dad was coming along for the whole wonderful ride. To play at the next level, I have to seek attention, I have to covet critics and spectators, not slink off to where I'll never have to worry about showing anybody my swing. So I tell myself that this is my opportunity to show Dr. Suttie the player I was instead of taking my usual approach, trying to hide the player I wasn't.

We head out to the first tee, Doc, the camera, and me—Doc and the camera is redundant, they are essentially one entity (Kubrick and Kurosawa combined didn't shoot as much film). On the tee we run into one of the cart boys, twenty-two years old, blond and tan

Chad from the Midwest, newly arrived in Florida for the season, looking to drum up sponsors for next year's Golden Bear Tour. He's got his Callaway tour bag, large and impractical for a cart-runner, "Chad Jones" stitched down the front. He's loosening up, slow and cocky, taking twelve too many practice swings. I've noticed Doc has been helping Chad from time to time—he stops by after his shifts for a quick lesson, during which he usually spends more time talking than Doc does. I've never said a word to Chad and I think he's pretty much a grade-A douche bag. I dig the club scrubbers, I used to be one, I might yet be if the golf thing doesn't pan out—but a club scrubber with tour attitude, I am not a big fan. So when Doc asks Chad to join us for my playing lesson, I nod with the phoniest golf smile I can muster.

"Tom's a writer," Doc explains. He points this fact out to most of the pros who hang around his studio, quick to explain that I'm a golf-writer, not a golf-golfer. *He might look the part, but he's not a pro. It's not my fault he hits everything dead right.* "Tom's spending a year to see if he can play at the next level. He's going to tell the world all about how I screwed up his swing."

Chad smiles and nods without hearing a word of what Doc said.

As Chad addresses his ball, Doc's camera angled on him from behind, Chad starts with enough commentary for a crew from the Golf Channel. "What I'm trying to do here is play a little cut off the left bunker. The cut is my safe shot. If I block it a little, I'll have plenty of fairway to work with. I don't need driver here, but with all that room out there, why not just tee it high, and let it fly?"

He bangs three drives out into the fairway, providing post-game analysis of each pass: "That was my three-quarter swing. Now I'll try to hit it a little higher; this is how I'd hit it if the fan was on" (that's douche-bag speak for "downwind").

Chad barely steps aside far enough to allow me some space on his tee box. I pop a sheepish driver out toward the fairway that ends up tailing into a fairway bunker. I get into our cart and listen to what Doc thinks is right about Chad's swing.

"That's a pretty solid golf swing," he tells me. "This will be good for you. You need to play with better players. You can learn from him."

Just to ensure that I do indeed learn from him, Chad commences a running commentary on *my* game—this twenty-two-year-old, crashing at my bud's place, dropped-out-of-school-to-clean-out-golf-carts wanker—just because he's parred the first three holes (as have I, though no one seems to notice), he feels qualified to stand behind me while I'm chipping the ball and explain, "I like to get the ball on the ground and get it running. I don't hardly ever use my sixty-degree wedge," as if I should take that as a cue to turn around and whip my lob wedge into the pond. On the green, Chad is of the opinion that my putting stroke "feels rushed. It's not tour tempo," and that's before he looks at my setup on the tee and accuses me of having the alignment of a Rent-A-Wreck. I keep looking to Doc, waiting for my attorney to object, but for the most part he nods about what future-tour-great Chad Jones has to say about the golf swing.

Chad makes a bogey on the fifth hole, and I make a par, giving me the honor on the next tee, a potentially awkward scenario that I am rather looking forward to. When we get to six, and when he steps up to hit before me, I stop him.

"Hey, Chad, what did you make back there?"

"Bogey."

"I had par."

"Sorry," he says, plucking his tee out of the ground. "Didn't think it mattered."

And it didn't, not for nine holes of practice golf. But for our own little match, it was key. Golf is the greatest game in that, for all its pastoral trappings and delicate facades, there can be so much spit boiling just beneath the surface. One polite question—what did you have on the last?—that translated to: *Hey, asshole, get the hell out of my way before I take this six-iron to that shit-eating grin of yours.*

I unsheathe my Mizuno hammer and I pound the ball like I'm making Titleist scaloppine. You can almost hear my ball whisper *oh no* as my clubface catches it hard and center, 335 yards, a good lob wedge past Chad's drive—that is, if he would ever stoop to use one.

There was no scorecard from that afternoon. It was practice, sometimes we hit a second ball, then a third so that Doc's camera could catch us from front, back, behind. And maybe because there was no scorecard that day, I flat-out outplayed future tour superstar Chad Jones. Maybe it was because there were no numbers to think about, no scores to get wrapped up in, that I just went out and hit golf shots, one after another, after another. I don't know if I would have carded a smaller number, we may have very well tied for the nine holes, but if you watched the video afterward, you might have gotten the golf-writer and the golf-superstar all mixed up.

But don't take my opinion for it.

Thus far, compliments from Dr. Suttie had pertained almost exclusively to my writing—I help him with his articles, and he is a big fan of the catchy titles I slap at the top of his pieces. But in the ninth fairway, I am standing over my Titleist with an eight-iron in my hands, Dr. Suttie set up behind me to get the perfect camera angle, straight down the target line. I'm an average iron-player, I am not nearly as comfortable with a simple eight-iron as I need to be, but I stand steady over the golf ball, and I slowly turn the club away.

Before it even happens, I know precisely what is going to happen—as the clubhead backs away from the golf ball, I am suddenly clairvoyant, I can see everything about the next three seconds of my life. *This is going to be a perfect golf shot.* A part of my body that is far away from my mind has decided that I am going to hit a golf ball the way it was intended to be hit. I feel my body fold into the positions Doc has been drilling into my golf swing: ninety-degree shoulder turn, ninety-degree right-elbow hinge, ninety-degree wrist cock (in the article, I called it 90 + 90 + 90 = 10 more yards).

I can see my silhouette as if framed in Doc's lens. It is a picture he has printed out for me a dozen times, that I've pasted all over my condo, the first thing I see in the morning and the last thing at night, that grainy photograph of myself frozen at the top of a perfect backswing, perfect because Dr. Jim Suttie is standing next to me in the picture, holding my hands and clubface in the perfect power position.

And as if he just stepped back out of that picture, as if time unfroze and started from that spot, I drop the club and gently turn my right side toward my target. I feel the clubhead hanging behind my hands, clipping the dirt with hard, crisp, contact, so perfect, I hardly feel involved at all.

I can tell from the divot, that perfect slice of bacon flopping end over end straight away from me—I know it's going to be tight. The ball lands next to the pin, hops once, and grabs the grass not ten inches from its home.

"Tom Coyne, that was an absolutely perfect golf swing."

At least with Doc, when the compliments do come, there's a pretty good chance you've caught it on tape.

On the drive home from TwinEagles, I reward myself with Outback takeout. This afternoon, I turned a corner. I am not worried about what these young bucks think about me. I think they should perhaps start worrying what I'm thinking about them.

This is why I came down here, to immerse myself, to get so intimate with the game, to maybe have just a few of those absolutely perfect moments. Leaving Allyson, burning through my savings in just a few short months—this was the point, to arrive at a place where I feel more comfortable swinging a golf club than walking down the street.

I think I'm there. I know I'm there. Compared to Christmas Eve, the filet tonight is so much sweeter.

I go to sleep that evening, feeling as satisfied as I had been my entire time in Florida. But it's very early the next morning when I wake up with an aching in my jaw, like I'd been sucker-punched in my sleep. By the afternoon, there's a swelling below my ear, tender, the size of (what else) a golf ball. The doctor at the clinic can't tell me what it is.

"I think we can rule out a tumor. But if it doesn't go away . . ."

He recommends a specialist, and when it doesn't go away, the specialist recommends a CAT scan.

In what was supposed to be a year without excuses, this is one I never considered. Forty-eight hours from that absolutely perfect golf swing, and I don't care if I ever pick up a golf club again.

PART THREE

The Internet has a brutal bedside manner.

It was no surprise I had lost an extra ten pounds in two weeks—do a Google search regarding your "swollen gland" and see if you can still eat. The particular gland my ENT (ear, nose, and throat doctor) pinpointed as the problem, the parotid gland—roughly between your ear and the corner of your jaw—is apparently a hotbed for nonspecific maladies. My Internet research has made it perfectly clear that I either have cancer, HIV, or cat scratch fever. And there's an outside chance that the corner of my face was swollen because of an infection in my salivary gland brought on by dehydration exacerbated by exercise, humidity, and weight loss, an infection that certainly would be erased with a hefty round of antibiotics. But when the antibiotics do absolutely nothing, and the second round of antibiotics does nothing, it's back to the Internet, calculating my life expectancy in html.

A little knowledge is a dangerous thing, and in terms of medicine, that's all the Internet seems able to provide. A whiff of science, combined with far too much time alone—I spent two weeks in the condo, alone, watching *The Price Is Right,* waiting for the golf ball on the side of my face to deflate, my paranoia breeding like mold on a lost sandwhich.

HIV seemed a stretch, but after two weeks alone with your thoughts, was it, really? My contracting AIDS would be a minor medical miracle. (SPOILER WARNING FOR CATHOLIC PARENTS: SKIP AHEAD TO NEXT PARAGRAPH.) Not that I have been a perfect saint in my first twenty-nine years, but trust me, my romantic history is a relatively short and neurotically safe one. If I have AIDS, someone would have had to slip it into my drink . . . but with so much time alone to wonder . . . What about the glasses in that sticky nightclub back in Cancún? What about that wet toilet seat I sat on in Manhattan? Or that night in Key West, with the cross-dressing bartender who kept pouring me free margaritas? If I had a job, if I were among friends, if Allyson had been there and I could think about something else, then I wouldn't have sat there taking inventory of every germ-swapping encounter of my last twenty-nine years, my mind racing off to my early death every seven minutes.

I take a blood test, and this greatest, perhaps most irrational worry comes back clear. But a CAT scan comes back inconclusive. A doctor starts talking about surgery. One afternoon in his office, he uses the expression "could be a deadly tumor" as if he's giving me a weather forecast.

I had never been sick before—"sick" meaning we-don't-know-what-it-is-let's-wait-for-the-tests-to-come-back sick. And as I sat around the condo sucking on Jolly Ranchers by the dozen (supposed to help loosen up the gland), I envision myself as part of this sad, stark, brutally honest collection of folks. The sick people's club.

It's a segment of society I would get to know better over the next month, hopping between specialists and radiology labs, sitting in waiting rooms and thinking, *Wow, these people, some of these people are really sick. I can't be one of these people. Can I be one of these people?* Waiting among so many brave souls, mothers and fathers and children just going through the daily routine of a sick person, picking up their new films and their new prescriptions, waiting for their next monthly appointment to hear if it's life or if it's death—there's a whole other world out there full of people who will actually *die*. Some people know it for years, some for a few seconds, but I had made it through twenty-nine years convinced I might never have to worry about it, that they would have a cure for death by the time I got to around to it. I might have nothing more than a nasty infection, but I realize that the sick and dying people, they're not the exception. Theirs isn't the exclusive club. They're the rule. They're the everybody. Those of us running around worried about our credit cards, dinner reservations, numbers on a scorecard—we're the weird little minority.

My being alone in Florida made these sorts of realizations all the more dramatic, revelations that varied from terror-sweats at three A.M., to lungs full of a sun and serenity, a *life is beautiful* epiphany, knowing that I'd had a great ride and could stomach any conclusion. But most of the time, I was just pretty scared. Take away my routines and my golf clubs, I became sharply aware of my surroundings, and exactly where I wasn't.

And one evening, I decided that I didn't want to not have control of the situation anymore. I didn't want to sit around waiting to get better, begging this little goblin on the side of my neck to go away, and I might have been risking my year and my chance and my one true shot, but I had to do something, anything, to feel like I was confronting the situation instead of playing doctor on the fucking Internet. So I packed up the entire condominium in forty-five minutes—golf shirts and shorts stuffed into trash bags, clubs and books and the computer mashed into the backseat, the pictures and scorecards and clippings all torn off the walls in a few furious seconds, nothing left but a dirty bathroom and a wall of mirrors, all covered with tape and glue.

I called and booked a trip home, with two months still left on the lease. A dozen more sessions with Mike, a good half-dozen lessons left with Doc—I didn't bother wiping the calendar clean before I tossed it into the Dumpster.

I was not surprised when Allyson said she wasn't going to let me make the trip home myself. And of course I let her fly down to accompany me on the ride back home—first, she had already booked the ticket to Florida before I decided to leave. And nothing morphs a proud and independent man into a needy thumb-sucker quicker than a little undiagnosed illness.

We made our way home, both of us not quite sure how we had found ourselves back on this Auto Train under such circumstances—it was such a departure from the plan, such a twist on our sunny expectations. The twenty-hour trip was marked mostly by my obsessively touching my face as I pondered my three weeks' worth of *Web*MD med school (80 percent of parotid tumors are benign; if it was malignant wouldn't it have become more painful instead of less?; would a tumor really sprout up overnight?), while Allyson begs me to stop touching and checking my face. It seemed as if the new antibiotic (my third round, this one a little more powerful) was having an effect on the lump, but it was impossible to tell—any change was imperceptible, seeing as we were staring at it around the clock.

I had imagined my triumphant re-emergence from Florida in strokes of Napoleonic grandeur. After six months in a golf-and-fitness cloister, I would return home as if on the back of an elephant, announced by trumpeters, a reborn scratch handicap with an eighteen-year-old's waistline. Friends would not recognize me through all my muscle; my command of the golf ball would make all the doubters beg my forgiveness, force them to look with loathing on their own unremarkable lives. With each dramatic entrance— into the pub, into the old pro shop, onto the beach at the Jersey

Shore—the jaws would drop like on some television makeover. *Hear ye, all you ex-girlfriends and erstwhile opponents, Tom Coyne is dead, long live Tom Coyne!*

And none of that happened. One morning I was in Florida, the next morning I had slipped into my hometown without telling anyone, embarrassed by the circumstances. And I didn't go straight to the country club or to my house, as I had hoped. I didn't call the fellas and tell them to meet me down at Maggie's. I called a hospital to schedule another CAT scan, and I stopped in to see my family doctor, who gave me my first full physical since high school—blood, heart, the works—and referred me to yet another ENT, who went from telling me that he wouldn't have even bothered asking for a CAT scan if I'd come to him first, to mentioning that I could very well have a malignant tumor on the edge of my face—but probably not.

The day I arrived home, ironically, my mom was on her way to visit friends in Fort Myers, so the next few days were just me and Dad around the house. He was excited to have me back, not nearly as shaken by my predicament as I was. And why would he be? He had been through prostate cancer, his stock market had gone to shit again, and my oldest brother's illness was daily inching his son closer to death. My coming home with a bump on my neck—even if it turned out serious, deadly maybe—would never be more than another thing we needed to accept. Money. Family. Cancer. Everyday life threw something at my dad that he probably didn't think he could handle, until he just looked it in the eye and said, *Okay. I'll handle it.*

When my dad first saw my neck, he said, "That little thing got you all shaken up? Mosquito bite."

If it didn't worry him, the less it worried me, and finally, after three weeks of antibiotics, the swelling went away, nearly overnight. The next CAT scan was again "inconclusive." There was something in my gland, but it was still too swollen to tell, maybe a mass, a cyst—whatever it was, it had gotten smaller since the last scan, a good sign, I was told. They didn't see a tumor, they didn't *not* see a tumor. Verdict: another CAT scan in three months, just to be sure. Just enough to give me something to think about as I walk down the fairway, wondering if that last drive stayed in bounds—*and by the way, that might still be a tumor you feel clicking in your jaw, don't forget about that date with the radiologist you're looking forward to.*

I attempt to transport my Florida routine to Philadelphia in March, with almost zero success. There is no Mike Willett here, no Doc Suttie, no tapes to study at night. There are friends who don't know the leaves I have turned over, a girlfriend who supports my golf but is happy to have a partner again for movies, dinners, a Sunday afternoon at the mall. There is no focus here. I'm back to paying for range balls; the courses are expensive and soggy and full of temporary winter greens. Forced to work at the rubber range, I spend forty bucks for three hundred balls—half the number I would have hit during a full day's work at Spring Run. And playing in the cold, with every ache in my jaw, every twinge in my neck, I get that shot of fear that pulls the breath right out of me—*what's wrong with me, what if something is really wrong with me?* I'm thinking about the meaning of "inconclusive" while I'm trying to remember what Dr. Suttie said about the angle of my right forearm, and I want to leave my clubs here for somebody else, somebody who wants them, because I cannot do this this way—not without my coaches and the cameras, not with no one to tell me where the hell I'm headed.

March, and I am uncommitted. Halfway there, and I'm already gone.

I won't be all golf. I cannot be all golf, not anymore. I have tried, and in the end, the game has proven itself to be just that—sticks and balls, a piece of paper to tally the score, a four-hour diversion and a pricy one at that. I am going to hit balls when I can, sneak out for eighteen when I get the chance and possess the means, but I am going to take Sunday afternoon off, and I'm going to go to the mall and sit in the bookstore and walk through Sears and look at stainless-steel appliances and wonder about a house we might someday own. I'm going to be that guy, ordinary and comfortable and far too intelligent to chance anything more on a proposition with such shit odds. In the disinfected air of a doctor's waiting room, golf dreams are easily forgotten.

On another cloudy Tuesday, I come home from the rubber range, having hit a hundred thoughtless balls out of sheer obligation. I didn't stretch that morning, I haven't done a sit-up in almost a month. In my limbo of either do this thing or don't, don't is making a better argument with every rainy day.

Until I step onto the back porch and find a package waiting for me. It's a huge cardboard box stood up on end. I find some scissors in the kitchen and I take my time slicing the tape, folding back the cardboard flaps. I reach inside the box and lift it out, and there it is—the most beautiful item to ever occupy a space in our kitchen, Christmas Eve lobsters included—standing there, beefy and balanced, all blue and white and turquoise leather. It was the Mizuno tour bag, the one they sent to their guys on the PGA Tour, a golf bag big enough to take a nap in. And stitched down the front panel, big white letters on blue, the name of their latest and most dedicated staff member.

The rubber range just wasn't going to cut it, not for a teammate of Luke Donald's.

By this point, the stewards on the Auto Train knew me by name. I had one month left on my lease, I had six sessions left with Mike, and I knew Doc would crank it up for the end of my time in Florida. I hadn't even selected a psychologist yet, the last member of a team that I was to have assembled before returning from Florida and jumping into my tournament season. I was going back. A return to recommitment.

Arriving back at Spring Run was like coming back to campus the fall after graduation. The only thing that had really changed was you, the way you looked at everything—connected, yet uninvolved, walking through a daylong déjà vu.

After months sculpting the perfect golf bachelor pad, the condo had been sterilized, returned to showroom status. My realtor had the impression, rightly so, that I wasn't returning, so the maids came in and cleaned it out, spices and ketchup and water jugs all gone. Rather than reload on olive oil and S&P, I would eat out for the next three weeks. I no longer enjoyed the condo the way I had before. It wasn't mine, it was just a place to sleep. No more concocting healthy dinners and falling asleep to *The Big Break*. I didn't like the look of the place, how everything reminded me of all the work I had done, morning after morning, the progress I had earned, and how, in just five weeks, I might have wiped it all away.

So my last three weeks weren't for making the rounds, a time to bid adieu to all my new Florida friends the way I had imagined it might be. It was time for panic.

Over a month without hitting balls, my swing had developed a whole new personality. Apparently, while I was at the doctor's office, my golf swing was at the bar. It came back to me like a drunk stumbling home at the end of the night, wild and unwieldy, uninterested in anything I had to say. My physique wasn't behaving much better. Couch-sitting wasn't listed anywhere on my customized Body Balance routine; a steady diet of fingernails was certainly not what the nutritionist had suggested. My new muscles disappeared as if I'd defaulted on my payments, and I had overshot my target weight by about a toddler. In *I Call the Shots*, Johnny Miller talks about the ideal golf body type, citing Ernie Els's build as having the perfect wrecking-ball effect—plenty of long, supple swing arc, combined with a little bit of belly mass to build the momentum. I was now well under-massed, I could fit into my Bugle Boys from high school. So during my last three weeks in the Florida sun, I run around town, scrambling to reclaim my stolen property.

Mike slowly works me through a quick Release phase on the therapy table, right back into Re-educate and Rebuild. There is no doubt I have lost a major step in the gym, I have to go back to my November reps and weights, but I gradually feel my cold muscles start to soak up the sweat again. I'm back to about 75 percent by my final trip to Body Balance, and Mike sends me off with the perfect going-away present—he photographs all my workouts and exercises, then fills my workout binder with pictures and notes and instructions, so that while I'm in Philly or on the road, I'll have my trainer there over my shoulder, reminding how to do that exercise where you balance on the ball and wrap the cord around your waist and the dumbbell through your legs . . . of all the things I will miss about Florida, my mornings at Body Balance are the top of the list. This was the first time I so fully committed to any sort of disciplined routine for self-improvement. It was also the place where that improvement was most evident, the results most dramatic, a place where my work couldn't be belittled by the whims of a golf pencil.

For those final three weeks, Doc Suttie invited me to hang around the studio almost every day. I didn't even bother scheduling lessons anymore—he would just take a look whenever he had a minute, which he really never did, but he invented plenty on my behalf. With a few reminders from Doc, a few nights poring over tapes of my last twenty sessions, I am able to re-tame my swing rather quickly. The time off might have actually helped my swing, flushing out some longtime bad habits, starting over from a place where I might only recall the good stuff.

We know that my swing is miles from perfect, but compared to the video from my first lesson, it's like two distinct people swinging the golf club. My before-and-after isn't so much a progression as it is a revolution—my posture, from C-shaped slouch to Iron Byron solid. My takeaway, frame by frame matching up with Peter Jacobsen. Perfect balance, no forward lean to my toes, clubhead staying in front of my body as I turn it away, then drops back my arms back down in front of my chest as I turn through the ball.

The swing-change I love the most, that the golfhead in me gets all tingly about, is that I came to Doc with a wrist-release that started about three days ago. Flip, scoop, slap was my usual game. No lag in my golf vocabulary, and trying to teach a player to lag the golf club—it's like teaching speed, people move that way, or they don't. But through five months of hitting half-shots, punch shots, a dozen drills to exaggerate my hands pulling the butt of the club through the ball . . .

"Look at that," Doc said, pointing at my wrists in my final videotape. "Look at that lag. What the hell is that doing there?"

"Must have your tapes mixed up."

"Must have." Doc said, shaking his head. "You couldn't do that when you walked in here, could you?"

"Nope."

I leave my final Florida lesson with one last tape to make a grand total of twenty-three Dr. Jim Suttie Golf Academy videos piled on my VCR (that's $5,750 worth of his time—no matter how many articles I might edit for him, there was no way I could ever re-pay him). Before I go, Doc's next lesson takes a picture of Doc and me together in front of his studio. I never did get a copy of it. One more reason to make his time and my work pay off, to score even a small place on Doc's wall (there's a spot below Doc and Tony Kukoc I've had my eye on). But putting another nail in that wall of bright awards and famous faces is going to take more than angry drives and soft hands around the green. I had fine-tuned my body, my gear, my golf swing—now it was time to get working on my most vital piece of equipment. Time for a golf lobotomy.

I have read all those books you've been given, the ones you received on some B-list holiday and sent straight to the back of the toilet, where you would find yourself reading the same single page every day for the next three years. I'm talking about one of golf's greatest markets, where the crossroads of publishing and golf instruction has been most bountiful, and effective, perhaps—in that space between your ears.

I have piles of thin journals sworn to improve my mental golf health, but I cannot help but be skeptical. Did Jack Nicklaus or Sam

Snead—would Bobby Jones—ever consider going to visit a psychologist? Can you teach someone a mentality, or is that like teaching someone to be coordinated, be athletic, be a winner? Maybe I'm too Irish, too settled in my cynicism, but I struggle to buy into the marketing of enthusiasm. I have a hard time warming up to the idea that I can effect the realities of the physical world with my positive mental attitude. As a writer, I'm sort of in the business of looking at things and calling bullshit-yes, or bullshit-no. I can't hardly get through ten pages of Zen-visualization-be-the-ball bollocks before I'm thankful that I'm reading this stuff on the toilet.

And yet I know I cannot afford to play the skeptic here. It is true, I have the golf mind of a rodeo bull. If I don't find some way to get my Dr. Suttie driving range swing out onto the golf course when it matters, I can write off a happy ending. Some guys out there, they don't soil their sheets like I do. Some guys don't make 9s. Some guys who can't hit it as far, or as straight, who look like they were built for spitball target practice, they can make the game look so easy. Some guys have never been there and they still put it together, guys like Jimbo Fuller, stepping out of the box in his first Q-school to fire that opening 69. I need to be like some of those guys, so on my *second* return trip from Florida, I take the long way home. No more Auto Train, this time I'm working my way up the east coast, taking my own mini-tour of America's golf head shrinkers.

My first stop is outside of Orlando at the home of one of the hot new names in golf psychology, made popular by the Golf Channel and plenty of warm publicity in the magazines. He is a college professor (as most of the golf shrinks tend to be), and I meet him outside the cafeteria of a college that had a much "warmer" student body than I recalled from my days at Notre Dame, when girls put on four layers for the walk to breakfast. The scenery kept me from being too bothered when he showed up late, damp from his morning jog, then asked me to again wait while he took a call on his cell phone.

The professor was young and shortish, handsome in a mani-cured sort of way. There was a Hollywood slick about him: *Nice to meet you, one sec, got to take this.* My original coaching search had taught me to be open to, even expectant of, overly ripened egos. I figured that being a fellow academic (I'm an adjunct at St. Joseph's, go Hawks) would score me some points with him, and that he might be interested in a touch of exposure—judging by the amount of TV he was doing, it certainly seemed he wasn't opposed to a little self-promotion.

"I don't need any more exposure," was how our lunch began. Tray packed with roughage and protein for the professor, bottle of water for me, his latest ex-student.

We sat at a cafeteria table, and one of his seniors whose thesis he was directing joined us for a slice of pizza, which was perfect, as I now had double the audience to bore with my pitch. In fairness to the professor, he's a busy man, and a pretty good listener, but the fact that he can't get ten minutes to talk to me alone does not bode well for the close attention my noggin is going to require. It con-firmed the overall message of the lunch: *Sounds great, but by the way, I'm really busy.*

I tap-danced for twenty minutes, anyway, and once he accepted that I was undertaking a real project with a real cost and a real com-mitment, his interested perked up a little bit. He spoke briefly about his approach to working with his golf clients. He had more stu-dents than he could handle, apparently, but when he did choose to work with someone, he taught them how to deal with the physi-cal manifestations of anxiety and fear, how to recognize emotions and inhibit them from affecting performance. It all sounded inter-esting and impressive, though less golf-specific than I was expect-ing. Actually, he didn't strike me as a golfer at all (he never said if he played or not), which, on the clipboard in my mind, is a bit of a red mark. Seeing as the shoes I'm trying to wear already feel so unwieldy, I might like to work with someone who has tried them on himself.

I impress him with my level of commitment—the leaving the girlfriend at home for golf really caught his attention. He admits that he likes the intensity of the project, the focus and the immersion, and by the end of lunch, I think I almost have him convinced that this is a good enough idea to fit into his schedule. And yet, as we walk out of the cafeteria he asks me to send him an e-mail when I decide what I would like to do—he's going to look at his schedule, and I believe that, if I can afford the time, he can find some for me. As we shake hands and say adieu, I know that pseudo-lunch was the beginning and end of our working relationship. Honestly, I have no real opinion about a golf psychologist's particular approach. I don't really care who they have worked with. I'm not terribly interested in their methods, or their track record. I'm expecting to balk at most of what they have to say, anyway. My only real criteria for selecting a mental game coach was, whatever philosophy you're peddling, whatever bullshit you are selling—go on and sell the shit out of it.

I wanted nothing but unabashed enthusiasm for the challenge I was undertaking. Tell me you love my project. Tell me how we can do it. Tell me why. And if it's all crap, than feed it to me in spoonfuls. My walking up to a golf shrink and telling him that I would like him to prepare me for the PGA Tour—that takes a certain amount of balls and exuberance that I would like to see my coach try to match, even just a little bit. And this is no judgment of the professor—he didn't know me from Adam, and I'd probably be more trouble than it was worth. I don't blame him for being busy, any more than I'm sure he doesn't blame me for never getting around to that e-mail.

My psychology mini-tour would include one more similar mis-interview. It was again a professor, and a meeting at his university that doesn't quite take ten minutes. The doctor was one of the big golf names, an original in the performance psychology field, someone Dr. Suttie considered the genuine article, fixing up tour players before it became a multimillion-dollar business.

He had just returned from the Masters, he explains, as we sit in a golf cart at the university's home course.

"The security makes it nearly impossible to get close to your students," he explains. "It was very frustrating."

"I can imagine."

You wouldn't have that problem at any of my tournaments, I think, but the conversation never really even brushes up against that possibility. Again, busy—which I am fine with. He has his own book he was writing, he has new students on the tour he already is unable to make time for.

"I understand, completely," I tell him—and I do. I am sort of psyched just to be sharing a golf cart with him, actually, this guy who has rejiggered the minds of some of golf's greatest modern players.

He is also leery of getting involved for another reason. He has been contacted by overzealous amateurs in the past, golfers interested in embarking on golf transformations of their own. He didn't know if they were up to the seriousness of the task, or if they could possibly reach their goals in such a short period of time.

"I don't know if you would be prepared for the time commitment I would require of one of my players," he says.

I want to grab his collar and tell him, *I'm different, I've already come so far, I've proven it, I'll do anything, hit a million balls, go wherever, do whatever—I practiced on Christmas, for crying out loud.* . . .

"Most people aren't prepared for the hours," he continues, "or the expense."

Ding ding ding. The ref jumps in, arms flailing, *It's all over, folks, the kid is out!*

The expense. The cost burden, the bloodiest of all the red flags. Not that the doctor isn't worth every penny and then some, but if cost has been an issue for some, it will certainly be an issue for me.

These last nine weeks were not built into the budget. Nowhere in the ledger was there space for all the unexpected travel, the doctors and the bills. I had writer's health insurance (which is to say, none), so the scans and visits and tests sucked about ten grand out of this story, leaving me with Visa and MasterCard to make it through the summer to Q-school. This is why I get a little sentimental about the Body Balances and the Mizunos and the Hideouts and the Raptor Bays and, especially, the Dr. Jim Sutties of the golfing world who have given me break after break. In case you've missed my subtle drift thus far, golf is too goddamn expensive. You can't even try to do what I'm doing without a few years' worth of good salary at your disposal, ready to torch it all. You know about the big-ticket buy-in for Q-school, but consider the cost of some of the anonymous mini-tours where young players sharpen their craft—one season on the Golden Bear tour (twelve events) comes with an entry fee of $13,500; the Grey Goose Gateway Beach Series (seventeen events) will run a tour hopeful $18,000. None of these numbers encompass the real cost of playing golf for a living, the travel, food, instruction, equipment—if I had to pay sticker price for every hour, every range ball, every piece of equipment donated to me this year, the price tag would be well past the $100,000 mark.

And now I head back home with no place to play, no home to hit balls, no club to keep a handicap. Golf handicaps are distributed exclusively via clubs meeting the USGA's "Definition of a Golf Club," making handicaps least accessible to the non–private club member (i.e., me), the exact golfer who could use the strokes most. (I can do my taxes free on the Internet, but to acquire a handicap that's blessed by the USGA, I have to find a golf club that will take my money.) Industry analysts estimate that upwards of 85 percent of the golfers in the United Sates are not members of private golf clubs. When my car crosses into Pennsylvania, I will be one of them, without the handicap and club affiliation I need to make me eligible for USGA and local section events. As a would-be tournament golfer, I am already barred from tournament play, clinically unavailable for competition.

But that is a problem lurking a few more days up I-95. For now, I have a different handicap that requires my attention, and that's the one between my ears.

I had suspected it was a tad more than coincidence that I hooked up with Jimbo Fuller at the Q-school, that I arrived at the time I did, to walk with the gallery I found . . . maybe it was for more than a free lunch. Maybe it was for that name, it's somewhere back in my notes . . . *from almost giving up the game, to the Qualifying school leaderboard.* . . .

You've got to love the name—*Championsgate*—the portal of future, past, present greatness. Pull off I-4 outside of Orlando, pass through the giant amusement park gates and into an entire zip code built by people like me, folks desperate to get a handle on the slipperiest game in the world. Doc Suttie's shop in Florida was the best I had ever seen, and I've heard his summer digs in Chicago are even more ridiculous. But you have to give this much to Leadbetter: The guy's pretty much got his own town.

Sitting in the lobby of the Championsgate clubhouse, fifty people might have walked past me, but I pick out my guy before he's two steps through the glass doors.

"Bob Winters," he says, extending a firm grip. He has that look in his eye, intense but not off-putting, not quite as prone to blinking as your average joe. He's not quite six feet but strong, a middle-aged yet striking physique that screams personal trainer. And the hair—

can't go further without noting the hair. It is magnificent. Or awful, depending on your style and station. For a guy who I am shocked to learn is fifty, I look at the thick, flowing locks, something out of a Renaissance sculpture, and I give him the benefit of the doubt.

We sit down for a Diet Coke, and instantly, there is an electricity—it might be salesmanship, it might be guru-chic, but it is intense, and it's working on me. He asks about the state of my game, we talk about where I want to go, and never for a second does he raise an eyebrow at the words "Q-school," the letters "PGA." He nods and listens, never interrupting to talk about his crowded schedule, and by the end of my first soda, I am fessing up about my anxieties in competition, my worries about being rooted out as a fraud.

"I can hit it just as good as these guys," I say. "I've done it before. But I can't convince myself that I belong, that I'm not just playing a part."

And that's when I first hear that story about Craig Stadler, the one that ends with, "All anybody here wants to know is, can you play stick?"

"That is what we have to get you to understand, Tom Coyne," Dr. Winters explains, pointing straight at me. "Nobody at that Q-school gives a darn if you played in college, or if you didn't, or if you were all-American, or if you weren't. Or if you were a writer, or lawyer, or a janitor. All anyone cares about—all *you* need to care about—is seeing your target, committing to your golf shot, and executing. From what you've already told me, and with my help, I am pretty confident that you are going to be able to do all of those things."

"Sometimes I am."

"And we have to get you to every time you are. Every. Single. Swing. One swing. Then the next. Then the next," Dr. Winters explains, piling sugar packets on top of each other, demonstrating his point. "You're not thinking about the next shot. Not thinking about the last. You're not wondering, what will happen if I hit this one right? The only thing Tom Coyne can think about when he steps up to the golf ball is, 'This is *my* time. This is *my* ball. And this is *my* game.'"

He's looking me dead in the eye, and in ten minutes has just about hypnotized the professional skeptic. I feel my head nodding.

"You have to say to yourself, 'I have a specific target. I commit myself totally to that target. I trust my decision. I trust my club, and yes, I trust my golf swing.' *You have got to get to Yes before each and every golf shot,*" he explains. "If you can get to Yes, and only Yes—with that mind-set, you are giving yourself an opportunity to succeed."

I'm close to throwing out a Hallelujah, or at least a high five. And as if he didn't already have the job, "Now, I have been through Q-school myself," he continues. "I understand what you're up against, I can tell you what you're going to be going through. What I teach you, it isn't all just words and ideas. I go out on the golf course with you, I play right alongside you, and shot by shot, we implement what I am teaching."

Dr. Robert Winters has worked with dozens of stars on the PGA and LPGA tours, scores of NCAA studs. He's the resident sports psychologist at David Leadbetter's headquarters, he has his PhD, studied under Rotella—and none of that is of the slightest importance to me. The enthusiasm pulsates from his eyes, his hands, through his outstanding hair. He makes me want to run out of the clubhouse and go shoot 69. He doesn't speak with reservations, he speaks with possibility—even if he should have plenty of reservations, which he should, what the hell good would they do me now, already six months' golf pregnant? And while he isn't free, he works out a deal that isn't cost-prohibitive, where I'll have access to him throughout the season, and 24/7 for counseling sessions on the phone, mid-tournament if need be.

I leave Orlando with a full and functioning squad. I have my mental point guard, and I'm not two weeks back in Philadelphia when I find out that I have a home court, even someone to make balls for the team. A great friend and Philadelphia golf-pro legend, Harry Heagy, has persuaded the owners of his club to take a look at my project, and in one afternoon I am set up with a handicap and a season's worth of playing privileges at Edgmont Country Club, not ten minutes from my house, with a driving range that goes on till tomorrow. And not only do the owners at Edgmont hook me up with a home, one of them makes a phone call to a friend at Titleist, and, voilà, it isn't one week before a beautiful cardboard box shows up with two pairs of shoes and more golf balls than I could have afforded with all the cash left in my account.

I never thought I would be so happy to see a pair of golf shoes. It's not something you think about being desperate for, needing new footwear the way you require food, water, cable—but I had worn my spikes down to the nub and last thread. And the thought of not having to pay for golf balls anymore, my number-one daily expense— some people have two-pack-a-day habits, mine was a twelve-dollar, one-sleeve-a-round addiction to Titleist. Talk about a company who doesn't need the exposure—and yet the biggest kid on the block, he has a heart, too.

Funny, the bigger the team gets, the more the focus feels like it is on one face alone. The more talent I surround myself with, the more suspicious I become of my own. And the more they teach me, the less I need to know—because it is becoming quite clear that the only question that matters is the one about the stick. And the answer to that question . . . through that long ride home, three days and a dozen stops, nowhere along the way did I quite arrive at yes.

"I 'm sorry. I didn't mean to say fuck."

I'm apologizing to my caddy on the third tee of the United States Open. Rather, my US Open. Which is to say, local US Open qualifying outside Harrisburg, Pennsylvania. In any oddsmaker's book, I would have been packaged in a sucker's bet along with the thousands of other unknown dreamers, soon-to-be also-rans who make their annual hundred-dollar donation to the USGA by entering local Open qualifying. With a certified USGA handicap better than 1.4, any golfer in the world can pony up and say that he or she played in the US Open. How far they advance through the sea of floundering dreamers remains to be seen—this year, a mere 9,039 players applied to qualify for the Open. Of the 8,726 players accepted, roughly 550 players will qualify from 107 local sites to compete in regional qualifying. There they will compete with a fresh batch of some 200 competitors exempt from local qualifying (tour pros, USGA winners), meaning close to 800 players duke it out at 13 regional qualifiers for 78 open spots in the tournament you will be watching on TV. And while that provides me a mighty .893 percent chance of making it into the final field this year, there is presently a 100 percent chance that I am even after one hole of US Open qualifying (after a booming drive, chubby sand wedge, and nice up-and-down on number one), and I have as fair as shot as any of the thousands of players around the country who changed their shoes in the parking lot this morning, the same way that I did.

And while I might be Dilinger money, none of the bookies know about this new Tom Coyne. None of my competition is aware that I am now a player who was going to focus, succeed, triumph in these throat-cinching situations. All these club pros and the kids from the golf team at Millersville and the club champions from all over central Pennsylvania, I recognize none of them from the range in Florida or from the weight room at Body Balance—the safest money in all the US Open was that no one else in this widest of fields had spent the last eight months of their lives quite the way I had. So what if there were only two spots for this entire field? That's plenty. I would just go out and play as if there only needed to be one.

So when we arrived at the second tee and I pushed my drive a touch wide, just a few steps into the right rough, I admit that I snapped at my caddy when, after a good five-minute search, we still couldn't find it—sure, the grass was thick and damp, green spaghetti, but there was no excuse for losing a ball that wasn't ten yards off its target. We stomped around the cabbage until I finally surrendered, humiliated to have the entire group and two marshals already involved in my round of golf.

"Goddamnit, where's the bag? I need another fucking ball."

Most caddies would have not even flinched. In my own former caddy lifetime, I would have lowered my chin and tucked my tail between my thighs and avoided eye contact for the next sixteen holes, bracing myself for a minimum-fee payday. But my caddy didn't do any of those things. The look on her face—she looks at me like I just told her that those shorts made her look fat.

I had warned Allyson that she might see a different side of me at work in the trenches, but she insisted that she was still up for it. *I want to caddy for you*, she said. *It will be fun.* Aside from never missing a chance to spend an evening in central Pennsylvania, she wanted to come watch me play and succeed and win—and in the US Open, now that *did* sound like fun. But I doubt that she expected me to start lobbing F-bombs in her direction halfway through the second hole.

The caddy-girlfriend/spouse/partner is a complicated new role in the game of golf. You'd probably have to look at Faldo's Fannie as the one who opened the door for wives and girlfriends who wanted to follow their lesser halves around the golf course. With a female caddy on CBS every Sunday, the stigma was lifted from a lady toiling beneath the weight of a tour bag. The dawn of the Ping carry bag probably didn't hurt, either. Cracked leather straps attached to suitcases were out, in came canvas and cotton and double straps as ergonomics came to golf bags, and lugging golf clubs became suitable for a pair of narrow shoulders in a skort. And the economics of the game—the money I was spending on entry fees, hotel, food, gas—a one-day tournament could quickly become a thousand-dollar enterprise, so taking a caddy fee out off the books becomes hugely important. And if you propose it as *I'd like to spend more time with you* rather than *I can't afford a caddy*, it's possible to kill those rarest of two birds with one stone: being the good boyfriend while being cheap at the same time.

It isn't long before she figures out that this isn't quality time, not in the capacity she was envisioning it. I told her it was going to be fun, exciting, the world's toughest golf tournament and we would take it on as a team. But my yelling and my sickly, ashen face, my tournament Tourette's—she had no idea that I harbored such a low opinion of myself, that I so sincerely believed I was the dumbest mother f-er in the mother f-ing world. She didn't know this new Tom Coyne who was doing his best to spoil her Harrisburg weekend.

I had always viewed players who had their girlfriends caddying for them as the golf equivalent of guys with No Fear stickers in the tinted windows of their IROCs. Showy cheese-balls—*so you've got a girlfriend, seriously, buddy, no one out here is impressed.* But it is kind of cool to play at being the guy in the muscle-T every once in a while, and no matter if I started looking a little goofy, a little profane, she had signed up for it. She wanted to see what this fancy golf was all about, and I wanted to show off a little bit, and whether it was good or bad, she was going to see what I had been up to, and what I was up against.

Here it was—this was serious, and I was pissed, and I needed another fucking golf ball right fucking now, so I could begin that longest walk in all of sport, the lonely stroll back to the tee box, driver in one hand, new golf ball in the other, the group behind us watching me approach like I'm a leper come to give them all a hug.

Just as I went digging in the front pocket for a new Titleist, the chorus came, lovely and triumphant:

"I found it! I've got it! Right here, I got it!"

And there she was, the caddy of the year, standing over a wiry patch of grass, surprise and joy all over her beautiful face. I could see it in her eyes, the thrill of it all—not just from finding the ball we had deemed unrecoverable, but from being involved, being a part of this game, being solely responsible for the salvation of three whole strokes in the United States Open Championship.

I have never partaken of cocaine or crack or heroin, but I can't imagine that any of the big-league opiates can do much more for your spirits than finding a previously abandoned golf ball in competition. The clouds of making eight were brushed away, the nightmare transformed into a laughable story for later, and I was back in the game, back to chasing birdie on this simple par-five.

I quickly apologize for the snip in my voice, begging forgiveness the way I had never heard a golfer apologize to a caddy in my fourteen years of looping. Then again, none of those caddies had long blond hair or lovely long legs, an ample chest that is downright distracting when pushed up and outward by a double-strap golf bag. . . .

"That's fine, don't worry about me," she says, laughing with a half-roll of the eyes, accepting that I'm golf insane and will continue to be so for the next three and a half hours, a split personality of spit-flying grass-stomper and birthday-boy on a sugar high.

"You do what you have to do," Allyson tells me.

And I do, taking intensity to a new level, cruising right past focused and heading straight to panicked, sketching my own caricature of the golfer who cared too much.

On the fifth hole, faced with a tricky fairway bunker shot, I revert to one of the most comfortable go-to golf shots from my childhood, the eight-iron hosel rocket. Dead shank, up and over the heads of my confused playing partners, my ball soaring in an impossibly lateral direction, finding a home in the middle of a fairway we had yet to play.

Even my caddy couldn't help herself: "What the hell? Did you mean to do that?"

With this latest turn of events, the one in which I would have to play two holes at the same time, our budding caddy-player relationship descends into country club chaos. There was a trap to rake, and I had suddenly decided to abandon this golf hole altogether, opting for a whole new hole populated by an entirely different threesome. There was the floppy-hatted marshal warning us about falling behind, and the pro in my group who thought this was the actual US Open, taking his time over every shot as if he might never hit another one—I have to move, so I grab half my clubs and run for the next fairway, leaving Allyson with a rake, a bunker, a terrified confusion all over her face. This is advanced caddying, and my shank had exposed her for the rookie she was. As I work my way up the parallel, yet incorrect golf hole, I wave to her through the trees— *Okay, forward, stop, now go, stop, wait, he's hitting, now keep going.* I was finally reunited with my clubs up on the green, after I lobbed a nine-iron over the pines, returning my ball to its golf hole of origin.

My blind shot over trees found the green—and like so many shots seem to do when you have no idea where they're going, it was stony tight. I tap in for par and look to my caddy for a good fist-pump or an exhausted look of relief, maybe even an *I love you, you're the best*. But she isn't watching. She's halfway between the green and the next tee, intently studying some object in her right hand—is that the pin sheet? My yardage book? And why would she be putting the pencil in her mouth, scribbling on her lips. . . .

As routine as golf had become, as predictable as my afternoons could be, once in a while something pops up that, in all the golf, I had never seen before. A caddy standing beside the green, staring into her compact, carefully applying an extra coat of pink lipstick.

Why not? If your player's out there designing his own golf course, one of you might as well look good.

The rest of the afternoon is spent making an unremarkable smattering of pars and bogeys, shooting an only slightly embarrassing 81. The driving, outstanding, the iron-play, average, the putting, piss-poor. On our drive back down the turnpike, we talk about a learning experience, about being close, about those handful of swings that kept me from going lower. But while my golf was average, uninspired, on her first day of caddying, she was an absolute all-star. Not once was she in the way, in anyone's line—she didn't cough or sneeze or do anything in anyone's backswing, aside from put on her lipstick, which she was careful to do in silence.

As payment for her fine services, it was my treat at Philadelphia's king of crabs and wings, the beloved Byrne's Tavern. We toast with frosty mugs, and on this day of my first big tournament, there was a winner in our midst, someone who had performed beyond expectations and proven the naysayers wrong, stepping into an unfamiliar arena and walking out triumphant. One of us went to the qualifier, and came back qualified. And she was sitting across from me, laughing at the way I nimbly deboned my chicken wings in one clean mouthful.

"81 isn't that bad, Tom. There were plenty of higher scores up there."

"Plenty of lower ones, too."

"It's all just practice for the Q-school, anyway. These tournaments are just warm-ups, right? This was the US Open—just think how much easier your next tournament will feel. What's the name of it?"

"It's a qualifier. For the Nationwide Tour."

"Nationwide? Like the insurance?"

"Yes."

"Nationwide Tour," she says. "Sounds made up. You shouldn't have any problem making it at that one."

My mailbox has been crowded with letters from the USGA and the PGA sections and the state associations, entries and confirmations from the dozens of tournaments I have entered for the summer season. I have spent north of $6,000 on entry fees alone, and if I were eligible for more tournaments, I would have spent more. Most big pro and amateur events require some sort of playing résumé, which, for me, someone whose most impressive tournament win last year was in the Paddy Rooney Pub scramble, was out of the question. Again, the outside-golfer looking in, the kid with heart who can't get the job because he doesn't have the experience, can't get the experience for not having the job. But even with being shut out of the invitationals, the summer schedule is plenty busy with chances to prove myself before October's Q-school.

It has also been plenty busy with doctor's visits. The curious illness and inconclusive tests stay with me through most of the summer, kidneys and blood pressure and cholesterol concerns keep me running around to hospitals all over Philadelphia. After never having blood taken in my life, I had it taken fourteen times in two months. But as my mom tells her seventy-year-old friends when they go out to dinner: No sick stories allowed, so I won't bother you with them here. Bottom line, I was back to getting the swing and the head in order. If once in a while I had something else to distract me, that just makes my day a tad more like everybody else's.

Allyson was right: All the tournaments are just practice for the big day, so that I can step up onto that first tee without wetting myself. And she was wrong: This isn't just warm-up, and this isn't going to be easy. A qualifier for the Nationwide Tour is as big a deal as the Q-school itself, perhaps even bigger. These are guys who are one week away from the PGA Tour. When my tee time arrived in the mail, it was almost enough to make me concoct a debilitating groin pull. I recognize a dozen names on the list. Ty Tryon would be in the group behind me—okay, it's not Fred Couples, but for a recovering twelve-handicap, it's pretty rare company. I didn't realize when I signed up for the two Pennsylvania Nationwide Qualifiers how much the field would resemble what I would be facing in October. I had plenty strokes left to shave, and I was on schedule to be ready by then. But with a signed check and a stamped envelope, I had pulled October right up into June.

Each stop along the Nationwide Tour hosts a Monday qualifying event—roughly 160 players, often spaced over two golf courses, competing for six to ten open spots in that week's field. As closed-door as the Q-school can seem, with its three stages and hefty fees, the Nationwide Monday qualifier is more reasonably priced ($300), but perhaps as statistically prohibitive an avenue as the October school.

There is a great deal of old-blood–new-blood tension in the world of professional golf that has probably existed since the first time a tournament field had to be trimmed. The "rabbit" system employed prior to 1983, in which touring pros and class-A PGA club pros would play in a Monday qualifier for a spot in that week's PGA Tour event, was largely criticized for the extraordinarily cruel odds facing touring pros of the 1960s and 70s. The old rules said

that spots in tour events were guaranteed only to the top-sixty players on the money list—everyone else had to go qualify, forcing a
mass of talented pros to live a week-to-week life on the edge of
sanity and bankruptcy, guys who, under today's conditions of full-
exemption, sponsorship money, and escalating purses, would no
doubt be golf millionaires. In the 1970s, they were borderline
homeless, a pseudo-cult of golf hobos traveling the land, desperate
for the one spot being offered in a Monday qualifier, field of 180.

Perhaps as a reaction to the unpleasantness of the rabbit system,
the all-exempt tour was initiated, offering full exemption to the top
125 players on each year's money list, with partial exemptions for
numbers 126 through 150 who, with the disappearance of the rabbit
qualifiers, were likely to get a spot in at least a handful of events, regardless of how well they might have been playing. Gone were the
weekly nervous breakdowns. A qualified player was now actually
qualified to go out and play—a far more amenable and fair working
environment, no doubt. But the pendulum of the golfing life seems
to have swung from too cruel to a tad too cushy (look at the Charity,
I mean, Champions Tour—they don't even have cuts, for crying out
loud). I think golf would do well for itself to bring back a little bit
of the luck, fun, and spirited desperation of the rabbit Monday
PGA qualifier and reduce the number of fully exempt players on the
PGA Tour.

One hundred twenty-five guaranteed spots—it feels a little
heavy when you consider the amount of new talent that is kept from
rising to the surface every season. There are Q-school and Nationwide grads not just surviving in golf, but tearing it up on the big
tour every year. As in all major sports, golfers are getting better by
the minute. The game needs fewer grandfather clauses, not more.
And I can suggest rolling back players' exemptions with clean conscience, knowing that there is still huge money available to mid-
and lower-tier tour pros. By scaling back the number of exempt

players—say from 125 to 100, or better yet, 85 spots—and reshuffling those positions into the Q-school and the Nationwide or into rabbit qualifiers, there would more opportunity for all this able new blood to find its way to the first tee. And if the player at 122 truly deserves his exemption, he can go back to Q-school and prove it against the new talents. As tough as that might seem to a journeyman tour pro who is able to squeak out a few cuts every year and keep his place in line, consider how talent evaluation and playing time works in football, baseball, basketball—if you are five minutes past your prime, you are wearing a suit. If there is a kid on the bench who could better fill your space, who could bring more fans into the building, you'll be sitting down before anyone even offers you a chair.

When I show up for my Sunday afternoon practice round at the Scranton Nationwide Tour stop, I meet a pack of these young studs, hungry and frustrated, thick-shouldered players who had driven through the night from the last tournament in Chicago. They don't have hotel rooms yet; most of them were using the clubhouse locker room for their first shower in two days. And some are around the putting green, clothes wrinkled from the drive, chatting on their cell phones with friends who had made the cut and are still back in the Midwest, fighting for their daily bread.

I play my practice round with a guy named Ron who doesn't miss a single fairway all the way around the golf course. Ron has a caddy riding in the cart next to him, a six-feet-five dude who looked like he could be running a bank if he wasn't covered in a fifteen hours' drive worth of stubble. The caddy takes notes like a teacher's pet. He scopes every yardage through laser binoculars, and he marks the next day's pins with a divot tool, giving Ron a spot to practice for. They go through their practice round routine with an arrogant efficiency—it was simple for them, rehearsed, earned over many tough Mondays. Me, on the other hand, I was half-scared to death just playing the practice round. I just grab a ball out of my bag and start playing golf.

It takes me five holes to realize that those little white dots on the green aren't big drops of bird shit, but a marking for tomorrow's pin. I stand around and try to look busy, check my phone, make a couple strokes in the fringe, count my tees, again, while Ron rolls putts all over the green. He tosses a couple balls into bunkers and hits to three different spots on the green. On par-threes, he hits a high shot and a low shot. On par-fives, he lays up, goes for it, picks a safe greenside bunker where he could land his second shot, then goes into that bunker and hits four, five shots from there. It was clinical. It was professional. And I watch it all like I had bought a ticket instead of paying for a greens fee myself.

Ron knew how to actually go about playing a proper practice round. He hit it a little straighter than I did, he had a bit more polish to his game, but that's not what I saw—he was a seasoned touring golf professional in the company of a masquerading golf dreamer. Again, the tournament had not even started, but the game was well on.

Of course, not everyone at the golf club saw us that way. When I come in and ask one of the cart boys to caddy for me tomorrow, you would have thought he confused me for Phil Mickelson.

"Really? Are you sure? I mean, I'm not, like, a professional caddy or anything."

Don't worry, I'm not, like, a professional golfer.

"I'm sure you'll do fine," I tell him. "I just need someone to carry the bag up and down these hills. I barely made it around today, and that was with a cart."

"Wow. Thanks. Wow," he says, face bright with his impending good fortune as he pictures himself in a white jumpsuit, someday strolling the fairways of Augusta. "Let me see if I can get someone to work for me. God, I hope I can."

I almost reach out to physically stop him—*Oh, don't take a day off for this*—but he's already hopping away. And he quickly returns with the good news: He has told everyone inside how he got the call, got tapped on the shoulder by one of the tour big shots. From the bag room to the big time, I think his hands were actually shaking with excitement. He would be there two hours early, he told me, waiting for me on the range.

The following morning, there he is, bright and smiling, towel in his right hand, tip already dampened like a seasoned jock. I think he's wearing a new shirt, young Michael is, a skinny sixteen-year-old who I could tell spent the prior evening thinking out yardages, planning hole-by-hole strategies with his pop, probably searching for my name on the Internet—*found some writer guy, didn't see any real golf pros.*

And not five hours from meeting him on that dew-brushed driving range, young Michael would look back on his experience with Tom Coyne as a day that changed his life. Because I took a young man's dreams and hopes, and with only fourteen golf clubs at my disposal, I bashed them into oblivion. I took a young man's idealism and his best wishes, and drowned them in a dark and sour cynicism. Rarely does one get such an upfront seat to a loss of innocence, but with each swing, it was like I was telling him that there was no Santa Claus, that the girls *did* giggle about his acne, that he would look back at this summer running carts at a Pennsyltucky Country Club as the high point of his life.

It started with the swing off number one, a drive over a small pond, through a shoot of towering pines. Young Michael insisted that it was only a three-wood, a bit of home-course insight he had probably been polishing since last evening—but on the first tee, the head of my three-wood looked about the size of a Tater Tot.

"Driver's too much. I'm telling you, you don't need it," he

insisted, but I pulled driver, anyway, solely on the grounds that it was the club I was least likely to whiff. Honestly, I might have pulled out a tennis racket if I'd had one.

Michael's feelings on driver turned out to be spot-on advice. With my *first* tee ball (there would be more), the ball gently fell off its intended line, soaring deep into the Appalachian darkness. Driver was, indeed, too much. But on my second shot off the first tee, driver wasn't nearly enough—like some 1960s rocket test, the ball left the earth for only a short time, knuckling off the inside of the clubface and diving into the pond in front of us, the one that was there more for ambience than it was for difficulty, at least when a field of Nationwide Touring pros was concerned. After I returned to my bag for my third golf ball on the first tee, my instinct about my driver proved to be just right, high and straight, my ball funneling deep down the tube of pine trees.

Hitting three balls off the first tee was not part of anybody's game plan. Not my game plan, and certainly not Michael's. Regardless of the fact that we eventually found the first drive—with the help of a search party of PGA marshals, my ball was located behind a boulder, nestled beneath a petrified root—the jig was up, and I played like it. The front nine was a mix of tightfisted golf swings and shit-awful breaks. It's amazing how when you're swinging well, your ball never ends up against the lip of a bunker, your drives never roll into a fairway divot. When I finally stuffed a nine-iron on the tenth hole (three inches, my first actual golf shot of the day), young Michael actually slapped the putter in my hand and said, "It's about goddamn time," with a look on his face like I owed his mother child support.

No need to thank me, Michael. Today . . . today you learned how the world really works.

When we finally arrive at the scorer's table—it's like kneeling in the confessional, only with a microphone stuck in your face—I put my mark on my bloated numbers and look for the fastest route of escape. Turns out, I wasn't the anti-medalist—a few brothers-in-pain hung up numbers in the 90s while I parred the last four holes on the back (after soiling two back-side birdies with an emphatic nine on the fourteenth hole) to shoot a hardly redeemable 89.

I meet Michael in the parking lot, and out of guilt and pity I pay him double what I was planning. I know he was on his way to the bag room to brutalize my game for his buddies (*dumbass hit three balls off the first tee!*), but I couldn't have him calling me cheap as well. Whether I was a cheap or a charitable loop, that was one thing in my golf game that I could control. What I apparently could not control was my season-long bout with the Big Number.

It started with a few Big Numbers here and there, just a few times a week, in casual company—a triple bogey here, a double bogey there—and ballooned into a full-scale sickness. When faced with a chance to add one more stroke to an already swollen score, I could not stop myself. I was powerless. I needed help.

In the Pennsylvania Amateur Qualifier, I would take my even-par round and sprinkle some quadruple bogey on it. It was a par-five that bent like a horseshoe, but the shoe I decided to play was for a bigger horse. My second shot went soaring through the fairway, deep into a Pennsylvania pine forest that was, lucky for me, chock full of massive igneous boulders. I ventured into the shadowy wood with my forged nine-iron blade, and proceeded to do battle with the rocks. And as I should have learned in grade school, rock beats steel. It kicks its ass. I would miss qualifying by four.

In my next appearance on the Nationwide scene, this time at the Hershey Classic Monday qualifier, one bad golf hole gets my round all fudged up. I had been paired to play with Kevin Stadler, son of Craig, who had mercifully won the Nationwide event that previous Sunday afternoon, making him exempt for this week and making our group a twosome. I was terrified and excited to get the pairing—of all the big names on the Nationwide, he was one of the guys who seemed laid back enough to not mind sharing some space with a greenhorn. After preparing my head to play in front of a small crowd, I was disappointed to hear that he wouldn't be joining us, no Monday gallery for Tom Coyne and a grinder from the Hooters Tour. But when I came to the fourteenth tee at five over par, and left the fourteenth green at ten over par, I was relieved that I was able to make my nine in quiet anonymity.

In Pennsylvania Mid-Amateur qualifying, I stand on the ninth tee box with a grin hiding behind my lips. I had just made a nice birdie to get back to even par, and my prospects for finally making a main event are looking good. Coast home, no train wrecks, and you're off to the big tournament in Pittsburgh. I was playing with one of the big-name amateurs in the section, and not only was he notably impressed with my game—*I'm surprised I've never heard of you before, Tom. You play a lot of these tournaments?*—but since the first hole, he had been hitting second. So on ten tee, I pull three-wood and rip it dead down the middle, out of range of his new R7 driver. My swing was in the slot, my timing perfect. It was fairway-green autopilot, and I was just along for the ride.

When we get to our fairway, I am surprised to find my Titleist with green dots behind his golf ball. I know he hit driver, but I was sure he couldn't keep it up with that last swing. I grab a sand wedge and punch my ball up onto the green, my playing partner does the same, and when we get to the green and kneel down to mark our golf balls, we realized that my first instinct was right: I had hit my drive past his. What I was wrong about was that I was the only one playing a Titleist with green dots.

Titleisist's dominance of the ball market has become such that 90 percent of the field seems to be playing the same ball—ProV1x—and as golf balls are marked with one of four numbers, there's a good chance that your ball will be playing exactly the same ball as a member of your foursome. Enter the Sharpie into the world of golf equipment—a good Sharpie for branding one's golf ball has become as common in a player's bag as tees and divot tools. And the hot color of the season? Lucky Irish green, apparently. So my partner and I make the long walk back out to the fairway, take our two penalty strokes, and try it again, this time playing golf balls that actually belong to us. Take away those two birdie putts, in their place insert double bogey. On the next tee box, I hit two drives so far off the property, they'd had to have paid a guest fee to get back in. I follow up my double bogey with a nine, shoot 80, and miss the cut by three shots.

And yet it wasn't until the qualifier for the Pennsylvania Open that I would realize the extent of my problem. If there was ever an intervention for a troubled golfer, the sixteenth hole at Bellewood Golf Club in North Coventry, Pennsylvania, was mine. After teeing off number ten and beginning my day par, par, birdie, par, par, par, knowing that all I needed to do was hang up your basic 77 to make it through to the finals, I came to the sixteenth tee with the honor, and all the confidence in the world. After all, I had toiled among the golf elite—I may have shot my weight in competition, but after experiencing the talent and pressure of a Nationwide Monday, this little local outing should be a piece of pumpkin pie. *I should be two under—no, three under! Why not four! Watch out course record, watch out PGA Tour, and heads up Tiger! If you only knew what it felt like to play my kind of game, to be able to hit the ball like this* . . . long and deep and yawning away from the center of the fairway, skipping through the right rough and hopping through two white stakes like they were goal posts.

But they were not goalposts. For you lucky ones who don't have the intimate knowledge of these posts that I do, they were out-of-bounds stakes—OB, to those of us on a first-name basis. And in this forgettable moment, this passing instance of unfortunate physics, it happens. The scorecard jumps out of my back pocket, blows up one hundred sizes, and is hanging there above my head like some giant bowling alley scoreboard. *My God, I'm not one-under anymore. I'm not even even. All this work and focus, all today's effort, and the best I can do now is scrape together a six, which I doubt I will, because to do so I'm going to have to get my shit together ASAP, and one thing I know on a golf course is when my shit is being lost, as it is now, and who cares, screw this, anyway.* I am instantly the child who, should you take away one of his toys, would consider burning down the entire house his most suitable form of protest.

The next ball off the tee was a fraternal twin of the first—two hops and another GOOOOOOOAL! Guarding against a third ball OB right, my next attempt turned left with unnatural-hooking spin. After a few chip-outs to the fairway, I stung a solid nine-iron dead at the stick, where the rest of my impatient threesome were each waiting on their birdie putts. Yet I failed to account for the pints of bloody murder pumping through my veins, how that might pump ten extra yards into the shot. My Titleist carried the green, trampolined off the concrete cart path, two hops and, you guessed it—*he shoots, he scores!*

What would have been that trick in soccer, in golf was a very stout 13.

It hasn't all been nightmares. I am growing more comfortable in my tournament skin. I'm trying to make up for years of missed experience, and there were going to be some bumps in the road. Wrong balls played from the center of the fairway, thirteens on 385 yard par fours. It happens. Once in a while I escape the clutches of the double-digit blow-up, and the hard work comes together in rounds of golf I could not have dreamt of eight months before. In the US Public Links qualifier (not that I was a true public course golfer at this point—in case you're keeping track of my status, I am currently a professional-amateur-public-course-private-club-member—if a tournament will take my check, I enter), Allyson pulled my bag around and watched me birdie the fifteenth hole to get back to even par. I birdie seventeen to go one-under, and as my putt bounced through the fringe, leaning right and dropping into the cup, I watch her actually fist-pump. Even cooler, standing on that eighteenth tee I was on the leaderboard and tied with *the* Michelle Wie at minus 1. She was an unlikely competitor in the Harrisburg Publinks quali-fier, but there she was in the flesh, two holes ahead of me, and I was on her heels. Okay, she's a fifteen-year-old girl. But she had hung with the boys on the big tour, and I was hanging with her. You've got to take your victories where you can get them.

I would go on to stick my last drive of the morning into the meat of the 150-yard bush—two yards off the fairway, and I some-how find an unplayable lie—how's that for God casting a vote against the golf career. After taking my drop and penalty, I nearly get up and down from 150 yards to remain tied with Wie, but I card an even par 72, one of the low five scores of the day, and for the few minutes before our second eighteen of the day, I could walk around the clubhouse like the real deal, a bonified, certified stick.

"Look at your name," Allyson said, pointing to it at the top of the scoreboard. "This is so cool. This is actually fun."

The second eighteen of the thirty-six-hole qualifier was a little less fun.

Consider a beautiful balloon slowly leaking over four hours un-til it was finally flaccid and empty. There were no big explosions, but a few wayward shots here, a fleeting focus there, and I topped my 72 with a very ordinary 80, and it was another long drive with my girl-friend with plenty of wishful golf talk.

There is a known phenomenon among the upper tiers of golf known as Golf Depression. Whenever I discussed my own Golf

Depression with a grinder or stick or mini-tour hopeful, they would all nod in agreement, eyes wide with recognition, thrilled that someone had finally given it a name and that they had not suffered alone. Every life-dedicated player I met knew that feeling of emptiness that comes when hitting a golf ball is your absolute everything, and you find yourself hitting it crooked. When you have nothing else in your life, when you walk out onto that bent grass plank only to find that, on that particular afternoon, you are just not good enough—it doesn't make you hate the game. You could never hate it. I don't know a less sentimental way to explain it other than your only love does an about-face and walks away.

Yet it didn't make any of them quit. And it doesn't make me quit. I keep to my new Philadelphia routine: mornings at Edgmont, midday in the gym with Mike's binder, afternoons playing eighteen at any course that will have me. The problem isn't my ball striking, it wasn't the way I hit it, it wasn't my work ethic. My trouble is that I am in a bad golf relationship—it's all giving, and no getting, and I am afraid to believe in this relationship anymore. Golf is telling me it needs more space, but I'm still leaving fifteen messages a day.

What I need for my real Golf Depression is real golf help. I need a professional, a counselor, a Dr. Phil of my own. Lucky for me I happen to know one, with a head of hair that would make Dr. Phil weep.

"This is going to be a great day," Dr. Bob says. "This is going to be super—we are going to have a super day, you are going to get a heck of a lot out of this."

I have to open my mind. I have to adopt that attitude that I take when Allyson picks the movie, or she ropes me into dinner with a crowd of insurance lawyers. It's not so much that I am a cynic, I just might take a bit too much pleasure in demonstrating why things aren't as rosy as they seem. But if I don't check even a little bit of that attitude at the door, I'm not going to get anything out of the next eight hours with the last and latest member of my team.

Dr. Robert Winters, or Dr. Bob, as his students seem to refer to him, is alive and well at nine A.M., whirling about this roomy studio here in the David Leadbetter Academy, hanging a giant paper tablet on an easel, handing me a binder with my name on it. The binder is full of essays, affirmations, and articles Dr. Winters had written on everything from getting off the first tee to learning how to score to how to warm up before competition. But this is all for later reading. We begin my full-day session by taking a personal inventory. Dr. Winters asks me to write down what I perceive my golf strengths and weaknesses to be.

When I am playing well, what is going through my mind:

I'm the best player here.

I have a great golf swing; I want to show off my game.

The next hole is another birdie chance.

I'll make this putt; I look forward to the chance to make another putt.

Few swing thoughts—easy swing, smooth takeaway—no mechanics.

And my thoughts when I'm playing poorly:

Do I belong here?

These guys are better than me.

My score should be lower, I should have made that putt, I missed an opportunity.

Don't hit it OB, don't hit it in the water, don't make another bogey.

I'm tired, I'm hungry, I'd rather be doing anything else right now.

Each thought goes up on the board, and, in their totality, Dr. Winters and I can see a glaring confidence issue staring back at us, more obvious and deep-rooted than I had imagined. I am playing with fear, and the only way to deal with fear is to look it in the eyes, welcome it into the room, talk about it, and turn it into something else.

"The great thing about the game of golf is that it challenges you to understand your doubts, and move beyond them," Dr. Bob explains. "You have to be smarter than your doubt and fear. When you to tee it up at that Qualifying school, it is no longer about ball-striking. It is about developing a one-shot mind-set, a positive attitude that allows you to play one golf shot at a time."

"You have to accept your anxiety, and then turn it into something else," he continues. "Instead of looking at the guys in your group and thinking how talented they are, think about how special a player you are—*you are Tom Coyne.* You are one heck of a golfer, you have worked as hard as anybody on any tour out there, you deserve to be there. You have to turn around the doubt, and tell yourself, it's these other guys who are lucky to be playing with me."

He says all of this with enough commitment in his voice that I can't help but believe him—*yeah, who the hell do those guys think they are?*

"It's not just a matter of telling yourself that you're not anxious. If you are going to believe, if you are going to have real trust in your golf game and eliminate the doubt, then you have to outsmart it, and outwork it. If you fear a particular golf shot, then that is the shot you need to go home and master. If you're afraid of tournaments, play a dozen more tournaments. If you're afraid of flop shots, hit a thousand flop shots. If you want to gain real competence in your golf game, if you want to master these anxious moments, then between now and the Qualifying School, you should always be *doing the thing you fear.* Worried about the Q-school? Then for every day from here until then, I want you to promise me that you will write down, *I will do well in Q-school. I cannot wait for the Q-school.* Remind yourself that that is exactly where you are headed. Don't let your anxiety enable you to think about anything else."

Doc slides me a sheet of paper titled "Dr. Robert Winters— Golf Tournament Readiness and Commitment Inventory." There are twelve questions with twelve number grades, questions designed to gauge a player's level of mental preparation, warm-up time, level of commitment, intentionality and purposefulness, trust, acceptance, emotional freedom, and fun.

"The Qualifying School is a school because it is a test. You are going to take an exam. When you had studied for your exams, when you were prepared and you knew your stuff, you didn't sweat taking a test. You looked forward to the chance to reveal your *abilities.* Players who have not prepared, they worry about their abilities being *exposed.* Do not look at Qualifying School as a chance to pass or fail—look at it as a chance to show yourself, to show off Tom Coyne."

Dr. Winters jots down notes and flips through sheet after sheet on the tote board in front of me.

"Sure, you are going to be nervous, everyone wishes they had more time to practice. Honestly, the Q-school is a little bit like a marriage: No matter how well you feel you are prepared, you can't really know what it's like until you're there in the middle of it. I can tell you from my experience, the Q-school is a cycle of hot and cold, short term and long term—in the short term, it's all go, commit to the shot, hit the target, drop the putt. In the long term, it has to be all about patience, focus, that one-shot mind-set. Everybody talks about focus. Focus, to me, means getting your butt interested in what the heck you are doing. In golf, that translates to 100 percent effort on each and every shot."

We talk about the parts of my game that aren't so good. I describe for him a few of my greatest hits, the one-under round that turned into an 83; the round that opened with four out of five birdies but eventually swelled to a plump 76.

"There are no flukes in golf, Tom. Get that through your head right now. If you open with three birds, then you make an eight, you'll tell yourself that the birdies were flukes and the quadruple bogey, that's the score you deserve. That mind-set is going to get you nowhere. There is no doubt in my mind that you are capable enough to play each and every golf shot with full and consistent effort. Effort, you can control. You cannot control results."

Up on the board in big blue marker: LET GO OF EXPECTATIONS.

"If you step up to the first tee wondering what you're going to shoot, thinking about how you're going to play, how you're going to finish against Joe Smith or Johnny all-American, then you have adopted what I call a Questioning Mind-set." Doc circles a giant question mark on the board. "And the only expectation that you can bring into a golf shot—the only expectation that works—is expecting yourself to pick a target with complete focus and clarity, and commit to that one, single golf shot. This is a Yes Mind-set, a Proclaiming Mind-set, not a hoping or questioning way of looking at your golf swing. You are going to have to accept your results and your scores for what they are. You have to start thinking about your success on the golf course as whether or not you gave your best effort on each and every shot, one at a time."

Doc and I discuss a European golfer's mentality versus how we think about our golf here in America. Americans tend to be more result-oriented—*nice birdie, nice five, good par,* always aware of the score, focused on the end result. You hear the broadcasters in the British Open talking about how a hole was *well-played*, or a putt was *well-holed*.

"We would do well to borrow a little of that attitude on the golf course, to get away from the fixation on outcome," Dr. Winters explains. "If you are out there on the golf course thinking about a certain score, it is almost an absolute guarantee that you will not shoot it. If all you can think about over a golf shot is winning a tournament, then you might as well pack your bags, because it isn't going to happen. But if you can get to the point where you do nothing but focus on executing one golf shot, then the winning often takes care of itself."

Doc returns to my self-evaluation sheet and where I note that I am almost always under par by the fifth hole, and rarely anywhere near par by the ninth. My everyday rounds have adopted their own predictable routine—two, three under to start, effortless opening birdies, all eventually overrun by unwieldy numbers at the other end of the line, a scorecard tug of war: 2s and 3s on the left versus 7s and 8s on the rights. The birdies never put up much of a fight.

"See, you play great out of the box because on the first tee, you don't have the weight of expectations. You don't have a score in your head yet, a number that you're fixated on. Then, all of a sudden, you let score creep into your round. You let expectations begin to cloud your focus. You're worried about the score instead of being in that particular moment, you start telling yourself what you MUST do. *I MUST make this putt, I MUST make this birdie.* And that is all wrong—the only thing you MUST do is be committed to each and every golf shot."

Doc explains the phenomenon experienced by tour players who are going low, players in the zone who are reeling off eight, nine birdies in a round. If you ask them what they shot before they look at their card, nine times out of ten they would have no idea, or would drastically underestimate their score.

"That's being in the moment," he explains, "when you have absolutely no idea what you might be shooting. In that state of mind, you're not thinking about birdie putts or bogey putts—there is no such thing as either. I want you to forget about birdies and bogeys altogether. That putt is worth one stroke, same as the one before, same as the one after. People say, 'Wow, I gave one back there,' or, 'I made bogey, I have to go get one back now.' And you know what I say to them? I say they are fooling themselves. I don't care if they eagle the next hole, they will never get a stroke back that has already been played. If you are focused on giving strokes up, getting strokes back, then you are certainly not playing golf in the moment. Don't think about birdies. Think about giving full effort on each and every golf shot. If you can do that, when you get to the scorer's table, the birdies will be there waiting for you."

I am tingling with possibility. The professional cynic is nodding and grinning and scribbling down notes while his teacher imparts insights with a preacher's zeal—the look in Dr. Winter's eyes, you can't get a PhD for salesmanship, but he has one. I don't know if I should head out to the range or sign up for active duty.

As good as it all sounds now, I still know that I will find a way to leave it all here in the studio, that I will continue my one-sided love affair with the out-of-bounds stake, unless I find a way to take all this sexy one-shot wisdom and take it out onto the golf course. And this is where Jimbo's advice and my instincts, were right. A psychologist who plays the game, who has teed it up in a Q-school himself, who knows what it feels like to be standing on a first tee, unsure which way is forward.

So after lunch we both strap our bags to the back of a golf cart, and we head out to the golf course to take it step by baby step.

It starts on the driving range, where Dr. Winters takes me through his "Pre-Tourney warm-up to provide stability and confidence." The routine takes roughly forty balls and is twenty-five minutes long, meant to be partnered with a twenty-minute putting routine. Like cultivating a good pre-shot routine, having a go-to warm-up routine is another way I might build confidence before a tournament. At the Nationwide events, I would stand up there beating balls for an hour, working on mechanics, hitting too many six-irons and not enough wedges, knowing, as I looked at the efficient work of the sticks all around me, that I was already out of my league. I would have liked to have had this simple routine then.

It goes like this:

Five sand wedges, just getting loose, no target, no judgment. Then hit three sand wedges to a specific target, using a full pre-shot routine. Then three pitching wedges, to a new target, using a full pre-shot routine. Three nine-irons, full routine. Three seven-irons, five-irons, three-irons, three fairway woods, and five drivers, all with a careful, precise pre-shot routine. With the last eight to ten golf balls, simulate your first three golf holes (driver, seven iron, driver, three-wood, pitching wedge).

We are loose and ready on the first tee when Dr. Winters tells me a story about David Duval on the first tee of one of his college tournaments. When young David stepped onto the tee box, he got under the skin of his playing partners by standing in their line of sight, by dropping his bag in front of theirs, by nearly bumping into one of them when he went to pick his target line. His threesome wasn't too crazy about Duval acting like the rest of them didn't exist. When Dr. Winters had the chance to talk to Duval later that afternoon, he asked him if it was a conscious bit of gamesmanship. Duval was a little embarrassed, because he didn't know what Doc was talking about. He didn't remember standing in front of them, or getting in anybody's way. He wasn't being rude or playing games—he honestly didn't remember them being there at all.

"Point is, you can't step up to the tee thinking about anybody or anything other than where your golf ball is going," Doc explains, teeing up a golf ball between the black markers. "You come to the tee confident because you know that you are physically and emotionally prepared to play well. What I want you to do is to stand behind your ball and choose your target. Create your plan for what you are going to do—here, I am going to hit it at the top of that third mogul through the fairway. That is my target, I can see how my ball is going to fly to that target. Then I rehearse my plan—take a practice swing, feel yourself hitting the golf shot that gets your ball going to that target. Commit to the plan, trust your plan. Once you are committed, once you have gotten to yes, then step up to the ball, fully committed. You cross the trust line," Doc explains, stepping over an imaginary line and stepping up to the golf ball. "Now all I think is target, and go."

Doc smoothly ropes one deep down the left side of the fairway, not two paces off his target hump.

"And the most important thing you do after every shot is accept the results, no matter what they are. Accept them, move on, and do it all again."

The whole crux of Dr. Winters's approach, the focus of his pre-shot routine and his on-course strategy, it all seems to be about trust. Faith, even, the power of believing in your abilities and allowing yourself to say yes. As I tee my own Titleist in the first tee box at Championsgate, I think about trust and how a shitty golf attitude, a whiny, blaming golf persona might just be somebody who can't trust themselves over a golf ball. Can I take that leap of faith, to buy into *Tom Coyne, touring golf professional*? I'm the sort who flips through the late-night gospel channels and sees all these adults smiling like babies, so full of joy and belief as they pray to some guy in polyester, and I think, *You suckers.* But who's the sucker? They may have left what I consider reality, but at least they weren't afraid to jump. Maybe it's all bullshit, but at least their bullshit is warm.

My swing won't always work. I won't always make a good gold decision. But if I can start looking at what's right with my game, the things I can control instead of looking out into the vast ocean of golf trouble before me, maybe some uncommon things are possible. Maybe this really can be a great day.

"Stepping up to the ball, you cross the trust line," Doc explains as I stand behind my ball and pick out my target. "And when you cross it, make no mistake about it—you are committed and ready to go. You are arrived at yes, 100 percent."

"How about 75 percent?" I say, unsure if I should be playing a cut down the left side, or planning for a snapper down the right.

"Then you back away, right now, step away from it," Dr. Winters instructs. "And you start again."

I step away from the ball and exhale, moving back behind the ball and beginning again.

"I don't mind seeing you step away," Dr. Winters tells me. "I like to see that. It tells me that you are thinking. You are not going to hit a shot until you are ready. Tiger Woods said there is never an excuse to make a mental mistake on a golf course, because the ball you're trying to hit, in case you haven't noticed—it isn't moving. We initiate the action. There's no excuse for ever hitting a golf shot and saying *I wasn't ready,* or *I wasn't committed.* And if you should make that mistake, then here," he pulls a rubber band out of his pocket. "My space-age swing aid. Costs a nickel, but out here it is worth a million bucks."

I wrap the rubber band around my wrist and I wonder about all the other players I have seen with rubber bands around their wrists—I thought it was just coincidence or superstition or they liked to keep things organized. I didn't know that, according to Dr. Winters, it is the greatest training aid in the world.

"You are on the golf course. You three-putt. You find yourself starting to think about your score. You hit a shot without being fully committed, just hit it, anyway, for the heck of it. I want you to snap this rubber band," Doc pulls back his own rubber band, snapping it against the inside of his wrist. "If you're standing over a putt, and you start thinking about what you're having for dinner, snap the band and start over. Think of it as a restart button—snap the band, refocus, clear your head, start again."

I slide my band around my wrist. With some of the numbers I make, I could use one made of barbed wire, but I stand behind my golf ball, find a target, try not to notice all the everywhere swamp-land, wonder if there's water in there or if its all just mud. . . . I back off, right there.

"Good, great, that's what I want to see. And why wouldn't you back off if you weren't ready? The guys in your group? The people in the gallery? The group behind you? None of that is your concern. None of that has anything to do with your next golf shot."

I begin again. *Target. Be clear about the target.* Not, *I don't want to hit it in that creek.*

"The body doesn't do very well processing negatives," Doc explains. "You say *Don't hit it in the water,* but your body hears *Hit it in the water.*"

So just by bringing the concept of water, OB, negative results into your mental picture helps guarantee their eventuality.

I rehearse my golf swing. And when I am ready, I step forward across that line . . . *commitment, trust, yes.* The golf ball will often have a mind of its own, not all the putts will drop simply because I had faith that they would. But if I can step up to the golf ball without doubt, I have done as much as I can to give it a fighting chance.

"One, no more than two simple swing thoughts from here on in," Doc had explained earlier. "If there's one mechanical point you're working on, take one small piece of it, say *tempo,* or *smooth-takeaway.* I'd rather you just think, *Swing to your target.* Just something simple to get things started."

Swing to the target. Swing to the target. Swing to . . . I finally get the club head moving back, still a little nervous to actually take a golf swing in front of this renowned psychologist whom I had been trying to sell on the fact that I was Q-school caliber, that I wasn't going to waste his time—*the target*—and suddenly I am watching my ball ride long and deep toward that particular spot. Not the left side of the fairway, or somewhere out there, but a focused, specific landmark (the more specific the target, the more your mind can do to communicate the idea to your muscles). In this case, the fourth green hump along the edge of the fairway.

"Instead of keeping your score, I want you to give yourself a letter grade for your level of commitment to each shot," Doc explains as we drive out to our balls. "I don't care where the ball goes. I don't care what number you make. Right now, I just want you to be clear and committed on every golf shot that you hit."

On my scorecard, I give myself an A (awesome, absolute commitment) for my first swing. The grades range from A to C (clear, committed) to W (wavering) to F (fuzzy). I feel slightly liberated letting go of expectation, taking on these new letter grades and forgetting about my score. Just hitting shot after shot, it's like I'm actually playing the game, as opposed to just keeping track of it. The end number had been so much bigger than the process, the result had been drowning out the progress. Commit to a shot, and hit it. Then do it again. *That's* playing golf, it occurs to me. *That* is playing the game.

My confidence grades fluctuate between quite good and slightly confused, but it's interesting how nervous I'm *not* around Doc Winters. It took me a good few weeks to settle down around Doc Suttie, and when I went to the Mizuno sales conference in Atlanta that summer and tried out all their new gear, hitting balls on the range next to, gulp, Billy Andrade, I was scared shitless. But I was settled in with Dr. Winters because I wasn't thinking about Dr. Winters. I was trying to think about the next shot. They weren't all perfect, but they were all respectable, and well within an acceptable margin of error. By trying not to impress him, the impressing-him-part sort of took care of itself.

It's the seventh hole when he decides I have a fair chance at the upcoming Q-school. I had been bombing my driver Jimbo Fuller distances, and I stuffed two ninety-yard sand wedges back to back, my onetime approach shot nemesis.

"I didn't know what I was getting here. But I am impressed," he says. "To have your wedges dialed in like that, you're a lot further along then I thought you would be."

He sends me home with a rubber band, and a little bruise on the MasterCard. The day wasn't free, but I am going to get unlimited access on the phone, as well the chance to come visit and work with him at one of his golf camps, free of charge. In the realm of top-flight golf performance consultants, it was all quite generous.

I flew back home that evening (in all my time back and forth to Florida, my first flight of the year, white knuckles the whole way), and I didn't know how long the love would last, how long the message would stick without the deep, soothing convincing voice of the messenger. It seemed great in Orlando, but everything seemed great in Orlando. I wasn't home twenty-four hours before I had the chance to see if the rubber band snapped the same way up north.

In my season-long quest to violate all possible tournament entry protocol, I was signed up for the professional qualifier for the Philadelphia Open—exclusively for club pros in the section who had either passed through or enrolled in the PGA program. I had done neither. As with all these tournaments, I went online, put my name in, I got a tee time. And I knew enough of the assistant pro vernacular—*How many guys you got in the shop? You're a first assistant, and you're still running carts? Ever get any lessons?*—that I could blend right in. I was paired with a head pro and a first assistant, and when they started asking how many hours I was pulling in the shop, I started hemming as I tried to do the math.

"Not too many, actually." *As in, zero.*

"Do you get to teach?" the head pro asks me.

"Well, I'm really just playing this season. I'm not really working at the moment. They just sort of let me play and practice."

In their estimation, I was the luckiest damn club pro of which they had ever heard. The assistant promised that he was sure to be calling over to—*where d'you say you were from?*—Edgmont, hoping to get a gig like that of his own.

The gentleman's game. Once again, it had brought me to duplicity.

My first swing of the day is cause for a regular rubber-band lashing. We shotgun-started on the number-one handicap hole (i.e., the toughest), a par-five with a hundred-yard carry over weeds, a moat of goo at 250 yards, and OB snaking down the entire left side. I was not committed. I did not get to yes. I did not even get to *Why not?* It was my first time on this particular golf course, and I didn't know what club was too much or too little or if I was carrying one that was just right—my first pass felt like I was swinging with handcuffs on. As the ball snapped left, my fingers snapped the rubber band. My wrist is raw pink by the time I got out to my second drive sitting in the fairway, and as I step up to a 270-yard shot, I pull three-wood to try and have some chance of saving bogie.

Snap. No thinking about bogeys or pars or score. Think about the golf shot. Commit to this shot, even though a three-wood off the deck with an oily pool twenty yards ahead isn't exactly your forte, you can almost hear the gurgle of your Titleist succumbing to the pond scum. . . .

Snap. Pick the damn target, and hit the goddamn golf shot. All that other stuff—in words that Doc Winters might not have chosen—tell it all to just piss off.

Sometimes, the game feels so simple, so cooperative. My Titleist kisses the softest bit of my three-wood, and it was barreling toward the green, where, 270 yards later, it rolled to rest a half-dozen paces from the flag.

Holy shit, I could make par on this hole after snapping my drive out of bounds, the number-one handicap hole, what a great start that would be, making eagle on my second ball. . . .

Snap. I picked my line. This isn't an eagle putt. It's not a par putt. It's one stroke on your scorecard, nothing more, nothing less. If it goes in, great. If not, I'll do it again.

I wouldn't have bothered telling you about my first hole snap hook out of bounds redeemed by a ridiculous three-wood if I couldn't finish the story off with this: a putt dead in the heart for an outrageous opening par.

The rest of the day, me and my rubber band fought the good fight around the golf course. The newborn mental approach is like working fresh changes into my swing. Sometimes they take hold, sometimes they take a quiet backseat to voices from the past—*You dumb suck, how did you turn birdie into bogey!*

The round was steady, on a tight and tricky little Downingtown track, and I kept it together. I didn't lose my shit when I three-putted, once from a strength-sapping twelve feet, another time from three miles away. I took my bad breaks in stride—fescue grass through the fairway that turned a seemingly ideal drive into a lost ball, a mis-clubbed safety layup that found the downward edge of a creek. I arrive at my final hole five-over par, knowing that four-over 76, according to my partners who had been here before, was the target score for the main event.

Our last hole is a par three, 180 yards downhill over water, the tee box situated beside the clubhouse and a veranda where a few dozen curious members nibbling on sandwiches had come out to see how the pros got it around their sneaky-tough golf course.

I pull seven-iron. Knowing that I absolutely have to make birdie, I let score go. All I think about is taking the club back in the right spot, and swinging at my target. . . . Okay, that's a lie, I *am* thinking about making birdie. I'm surprised I don't scream it halfway through my backswing: *Come on, birdie!* But after a good day of ball-striking, I'm able to take tight aim and trust it, to call on a shot and hit it. No more *Please go in the air.* Or *Anywhere on the green would be wonderful, my firstborn for something on the green.* The ball jumps off my clubface and climbs up the breeze, crashing down far below us onto that green, grabbing ten feet past the pin and twirling backward to five.

Soft applause from the gallery, a nod and a smile from the pro from Edgmont as he mouths *Thank you, thank you very much.*

I make the birdie putt for a highly respectable 76—even though the cut ends up at 75, in my mind, I had qualified. I hit the shot I needed to make the number I needed to make. That was plenty good enough, especially considering that if I did actually qualify, the PGA section would have fingered me as a total imposter.

I do succeed in making tournament alternate, however. At 76, there is a play-off for an alternate position between myself and a young pro from New Jersey. The play-off hole is the same par-three I had birdied a few minutes before. And this time, with a slightly larger gallery hanging around the scoreboard, as I watch an almost identical seven-iron fall for the pin, I think for a second that there may not even be any need to walk down there and putt out. But we do have to make the walk down to the hole—my ball mark is three inches from the cup, and I tap in to finish the day with near twin birdie 2s.

And another wave for the gallery—*Thanks a lot, folks, thanks for coming out.*

"He's trying to not be result-oriented."

My father laughs as he explains my awkwardly laconic golf demeanor to his office buddy, Dennis. We're playing an evening eighteen at my dad's home track, Rolling Green. Dennis had asked how many over I was, and I told him I didn't know. I was trying to let go of that score, but I knew precisely—a lackluster plus-five through fifteen, standing on the tee of an easily reachable par-five seventh hole (we started on the back, a detail which, in this case, actually matters). I told my dad not to tell me what I was shooting, not to add it up at the turn, because I was trying to stop thinking about score and results.

"I'm trying to let go of expectations," I had explained. "I don't want to be result oriented."

My dad gave me an amused look, like I had confused this twilight round for Augusta Sunday. He cracked his Budweiser and said, "Sure, Tom. Whatever."

It was a simple thing, but it was also a tension that I fought most of the year: the need to take this game too seriously, when I had grown up with the game as my family's one great diversion.

Golf could too easily descend into playtime—it was either hyper-intense alienating focus, or *ten bucks I can hit this over that house*.

Perhaps I should have found more players to push me, spent more time immersed in that *golf-is-my-business* world that the grinders and the Jimbo Fullers occupy. But that was not a world entirely open or affordable to a newcomer like myself, a milieu that I was not prepared for in one year. Those guys, I don't think they played slap it around golf with their dads on Thursdays, or played in a nine-hole bar league on Tuesday nights at the local cow pasture. Mess-around golf—maybe it was something I should have cut from my diet coming down my home stretch, but let's be honest, and not sentimental: Strip away all the other stuff, and if there is an actual point to this silly game, if it is ever really meant to make sense, then twilight golf with Dad is as close as it gets.

That didn't mean I wasn't trying to hang up a good number. On these relaxed rounds, I would find myself pushing even harder, trying to show off as the conspicuous A-player, and ending up far more frustrated than relaxed. On the tee of eagle-friendly seventh, I go after my golf ball as if it owes me money. I turn eagle into eight, and I come to the last hole eight shots over par. And honestly, I would skip the final hole if they would let me. Nine is that legendary par five, 600 yards uphill, side hill, and forever, and today it looks like a saltwater Slip-'n'-Slide to my newly opened wounds.

"Come on, finish strong. Let's see that smooth swing," my dad says, and I stand there pouting, like I'd dropped my lollipop in the dirt.

"I don't even care. What's the point. I'm a million over."

"That doesn't matter. Try and get one back here, come on."

He wants me to finish well, and he wants me to stop acting like a twenty-nine-year-old country club brat who could look so miserable on one of the most beautiful golf holes in the state. So on my walk from the cart to the tee box, I shake off what cobwebs I can. I'm not wearing my rubber band (mistake), so I substitute a punishment, tugging the hair on my arm. *Wake up*, I tell myself. *Put one in the damn fairway.*

Number nine at Rolling Green is just one of those tee shots—maybe it was the way the shadow falls in the late afternoon, how I could always watch my take-away in silhouette—it was always host to my day's best swings, and in this case, one of the best golf swings of my life. Just when you can't see a reason not to quit, golf throws you a little bone to suck you back in for tomorrow. This drive is born of the perfect confluence of meticulous mechanics and arms-race technology—it's the sort of contact that makes you sympathize with the folks on the USGA and the R&A equipment committees. I am shocked to watch my ball soar beyond a fairway mound that I rarely reached with forty yards of roll. I turn to Dad for his reaction, expecting to see his jaw brushing the tee box, but he just looks at me, confused.

"Where the hell did that go? That go right?"

"No, it's pretty good," I say. "It should be in the fairway."

"You're damn right it's pretty good. Holy shit," Dennis says, smiling with his whole face.

After playing and toting two golf bags up this same fairway for eighteen years, I knew when I got ahold of one. I can tell by the sprinkler heads, or which mound the ball had rolled up against. But on this occasion, I am in virgin territory. I have never been up this far, except on my third or fourth shots, and it was the first time I had ever even heard of somebody having a marked yardage on their second shot on number nine—246 to the hole, uphill all the way.

To my knowledge, since the club opened in 1926, number nine had been reached in two by only three players, all golf professionals, only one of whom went on to make the putt. One eagle in eighty years, and I'm standing over a flat lie with a Mizuno hybrid in my hand that had arrived two days before (not working in a plug, just pointing out that I didn't quite need a three-wood), and I am nervous. *Holy shit, I have a chance to hit number nine in two*—at Rolling Green, this was far bigger deal than a hole in one. My dad had three aces of his own on this course, but here, sun-setting on a Thursday night in August, here's a chance to make some real club history, to conquer this old golf course's last unconquerable.

I back off. I look at Dennis waiting in our cart. His usually bouncy countenance has gone US Open gallery steely. My father sits in his cart with his playing partner, a client named John, and though Dad is usually a rabbit-speedy player, here he is frozen still, foot nowhere near the gas pedal as I eye up my target. . . .

The pin. Red flag against the shadows of the trees. I step into my shot, and hearing one swing thought, I take Dad's one bit if advice, and I swing smooth. The funny thing is, as I watch the ball move toward the pin, not cutting or drawing a hair, I think to myself, *I wonder if anyone has made two on this hole.* I would be elated, but not surprised if that golf ball goes into that hole.

I am not disappointed when it doesn't. The ball lands on the green after a 240-yard carry—I didn't bounce it up, there was a proper ballpark on the elevated green, the ball rolling to a spot ten feet from the hole.

When the eagle putt dropped, you could have heard my dad's voice on the driving range, in the parking lot, in the men's grill, all those sleepy faces turning to look at what happened out the window, a foursome of grown men high-fiving like they'd just received a snow day.

We sat down in the grill for a toast, and there wasn't a member who was able to pass within ten feet of our table that didn't hear about the last hole of our round.

"Hit it in two. Made the putt. First amateur to hit the green in two, ever. Only second eagle I've heard of in, what, eighty years?"

My father isn't a long hitter, barely gets it out two hundred yards now that he's passed seventy years old. Number nine was getting tough for him to reach in four good pokes anymore, so while a course record would have been nice, there was something about my playing that signature hole he'd been playing for thirty-five years, to play it in a way that few considered a possibility—it was significant in a way that I think surprised all of us.

When Dennis and John left and it was just me and my dad, we sat there a little while and just smiled to ourselves. We weren't the sort for big conversations, mostly we just checked in on each other, usually both deciding that everything was fine—*Everything here is good, how's everything there?*

That cancer? It's fine. Your brother? We'll handle it. The market? Nothing to worry about. It wasn't that we couldn't talk about touchy realities, or that either of us were dismissing any of it. Everything *was* fine—it was always the truth, and the truth with Dad was simpler, and oftentimes a little sweeter. So as we got up from our table, he was almost saying too much when he patted me on the back and told me, "That was awesome, Tom boy. Just awesome."

USGA Handicap Index: 0.0
Weight: 197.4 pounds

When Padraig picked up the new handicap sheet at Edgmont and saw that my index had dropped to zero, it wasn't five minutes before he was on the phone setting up a match for Saturday, telling me that "There's no fucking way I'll be taking strokes from the likes of you."

He would feel differently on the back nine.

As we watch my drive on the fourteenth hole at Tattersall in West Chester take a very aggressive line, carrying the far bunker and just steering past the out-of-bounds, Paddy says, "I'd tell you that was a good shot, if that was at all what the hell you meant to do with it."

"How do you know that wasn't where I was aiming?"

"Well, if it was, then you've got the course management of a donkey. You're one up on the match, and you go flirting with the out of bounds."

He's right, I was aiming thirty yards to the right of where my ball had ended up. However, as I point out to Paddy, "It ended up perfect."

"Sure it did. Just like it did at the Pennsylvania Open," he says. "Wasn't that the tournament where you decided to play with an OB stake stuck up your arse?"

But there isn't much else to say about my driving except that it had been pretty damn special. I hit two par-fives in two and drive the fifth hole par-four, three-jacking each of them to re-create one of golf's saddest scoring decisions, the three-putt-par. I don't know if it's my putting stroke, or my mental block about golf with Paddy, but if there is a chance to be generous with strokes and keep him in the match, I'll find a way.

He two-putt pars seventeen, and as we come to the final hole of our match, we are all square. Again.

After his best drive of the day, Paddy stands over a two-forty shot into the finishing par-five green guarded by a pond bubbling with stagnant green mucus. I have a three-iron to get home, so he steps out of the cart and, although the ball is slightly below his feet, he doesn't look at me as he unzips his three-wood. But I'm certainly looking at him.

"Wow, Rossie, he must really be worried about going to extra holes with young Coyne. He's trying to win this match right now. He's trying to end this with one swing."

Paddy backs off his ball, eyes on his target as he tells me, "We're gonna play that game, are we, fat boy?"

"He's reverting back to the old classic, right back to the fat jokes. I'd have to call this an all-time pot calling the kettle black, Rossie, seeing as Coyne has slimmed down quite nicely, while Paddy couldn't tell you the color of that belt he's wearing."

Paddy makes two unsure-looking practice swings before the slope of the fairway takes his final swing of the day deep right, cutting foul into the upper deck, plopping down deep into the pea soup.

"Oh, that's got to be one he'd like to have back."

Paddy looks at his clubface as if it lied to him. He drops another ball out of his pocket. "Must have a generous sponsor to be so careless with the golf balls," I continue as we watch the next ball go looking for its twin.

Paddy doesn't even stop at my ball to let me hit it. It's right to the pub, where he might yet save some face.

"You've got to give yourself that credit," Paddy tells me over a bucket of light beers. "No matter what happens at the Qualifying school, you gave it your shot. You'll know, either way. Most people just talk about it in the pub, then go home and get up for a job they despise."

"You're not the player you were," he continues, "but I don't think you have the confidence with your irons that you need. I don't think you go grab for that four-iron with any love in your heart." He's spot-on correct, and he's right again when he observes, "Your putting is for shit. It might be okay for mucking it about in the scat game at Edgmont, but for someone going to the Q-school, you can't be hitting greens in two and three-rolling them. You spend five minutes lining up a putt, and you misread the thing by nine feet."

"That's not an exaggeration?"

"Did anyone actually teach you how to read a green? Do you know how to plumb-bob and look for break?"

"Plum-bob?" I say. "Plumb-bobbing went out with orange golf balls."

"Well, you could use a few dozen of those as well, I think. Maybe this way you won't go hitting the wrong ball anymore from the middle of your own fricking fairway."

That's what I get for making him my golf confidant. And I might just be opening myself up for more, but I think he is the man for the job.

"Then why don't you come with me to the Q-school and read the greens for me?" I ask him. Paddy takes his eyes off the television, cashes out his cigarette.

"I can't be walking around reading the greens," he says. "You're not allowed coaches out there, only your caddy can read putts for you."

"That's what I'm asking you. Do you want to caddy for me?"

I've been going back and forth this year about finding the

perfect Q-school looper, some veteran jock or some on-course genius, or, as Dr. Winters suggested, someone who really knows me, who will make the strange environs of a Q-school more familiar. I take Doc's advice—even if Paddy busts my balls all the way around the golf course, it will feel just like home.

"Out of your mind." He laughs. "Me? Carrying your bag?"

"Like you couldn't use the exercise. I've got the carry-bag, with the two straps. It's just like walking around with a backpack on."

Paddy turns his attention back to the Phillies game on TV. He watches a few pitches. It's unusual—I've put him in a spot where he's got nothing to say.

"Well, it damn well better be the carry bag," he finally relents. "Because if you think I'll be lugging that blue coffin of yours around the golf course, you're out of your fucking mind."

It was my putting that brought me back to Florida for a weekend visit with a short-game specialist at Grand Cypress. Throughout the last year, my putting has taken me to several exotic locales—places like Clearwater, Florida, where I made a pilgrimage to meet the Bobby Grace in person at his MacGregor headquarters. Bobby Grace's putters have long been a hit on the PGA tour, akin to Mizuno in a way—not as many billboards, but the choice of those in the know. I played his Fat Man when I was a junior golfer and a good putter, and his new MOI putter (moment of inertia, designed to move the center of gravity back in the clubface, making the clubface more stable when it meets the ball) was quietly cleaning up on tour. The likes of Vijay and Retief could regularly be spotted using one. Padraig Mahoon had himself recently gone to a Bobby Grace long putter and, per his estimation, was "making every fucking thing I looked at."

When I met Mr. Grace—who was younger-looking than I anticipated, Florida handsome, not the back-room metal tinker one might expect—he was kind enough to take a chunk of time out of his day to visit with me and explain his philosophy on the long putter. While I don't get the impression it's something he would put in his own bag (he's a self-described pure putter, which, for a putter guru, I would imagine to be true), he agrees that, "The more upright you can get, the less talent it takes to putt." The more the putter can hang straight up and down like a bellcock, the less coordination and touch the putting stroke requires. It's just a matter of pulling the shaft back, and letting it swing. And over short putts in competition, where my hands get especially goofy, where I tend to forget which direction is back, the long-putter is especially useful in taking the jiggles out of one's hands. It's easier to hold a cannon steady than it is a revolver. While it may be more difficult to gauge distance and speed, the long putter rules for steady consistency. And I went to Clearwater and found the best—Bobby Grace fit me personally, wrapped the MacGregor sticker around the shaft himself, and sent me on my way.

It is a gorgeous putter, and for weeks I hardly missed from inside five feet. My only problem was that most of my first putts were rarely getting that close. I believe that the long putter is a scientifically superior way to putt the golf ball (the belly putter, where the butt of the club is planted in your stomach, holding the club like a third hand—that sort of feels like cheating). The long putter may itself someday be outlawed, but if it wasn't, I would buy every beginner a long putter before they ever stepped foot on a putting green. Players will putt like robots someday; someone will shoot 54 with a long putter—but only if they putt that way their entire lives. For me, I cannot get comfortable with the big stick, not halfway through my tournament season. Ultimately, the long putter goes the way of so many of my flat blades, becoming the easy scapegoat for shooting 81.

It had nothing to do with Bobby Grace or his craftsmanship—

it was worth the trip to meet the man and pick his brain. *It's not you, it's me,* I'd tell him—but in this case, it really is me. I have a problem. I am an absolute putter slut.

I commit to putters like a day-trader commits to stocks. Two weeks with the same putter was a common-law marriage for me. During one round at Rolling Green, I bought a putter before the round started, traded it in, and bought a new putter *during* the round (three-putted a green that happened to be near the pro shop), then returned that putter and bought an altogether new club after finishing up eighteen. I went from the Bobby Grace V-Foil MOI long putter to the Cameron Futura, from the Cameron Futura to the MacGregor Bobby Grace M-series, to the Ping EZ, to the Never Compromise Stubby (this was my most desperate hour, switching to a putter with a club head the size of a grape—you can't miss the sweet spot, because there's nothing else). I needed help, so I wrote to my pals at Titleist, telling them my sad story and inquiring about the healing properties of this new Cameron Red-X I had been hearing about, hoping they might be able to send one along to shepherd me through my final tournaments.

As we used to say around the caddy yard, *It ain't the arrow, it's the Indian.* I know deep down that it's none of those fine putters' fault, so I make the trip to Orlando to see a pro who had been recommended as something of a putting specialist (no offense, Dr. Suttie, just taking some time for a second opinion).

We spend an hour and half working on my putting tempo. Rhythm, tempo, cadence—it's the whole ball of wax, according to this young teaching pro who's a disciple of the bigger name I was hoping to visit with (again, the bigger the name on the marquee, the less likely they're actually there). The pro actually clips a digital metronome to my belt, and I putt to a repeating 1-2-3-4 rhythm. Luckily, I have an uncommon amount of rhythm for a gangly redhead, so putting to the beats resonates with me.

One, two, three, four . . . look at the hole, look at your ball, take the club back, hit . . . one, two, three, four . . . hole, ball, club, hit . . .

The speed and length of the takeaway vary for the length of the putt, but the rhythm and pacing always stay the same. I found it amazing how that four-count rhythm frees up your stroke. If you think about the rhythm and the numbers and forget about making the putt, it's amazing how many putts hit the putter face dead center (I think the most common reason for missed putts is missing the middle of the putter), taking off with a perfect end-over-end roll and finding the dead center of the cup.

Try making twenty-four-footers in a row. Not that easy, especially when you get to sixteen, seventeen, and start thinking about what you're doing. In come the hands, in comes the golfer trying to steer the ball, and here comes the golfer having to start over from one. But if you sit there over a four-footer and rehearse that rhythm in your head—*hole, ball, stroke, hit . . . one, two, three, four*—making twenty in a row is like gobbling bon-bons. It's like Dr. Winters said: letting go of the result, getting into the process. It's under pressure that the cadence would come in most handy, giving me something to fill up my head aside from positive thoughts like *Don't you dare miss this, moron.*

Two weeks after flying down to Florida, I am off to Chicago to work on the exact same putting concept with Chip Beck, a player who obviously knows a little bit about getting the ball into the hole, having helped win the Ryder Cup for the US, and having shot a 59 on the PGA tour, a feat accomplished only three times in tour history. He had been working with Dr. Suttie, preparing for, I suspect, a run at the senior tour.

When I arrive for my week of work at Doc's summer spot, the Dr. Jim Suttie Academy at Green Garden Country Club, not an hour outside of Chicago, the first thing Doc does is send me out to watch Chip Beck give a few of Doc's students a short-game clinic.

Chip's putting routine is almost identical to the one I had brought back from Florida, a four-beat putting rhythm.

Now some people talk about Chip Beck as a tour player who famously fell off the wagon of golf greatness—when you have the success he had in the late 1980s and early 90s, you don't have to slip very far to be considered less than the player you once were. But after watching Mr. Beck that afternoon, I don't know how ridiculously good you have to be to stay on that wagon. In five hours on the putting green and in the bunkers and in the fairways, I watch Chip Beck, a shortish pro, thin with strong, dark features and an accent that was more south then Chicago—I watch him hit a hundred golf shots, and not one of them wasn't so gorgeous that I wouldn't have put it on tape, downloaded it, and fired it off to Paddy with the subject line *How f-ing good is this?*

He moves around the property, demonstrating his short game arsenal. *Key to the fifty-yard bunker shot?* He knocks five of them stony. *My approach to lagging a forty-foot putt?* He drains half of them. *What's my strategy on four-footers?* He bangs ten into the back of the cup, a steady *one-two-three*, his putter in perfect rhythm.

Dr. Suttie had told me about his Midwestern digs, and they lived up to the billing. His nook at the Green Garden Country Club is an embarrassment of teaching-pro riches. As he shows me around the facility, I feel a sadness for all the golf pros everywhere else, teaching on tiny patches of Astro Turf and dust, no shelter from the rain or cold. Doc's one gripe with his new summer setup (his old, and possibly future, Chicago home was Cog Hill) is that it it's a good forty-five minutes outside the city—though, as I pointed out to him, to find enough property for a teaching mecca like this, you'd have to be pretty damn far from any city. The club itself boasts two highly rated daily-fee courses, but it's Doc's setup that is really worth the trip.

He has the first *indoor* driving range I have ever seen. The first thing you see of Green Garden as you come over the rolling cow pasture is the massive white dome, like half a giant golf ball rising out of the amber waves of grain. We used to have the exact same kind of dome in Philadelphia. The Eagles practiced in it. I'm not sure how often Doc even uses this golf thunderdome, because just down the road from the clubhouse he has his own indoor facility that you can't miss. THE DR. JIM SUTTIE ACADEMY as big as a billboard, painted across the side of a tractor trailer. His two-story studio has offices, a board room, a studio for having your putting stroke analyzed, and two hitting bays stuffed with more lighting and cameras than they had when they shot *A Gentleman's Game*. The hitting bays overlook a sprawling driving range, one entire side of which is covered by a green tarp. It's a giant sort of twenty-person golf umbrella, so as to bring the cliché to life that it never actually does rain on a golf course. And the range has more targets than any tour pro could ask for—flags every color of the rainbow planted in faux greens, yardages carefully measured from each flat to each spot along the range.

There are three different short game areas—you can play bunker shots from any conceivable lie and distance to a half-dozen different pins. The practice putting green is the size of Lake Michigan. And there's a second putting green tucked back amid one of the *seven practice holes* that Doc has entirely to himself. Each of the holes was brand-new, stunningly beautiful, and all of them more empty than the time I got to play Pine Valley.

And for a week, it was all mine. When I arrived on a Monday morning, Doc introduced me to his staff with his warmest, "This is Tom Coyne. He's going to be here for a while. Let him do whatever he wants."

Which included hitting a thousand balls off a driving range as tender as peach fuzz, or slipping off to Doc's practice course with a shag bag full of Titleists, working on those little shots that you can only get out on an actual golf course. Bump and runs from thirty, forty, fifty yards out. Chip shots from tight fairway lies, making the ball grab and release to the hole. I was in front of Doc's camera at least once a day, and by this point, I was breaking down my own film, cutting together my own tapes on the V1 for Doc to look over when he had a minute. For a guy who was afraid to fart in his studio in Naples, I swaggered around the spot in Chicago like I was one of the gang.

"You're still hitting the big right ball," Doc was surprised to find as we went over my first afternoon's tape.

At impact, my clubhead tended to get just a hair outside the line, wiping the ball with cut-spin. On good misses, it was perfectly playable. On bad ones, it was two strokes and re-tee. And take after take, rewind and rewind again, I could not figure out why until Doc pointed to my right shoulder, the way it was rotated forward at address, forcing my shoulders to angle left.

My feet and hips were dead square to the target, but, "Your right shoulder is pronated," he explained. "That gets your clubhead moving left with an open face."

I could have looked at the tape all day and never seen it. I'm sure nine out of ten pros would have looked at my posture and given me a gold star. But Doc, he pulls my right shoulder back, and he convinces me to work on keeping my right elbow a little lower to help my swing stay more connected, keeping my club out in front of me on my downswing.

We get a chance to sit down and talk over some of his article ideas—the golf magazines have, incredibly, yet to take one of our gems—"One Good Turn Deserves Another," "The String's the Thing," "Keeping up with the Woodses." We've tried to make them shorter and sweeter and simpler (dumber, really)—as they say they want them—but the publishing dice have yet to roll Doc's way this season (translation: Our little barter system is even more lopsided in my favor than I'd thought). When we get to talking about how I've been doing in my tournaments, I mention a few highlights, being tied with Michelle Wie, my ever-shrinking handicap, holding my own in the Philly Open, and a dozen other character-builders along the way. I tell him about the US Amateur qualifier that I would be playing in South Bend in three days' time—a big field of college sticks with two, maybe three whole spots for qualifiers.

"What do you think you need to shoot for that?"

"For thirty-six holes . . . it's a tough course. If I could keep it around par, maybe one-over, that would make it, I think."

"That shouldn't be a problem. Even par, you can shoot that, can't you?" Doc says, expecting one of his longtime students to be able to answer that question confidently in the affirmative.

And with all the hope I can muster, I nod. "Absolutely."

"And how are the plans for Q-school? Do you think you'll be ready by October?"

In all the time we had discussed what I was doing this year, or he had mentioned my project to a third party, he always left the part of my ultimately actually attending Tour Qualifying School undiscussed, as if that was a cart so mightily ahead of my horse. He vaguely described my goal as *trying to play at the next level*, never *getting ready for Qualifying School*. And that was fair. Sure, mine was a pipe dream, and I would never expect otherwise from someone who knew so much about the game, who had seen so many players walk through his studio with loads more game and never even sniff passing Stage I. I didn't expect Doc Suttie to say anything otherwise. He didn't blow smoke. But there was this one thing. . . .

"Actually, about the Q-school. I'm going to play in three of them. The Canadian Tour, and the Tour de las Americas . . ."

"The what tour?"

"It's the Latin American tour, around South America, the Caribbean."

"But you're playing the PGA Q-school, aren't you?"

"Of course. I want to play these other schools as sort of a warm-up, get used to playing a four-day tournament. I've never played one before, so . . ."

"You've never played in a four-day tournament?" He smiles, like I've told him a joke he wasn't expecting to be funny.

"No. But by the time I get to tour school, I'll have played these other two."

"Well, that's a good idea, then."

"Right. But, the thing about it is, for the PGA Q-school, I think I need a recommendation."

"Hmmm," he says. It's not as comfortable a *hmmm* as I would have liked.

"Actually, I know I need one. And I thought you would be a good person to ask."

"Well," he says, with a shrug of the shoulders. "I'll see."

I have been to Augusta National, and it's the only experience in my life where physically stepping onto the property has actually given me chills, where I have literally felt my steps grow lighter—the only time, of course, aside from every single time I revisit Notre Dame.

I am not the obnoxious rah-rah Irish guy you knew in high school. I find some ND fans tiresomely elitist, and I think it is far from the perfect university. But when I make that turn off the Indiana turnpike at exit 77, it is chills every time. I roll down the window, and the air, it smells like nineteen again, and though I've arrived in this weird little corner of Indiana, I can't imagine a more perfect place on this planet, a world where the sidewalk is always clean and the strangers all say hello and the biggest thing you have to worry about is how the coach is getting along with the quarterback.

But on this trip, there's no nostalgic stop at the grotto—not that I couldn't use the prayers. This time, I'm back to campus to get a job done, to show something to these college boys I tried to hang with ten years before, when they didn't quite seem to have the room for me at their table.

The U.S. Amateur Championship has essentially become an NCAA tournament. I don't remember the last winner who was older than twenty-two, and all the way up and down the driving range at the Notre Dame golf course, that's what I find, bags from Michigan State, Indiana, Ball State, and of course, ol' Notre Dame. There are a few of us without college colors, and we look ancient by comparison, regular old-timers with niblicks and hickory shafts, come out to see what these whippersnappers were up to.

I could have picked any qualifying site in the country, but I wanted to come back home and see what has changed since I'd three-jacked my way off the golf team. First off, the golf course has gone from eighteen landing strips out the back windows of my room in Fisher Hall to a new Crenshaw-sculpted serpentine at the far corner of campus. The facilities have changed the way everything at Notre Dame seems to have changed—small scrapped for big, old elegance replaced by new, the campus bulging into something immediately and relentlessly impressive. The Notre Dame golf team seems to have its own practice facility at the far end of the range, where a half-dozen Irish players are showing off their home-court advantage, trying to reach our visitors' end of the range with their drivers.

I watch them chat and point and wave their buddies over to watch them try to reach us, running their golf balls up to the front of our tee—gracious hosts, indeed. When one of them rolls a ball not five feet from the where I and half the Big Ten are hitting balls, I calmly walk over to my golf bag. I casually peel the Mizuno cover off my sleeping driver and I tee one up a little higher than usual.

I don't know how deep this range actually goes, if I would actually be able to get one near them or not. I just take a smooth swing, and loose the ball into the late-day sun. But when I watch all five of them spin around at the sound of something crashing through a tree behind them, I figure I had taken enough stick to get there.

Like a street gang called to duty, the five of them hurry to grab their drivers and start ripping balls back at us as fast as they can tee them up. I go back to knocking down peaceful seven-irons until one of the balls takes two big hops and rolls to a stop at my feet and I decide that maybe it is time to get working on that driver swing again, keep those shoulders square. Three hard blasts with all the attitude of an alum who can't believe these spoiled brats are hitting balls at him. And they are spoiled—they are smarter, more accomplished, certainly better players than when I was in college. Everything here has gotten so much *better*. But with better, it seems everything has gotten a bit more smug about it. I don't know, maybe it's just me. Maybe I'm just pissed that I'm not eighteen anymore, dumb enough to hit range balls at total strangers. Then again, that is precisely how dumb I am today.

When I arrive the next morning, I already know I have to go low—the first group has already posted 68 and 70, playing quick before the breeze kicked up, that flat Indiana wind that blew nastiness into this 7,000-yard track, caused the fescue to spin and grab at golf balls like little fingers. I start off with a par, make an absurd birdie on a 240-yard par-three, but from there I have a hard time drawing on everything Doc and I had put into practice just that week. I don't quit, I don't freak, I make one triple bogey when the fescue ingests one of my golf balls. But the swing feels like it only partly belongs to me at this point. My excuse of the week: coming off a bunch of lessons, hard to trust your swing when you haven't quite earned it on the range yet.

I shoot a regular 79 and get fescued out of the cut to play in the second day, set at a rather stingy 76.

The drive to Chicago is twice as long as the drive to Notre

Dame. My trip now has an unexpected free day, but I don't go back to Doc's place. I stay in the city, watch the White Sox win, have a couple Old Styles with the college roommates who don't quite understand what the big deal was about this golf tournament.

It isn't a big deal—not any bigger a deal than the dozens more I could already chalk up to experience. What I am doing, it is hard. Doc was right. It is hard to play this golf, among this talent, when you aren't allowed to hit one sideways from time to time and say *Just give me a double bogey.* Dr. Suttie, he had no doubt that I could make that qualifying number, and yet, with everything I have, the work and hours and dollars, I knew in my belly I still wasn't that kid. Not yet. Just like every other August at Notre Dame, never the player, only the fan.

When I arrive home from Chicago, Q-school season is upon me, lurking over me, dangling a finger in my face. My applications are sitting on my desk—the Canadian, Latin American, the PGA Tour Qualifying tournaments, filled out with my name and my shrunken handicap, each attached to my rubbery signed checks. I don't have any recommendations to send along, which is about what I deserve for delaying until the last minute, too nervous to ask my coach, hoping and waiting for that magic round to come along where I would wipe away all his doubt with two small digits sitting side by side.

Those numbers didn't come. And for once in my year of golf, the numbers didn't matter. Next to my bills, sitting in the mouth of my fax machine, I find a paper waiting for me. The phone number was from Illinois, and the letter read:

August 19, 2004
To Whom It May Concern:
    I want to take this opportunity to recommend Mr. Tom Coyne to you as a candidate for Tour School Qualifying. Tom has a good

character and is an extremely hard worker. I have worked with Tom for the past year as a golf instructor. Tom has a game that is equal to, if not better than, the players on the PGA Tour, European Tour, and Canadian Tour. I would expect him to do well on whatever golf tour he decides to pursue.

If you have any questions on Tom's ability, how he would perform, or his character, please don't hesitate to call me at any time.

Thank you for your consideration of Tom Coyne.

Sincerely,

Dr. Jim Suttie

2000 PGA Teacher of the Year

PART FOUR

D*on't miss it.*

    Stay balanced. Keep your knees bent, low center of gravity.

Don't miss it, you asshole.

Four-iron off a tight bunker lie was about the last shot I want to hit at 7:36 in the morning, Toronto time. In a year of one million golf shots, on my first hole of my first Qualifying school, I found myself with possibly the one golf shot I had yet to practice.

My rip at the ball was hit and hope, one of those swings where I can't quite decide how to do this right and it's the passing minutes that force me to finally take it back and throw it through, explaining to Mr. Golf Ball that, should he like to upgrade his current surroundings, I encourage him to get in the way of the clubface.

And in a half-second, without looking up from the salty bunker floor, I know all would be well. I can feel it in my fingertips, the thin, clean contact off the bottom groove, and a bullet firing over the lip of the bunker, my ball skipping to rest just fifty yards from the par-five green.

"Great shot," from all three of my playing partners.

"Thank you," I mumble, understated in my appreciation.

Reacting to good golf shots is all part of that other game being played, the one that has nothing to do with actual golf shots, but can, for the neophytes and the mentally fragile, dictate every other shot of the day. Players try to boost the appearance of their abilities by remaining consistently disappointed with good shots, or by being dismissive of compliments. A smug *Yeah, thanks a lot* is meant to suggest that, one, a player is capable of far more remarkable results, and, two, the payer of the compliment is a lesser player of lower standards. A great shot for you is merely a passable attempt up here on my playing field.

As we make our way down the fairway, one of the members of my foursome asks, "Philadelphia?" as if I have something to fess up to. His name is Charles, and he's about my height, six foot three, narrow in a way that makes you want to buy him a sandwich.

"Yeah, Philadelphia."

"You play this Q-school before?" he asks.

"No. This is my first."

"Your first Canadian?" he says, looking at his shoes as we walk down the fairway. I see the faux concern in his temples.

"First Q-school period," I answer. "This is my first time in Canada, actually."

Actually, it's not, but I feel the need to bluff him on this point for some reason, as if it makes me cooler, unexpected. Too cool for Canada, that's me.

He doesn't say anything else, just smiles to himself, holding back some secret about Q-schools and/or Canada that he's not going to share, like he's sticking it to me for Iraq. I appreciate the conversation, even if he is smug and seems about as much fun as a kidney stone. I know his type—I have been Econo Lodge-ing it the last three days here in Canada, up here in Yonder Ho, the land of impending hockey strikes and outrageous gas prices (seriously, in a nation this vast, it seems uncommonly cruel that you burn five bucks of petrol going through the drive-thru). Every sunlit hour of the past three days has been spent getting cozy with the Royal Ashburn Golf Club, site of the Fall Qualifying School of the Canadian Professional Golf Tour.

The course is immaculate, cared for as if it's a real source of pride for the folks in this part of Canada, just far enough outside Toronto to feel remote. Through three practice rounds I never did quite get chummy with the layout—too much water, too many trees, too many edges marked out-of-bounds. To be fair, a common theme to my evaluation of golf courses seems to be the overgrowth of trees, an overabundance of water, a superfluous surplus of out-of-bounds markers. My view of a golf course is often not the perspective a course designer takes into account: *That pump house down the hill past the trees forty yards left of thirteen fairway? Totally unfair, blocks any chance of getting to the green. Those white stakes on the other side of the parking lot? Arbitrary, totally at odds with any semblance of classic course design, makes it impossible to save par should you decide to shank your four-iron.*

But Royal Ashburn is a little tricked up, even by my uncommon standards—tricked up in the sense that most courses built in the sixties feel tricked up, lacking that organic feeling you get from golf courses built before architects could really push earth around. Royal Ashburn has a little bit of that manufactured feel, ponds dug where God never intended, creek beds plowed where they're not needed, low-limb evergreens planted around the course to add colorful borders, when, in this player's opinion, pine trees are the daffodil of the golf world—fine to look at, but little more than overgrown weeds. But aside from my few classic objections, Ashburn is a good golf course and a serious test of golf—7,000 yards, with the slipperiest greens I have seen in a very long year. Young men from all over the world have come to play here, and the course is going to give them their money's worth.

Of the hundred-plus players in the field, I have come to know and understand the various species of young players who have travelled to Canada in search of their professional tour card. They might all be members of the same species, but after a few dozen hours observing them in their native habitat, i.e., the Royal Ashburn driving range, the colors of their particular breed have become unmistakable.

The first group to jump out at you are the In Guys. You can tell them by their conspicuous senses of humor and their J. Lindeberg slacks—to stay current on the latest in golf fashion as well as the changes in technology and the changes in their own golf swing— the recent vintage of their getups can be intimidating enough, proclaiming they are skilled enough to spend time worrying about that season's colors. Their chitchat on the range is schoolyard loud, and they are obnoxiously buddy-buddy. The In Guys know the right motels to say in, they share rooms to save money, they get shit-faced together between practice rounds, go to the Indian casinos and lose their sponsors' or parents' money (usually the same thing). They beat balls and hold intimate conversations, even though they are talking to a pal three players away:

You remember the cart girl in Ann Arbor?

The swimmer?

Shit yeah, the swimmer. I got so fucked on those Molsons she was throwing at us, I think I tipped her forty bucks.

She wanted it.

Like you wouldn't believe. I woulda, too. Man, I woulda raked her bunker. But I was too shitty to speak by seventeen.

The stories tend to be similarly sophisticated, usually involving tails of a young lady's fun-bags and/or the gluttonous dispatching of a thirty-pack of beer. There was usually some mention of love that got away in some town, on some golf course, same place out there in North America where everything was fun and wild, as long as you were just passing through.

Aside from illustrating the fact that young men who dedicate their lives to a sport, even one as genteel as golf, can lack a certain social polish (overdeveloped golf swings tend to partner with under-developed social skills), the way these players bullshitted back and forth had a very specific purpose. First, it emphasized that you had friends. You weren't here alone, you'd been here before, which telegraphed the message up and down the range that, at one time or at one place, you could play. And it sent out the vibe that you were not nervous. You didn't care, this was shits and giggles, no big deal to a player like yourself, a young man who has gone places, lived a big wild life because of your estimable golf swing.

It was invisible unless you were standing there beside them, thinking about your own first tee shot, but the preening and the posturing, the tacit jockeying for position, it was all there. A regular dog show, young guys showing off their lustrous coats on the range and around the putting green. The game was on the minute you stuck one spike into the property. The first tee, that was just when you started keeping track.

Some of the In Guys were more amusing than others, and some could really stripe it between all the banter, but the story of the In Guys was that they weren't going to put it together when it counted, as if their big personalities were a soft cushion upon which to drop a big score—they could laugh it off, blame a hangover, commiserate with one another about the shit conditions or the shit course, how they could all really play were the greenskeeper not a crack-smoking simpleton. To see them in the lounge after a tournament round, pumping up one another's spirits, I can't help but recall wisdom from a former life, Oscar Wilde's estimation that "Bad artists always admire each other's work." They were in it for the life, not for the living. If they could really play, I mean, *really* play, you wouldn't even notice them, you wouldn't hear them preparing excuses, cursing their clubs and commiserating about missed chances the way the Sticks never did.

There were a few Sticks at every tournament. Never too big a

number, by definition of being a Stick. It was an uncrowded category of golfer. They might know the In Guys, but it rarely went further than a smile or a nod or a chuckle at the story about the girl
from Ann Arbor. The Sticks were too busy with their own crowd of
handlers—a coach, a caddy, a girlfriend or a father. They were tech-
nically standing on the same driving range, hitting the same practice balls, but there was something about the effortlessness of their
presence, it was as if they were operating in a whole other space,
separated from the rest of us by a thick velvet rope. They didn't
shout out to friends or joke about last night, because they were more
interested in birdies than in buddies, and last night they went to the
gym, loaded up on carbs and protein, studied their yardage books.
Whatever they were talking to their father or their coach or their
caddy about, that's what we wanted to be talking about, too. It
could have been their first Q-school or their tenth, it didn't matter.
They weren't using our math. Walking down the first fairway, they
would have never asked you if this was your first Q-school—not because they were rude, or because they didn't care, but because they
almost didn't see you. Sounds cocky, but it was the In Guys who
were cocky. The Sticks—they made cocky look classy. They were
just fucking good.

And then there was us. Rookies. Not familiar enough to pretend to be an In Guy, not good enough to glide around like a Stick.
So we kept to ourselves and acted like we'd been here before, nervous to the point of total arrogance, pretending to be above our
situation, pretending to be Sticks. But the differences, they were obvious. You could call our class of player the Twigs.

We the Twigs were lost most of the time—*Do you know where
we're supposed to register? So why did I pay two hundred bucks a night
for the Motel 6? Where did you get those tees?* We didn't have caddies,
or coaches, and if we had girlfriends with us, they watched us hit

balls with a cutesy smile on their faces as if it were Halloween and their guys had found the most precious golfer costume. We ended up playing practice rounds together, because by the time we figured out how and where to sign up for a practice round, we were the only players left. We were the ones most likely to leave a putter behind, or to not have a pencil. You never see a stick asking if you have a pencil he can borrow. Funny how big confidence takes care of all the little things.

And yet there were some moments and some places at a golf course where all types of golfers were truly the same. The clubhouse bar after the final round was a great egalitarian setting, when the work had been done and the scores couldn't be changed, when there was no one left to impress, just a handful of guys who were there to buy, and a whole lot more there to accept. And there was another spot where every tournament participant was created equal: on the first morning of the tournament, atop, beside, or kneeling before the porcelain throne.

Day one, I pulled into the parking lot while it was still dark out and I spent most of the morning trying to appear as if I had just arrived, like I wasn't so nervous that I was putting four-footers at five A.M. in the glow from my headlights. I overstretched, hit too many putts and too many range balls, and went to the lounge to stare at half a bagel for a while before I decided that my stomach was not the least bit interested in calories. I checked my watch every two minutes, convinced that at any moment I would find that we had suddenly shifted time zones and I had missed my tee time.

Thirty-five minutes to the first tee. Stroll to the putting green, carefree look about me, roll a few more putts, unconcerned if they drop.

Twenty-seven minutes—okay, a few more, hit a few flop-shots—but do I have time to go over to the bag for my lob wedge?

Twenty-three minutes till, okay, I'll run over and bang a few more drives, careful to save my tees because they gave me only a handful in the pro shop and, wait, twenty-two minutes, will I have time to go back and ask for more?

Nineteen minutes, first sign of the nervous grumbles. I'm not sure if the noise is coming from north or south, I don't think an exit strategy has been decided yet—okay, definitely south. Eighteen minutes and my first hard clinch of the morning. Not to be distasteful, but it is impossible to detail a big tournament morning without discussing the detail that players of all abilities wrestle with at some point or the other—namely, the need for the cooling comfort of Kohler. I've been wandering about the clubhouse for three hours trying to look relaxed and full of purpose, and with sixteen minutes to my tee time, I finally have something that I absolutely need to do.

It was as if Bobby Jones were giving a short-game clinic inside the men's room. Golfers were lined up three deep at the door, doubt and concern weighing heavy on each and every face. We had all carb-loaded the night before, and many of us had shoveled down an eggy breakfast as instructed by our coaches and our mothers, and now we were all going to stubbornly make the point that, no, we weren't joking, we really didn't feel like eating.

When I finally work my way inside, there are eight guys waiting for five stalls—funny, the urinals are all free—and under each dividing wall, feet, knees, hands are pointed in all sorts of directions, like some yoga class run amuck. And the sound—I'll spare you my first five descriptions—just think *1812 Overture*, played underwater. The nerves, they were everywhere, and that knowledge, that everyone was in the same leaky boat I was, gave me just enough peace to skip the line and head to the first tee. I gobbled three Pepto tablets out of my golf bag, and in a moment I found myself stepping down the first fairway, floating almost, the deadweight of that morning, that year's anticipation burning off like the early dew.

To quickly and unfairly stereotype my foursome, we had two In

Guys, Charles and George, both proud Canadians with red Maple Leafs on their golf bags, their putter covers, the heels of their shoes. Our fourth was a stick, a young Guatemalan named Jorge, whose affected English only ratcheted up his playerly persona. He had a dark and quiet charisma, a nonchalant intensity. Some of us had to remember to turn it on, to stay focused, but not this guy. Focus became him; he wore it as naturally as he wore his black pants and black sweater and black hat—he had a Zorro thing going on, but it was more than show. The two-iron he muscled off the first tee pissed on all three of our drivers.

And then there's me, thinking far too much about everybody else. *Just hit the shots.*

It's not that Dr. Winters didn't coach me well. He told me there is no substitute for being there. You can train yourself to be focused, but you can't fake comfort. So I hit an uncomfortable lob wedge over the green into a nasty pot bunker, then show off my supposed golf specialty by blading a sand wedge back across the green. When it finally stops fifty feet from the pin (it grabs with tight pro-spin, as if to mock me), I three-putt a green that's greased like a bowling alley, and I begin my Canadian Tour career with a lucky number seven.

On the second hole, I earn a resilient bogey. My "safe" three-wood takes an unintentionally aggressive line, ducking into a little stream. After a drop, my nine-iron settles within ten feet of the hole, and I lip out an improbable par to start double bogey, bogey. On three, a par-five as wide as a grocery aisle, I stuff a sand wedge and tap in for birdie. Back to earth. I spend the rest of the front nine trying to shoot myself dead on the first day. No one in the group is going low—we are mostly playing defense on a nasty golf course: trouble off every tee, slippery greens with comical crowns. The twelfth green in particular comes to mind.

Canadians are supposed to be warm, kind-hearted folks.

Americans are the bulls, boisterous, bulldozing and short-sighted, while the Canadians are supposed to be fuzzy wuzzy bears. I don't know if it's the impending hockey strike that has the superintendent bent, maybe the architect's dog ran away the day he came to this particular green, but on number twelve, a green that has more shelves than an IKEA, the flag is parked tight on the left edge of the green, placed atop the peak of a hill as if stuck there by a triumphant mountaineer.

My wily, wizened Canadian partners take the boring approach, playing out to the right of the green, leaving themselves long but safe putts, settling for par.

I am not in save-par mode. I had made the turn in an ego-squashing 43, and have since then attempted to hole every golf ball I came across. Two-thirty uphill, wind blasting out of the east? Better damn well go in, or by God I will lose my shit and throw this club and fire up another one of these crazy Canadian cigarettes that are making me want to nap and barf at the same time (single biggest difference between Canada and the rest of the civilized world: no Marlboro).

So I fire at the stick on twelve, and the ball behaves predictably, rolling off the top tier and curling into a tightly mowed collection area beside the green.

Jorge finds himself in the same predicament: As spotless as his swing was, he could sometimes overcook it left. I'm positively thrilled to see he has to go first—we're both faced with a shot that is like trying to put the Skee-Ball into the 50-point hole. Jorge goes first, and his nearly perfect bump into the hill rolls up to the pin, then makes a timid U-turn and comes rolling right back at us.

"Dios mio, que es eso? Vamanos, Jorge!"

Berating yourself in a seasoned Spanish tongue is cool. But after watching my own attempt come skipping back down the slope, my rant of choice is to accuse myself of being a "dumb whore mother humper." Not only does my exclamation lack any real style, it makes zero sense. Gibberish, I am neither of those things, but *you underachieving yet nonetheless dedicated golfer*, it lacks bite. So by my *fourth* attempt to get my ball up this malevolent slope, and to Jorge's pleasant surprise, I am belittling myself in high school Spanish. *Stupido, stupido. You dumb fucko.*

It was a golf shot that offered a myriad of alternatives, the sort of creative opportunity a golf purist might look at and salivate, the genius of chipping areas with all the short-game options they present a player. There were, indeed, many options—flop shot, chip shot, pitch it into the bank, putt it even—but no purist would have recommended I sample each of those choices in succession in a professional golf tournament.

My greenside buffet begins with a lob wedge that I attempt to pop to the peak of the plateau. It checks about six inches short, quickly begins moonwalking its way back as I scramble to get myself and my clubs out of the ball's way (there is no graceful way to do this, by the way, escaping the path of a ball you intended to advance, yet has returned for you like a golf ball buried in a Stephen King cemetery).

Following the lob wedge, there's a pitching wedge meant to release through the collar and dig for the pin. Yet the most important part of this game plan, in which the ball would release through the rough with the perfect bit of hook-spin, tumbling into the hole for a most improbable par—the whole thing really relied upon my golf club making actual contact with the golf ball, as opposed to thrusting the iron face into the earth as if I were planting tulips. Stubby Kaye. The ball lurches forward, but doesn't bother humoring me beyond that.

I grab my last resort, the putter, and I give my cheeky golf ball the firmest of whackings. But talk about shots I had not practiced this year, a twenty-yard putt through a ten-foot wall of fringe—the ball runs out of steam shortly after reaching the green, its progress thrust backward like a French army. I think of the greenskeeper draped in his Maple Leaf sweater, laughing himself to sleep, tears in his eyes but a smile from ear to ear. It's clown's mouth golf, kiddy stuff. And yet, Jorge had saved his bogey. The Canucks had worked their pars. There are goofy numbers to be found out here, but I guess not everybody takes it upon himself to play explorer like me. Nobody but myself to blame for not knocking the ball good and hard, clear to the other side of the green, if need be—which, on my fourth attempt, is exactly what I do, burning a Titleist across the bent grass and into the back of a greenside bunker, nestled up against the lip to where I have only the most remote chance of making contact.

If you go online and look up my score for that hole, it says that I scored a 1. They make room for only one digit on the computerized scorecard. They didn't have space for the whole 10.

It had been a lonely week of not knowing too many folks and not making too many friends, a lot of driving and plenty hours of timid practice, not knowing what I should expect. And then, on my first day of competition, my friend comes all the way from home to keep me company. My old pal, the Big Number. In the middle of the Canadian nowhere, he made me feel right at home.

"Your first time is tough."

Charles the Canadian is adding up my numbers, holding my card as if I'd sneezed on it. It's backhanded sympathy, and if I hadn't shot 92, I might have told him to stick it up his ass. But considering the level of mathematics I was requiring of him, I just hang my head and answer, "Yeah."

"It's brutal. Tons of pressure. First time's the toughest. You don't know the pressure until you've done it before."

It's our longest conversation of the day, but I appreciate even this much banter. I'm glad he'll talk to me at all after my toxic dip into the double-digits. We sit down at the scorers' table, where three old ladies check our cards, ticking the numbers like teachers checking a pop quiz. I am licking clean my pan of humble pie as I sit here, watching them cringe at the bogeys and the doubles and that bulbous, festering 10—I watch as one of the ladies seem to jump in her chair when she gets to it, as if I'd suddenly kicked her under the table. On the wall behind them, the scores are all posted in big blue marker, actual tournament numbers like 73, 75, nowhere a 92, no other neighbors in the 90-something neighborhood where my bloated digits might blend in and hide. The scorers glance up at me from time to time, and while they are trying to be officially disinterested, I can see the old ladies' minds working: *Jeez, if I had my clubs with me, I could give this Yank a run for his money.*

In golf, there are a small number of scoreboard abbreviations: NC (No Card), WD (Withdrew), DQ (Disqualified), DNF (Did Not Finish), DNS (Did Not Show). And then there's me, adding some new initials to the last. After the first day of the Canadian Tour Qualifying School, Tom Coyne from Philadelphia was DFL.

Dead Fucking Last.

"You can't quit," Allyson is telling me. "This is practice for the big tournament—that's what you said that it was, so that's what it is. You're just preparing for when it counts. You've never played in one of these things before. This is a great learning experience. It builds character."

Learning experiences, character-builders—I've had my fill this year. They should have a Q-school for golfers with character—I'd be the medalist, no doubt. From the mighty 13s to the Nationwide death marches to my tussle with Canadian gravity—Gandhi did not bank as much character as I've piled up this year. I have character in reserve, to the point where I can make a 10 on a golf hole in a qualifying school and still contemplate returning for round two the next morning.

"If I wasn't in Canada, I swear to God I'd be on my way home right now," I say.

"You're not quitting," Allyson tells me. "You've been through this before, and you never quit before."

"I quit that one time. When I ran out of balls," I tell her, recalling my early exit from the Pennsylvania Open qualifier (after making that 13, things didn't get any better).

"That was different. You were disqualified," she reminds me. "You're not quitting, and you're not coming home. You had one bad day, you've got three days left."

I whine like a baby for a little while longer, and Allyson plies me with the requisite ego-boost: *None of those guys have done what you've done in the last year, it's an accomplishment just to be there, at least you're not sitting around talking about doing something, you're giving it a shot.* And after a hearty fried lunch and two of Canada's coldest malt beverages, I leave my ego in the car and I head back out there, ready to not be a quitter.

Posting that number was baring my darkest golf soul to the world. My worst was up there on the wall for all the field to point at and feel better about themselves. The score was posted on the Internet for everyone at home to download and forward in e-mail batches, each attaching their own e-banter: *92, is that lower in Canadian? Is that 92 in metric? Thank God he practiced for a year, or he might still be out there.*

It's mildly liberating having your dirtiest laundry out on the clothesline. The toughest part was doing the deed and fessing up to it. Now that I'd come clean, I was free. Free from having to shoot a number. Free from having to act like I wasn't a rookie. Free from worrying about what anybody else was thinking. Free from expectations.

Dr. Winters hoped I would tee it up in round one with that mind-set, but I didn't. While I shouldn't have been thinking about score, in reality, I was doing more math in my head than a card counter at a six-deck shoe. But on day two, I would let it go. I had beat the bad thoughts out of my head, pounding them into oblivion with 92 stinging blows.

So instead of going back to the motel and weeping into my foam pillows, I leave lunch and drive back to the golf course at four in the afternoon. I hit balls until I find a swing I can trigger with one swing thought, which pretty much takes me until dark. My swing had gotten quick and handsy, I was trying to place the golf ball instead of swing the golf club, steering the ball away from trouble, which inevitably brought the trouble into play. I work on tempo and balance and a smooth takeaway, the first fundamentals Doc Suttie put on his tape. For the first time in my four days on that range, I am actually practicing. I'm not worried about looking playerly or fitting in, I'm not tattooing drivers over the fence for no other purpose than to impress the dude next to me. Now, it's about my game, and I'm unaware if anyone is hitting balls next to me or not.

When I finally take a break, there's nobody else here, all the players have peeled off to their motels, maybe making a run to the casino. I hit balls until the ranger kicks me off, and then I go to the putting green where, fourteen hours earlier, my day had begun in the twilight. My legs feel bruised, my heels are numb, the palms of my hands are covered with torn bits of black rubber. And it is brilliant. It's Florida, empty golf course, putting until you can't see the ball at your feet, heading home with the knowledge that tomorrow and the next day there would be more. There would always be another hole.

Back in the hotel, I call the tour players' personal chef—Pizza Hut—and spend the evening working with three different putters on the hotel room carpet. It's a motel cliché, middle-age business traveler knocking Titleists at an overturned water glass, but my putting had hurt me, and I needed the work. All day, the stroke was petrified, I was begging for two-putts, and, of course, I wasn't sold on my Ping putter.

I now understand: It wasn't the arrow, it was the Indian. I would never find a putter that was good enough, that I could love with all its faults, that could love me for all of mine. I need to commit, then and there, I need to know that no happiness will come from playing the field, keeping my options open, that a lot of great things can come from investing in a mature, long-term relationship. So that evening I go out to the car and retrieve my newly arrived Scotty Cameron Red X putter from the trunk. I take out the Ping and put it in the closet. We don't say much. It's easier that way.

I roll the Red X back and forth across the carpet for a half hour, trying to recall some of the putting wisdom Dr. Winters had tried to impart during my last visit with him at his Nike Junior Golf Camp at Williams College. We had a Q-school specific therapy session where we chose my sight for Stage I (Florence Country Club, in South Carolina, was my first choice: manageable driving distance from home, a golf course closer to what I was used to in the Northeast, and a passing score that usually fell around a makeable even par), and Doc gave me a CD-ROM for my computer titled *Putting Genius*. When I'm done working that night in my hotel room, I turn off almost all the lights, get into bed with my headphones on, and I get the CD spinning in my laptop. It's about as close as you can get to combining a putting lesson with a massage.

A woman's voice comes over the earphones, relaxing you into a deep, suggestive state. On the computer, a golf ball is floating on the screen, turning end over end, and as your eyes watch the spinning ball, and the words coax you to rest . . . it's a sort of electro-hypnosis. Once you've been settled down and put in the properly softened mind frame, she begins humming putting affirmations, whispering positive putting strategies into your ears that seem to drip down into your soul.

I am a great putter. I take pride in my putting. I look forward to putting. I enjoy the challenge of putting. I accept the results of my putts. I think about only one putt at a time. . . . Before I putt, I stand behind the ball, and see a long green line behind my ball, stretching from my ball to the hole, from the hole to the ball, from the ball to the hole. . . .

The voice is downright sexy. And there's nothing like being alone in a hotel room, relaxed in bed with a gorgeous voice tickling your ear to make you want to believe every damn word that's being said. I don't know if that was Dr. Winters's intention, but either way, I'm buying into each line she is feeding me, letting the words wash over me, hearing myself agree with her. *Yes, I am a great putter, a great, great putter, I'm the best, you know it's true. . . .*

As I lie there wearing headphones in bed, eyes glued to a floating golf ball, a voice whispering in my ear, I think I might have finally lost enough of my mind that this ridiculous game might start making sense.

Shaking hands with the same foursome this morning (we don't reshuffle groups until day three) is about as much fun as apologizing to the stranger whose party you ruined with your beer-bender. But I don't let the awkwardness of the greeting last more than a minute. Once it's established that yes, I have returned, I have yet to quit, and we are four more hours a team, there is nothing left to feel ashamed of. And their bags aren't exactly stuffed with magic tricks. In spiteful conditions, they had shot in the mid-70s: 75, 76, 77. Solid, but nothing to make me wilt.

And I do not wilt. On number ten tee, our first of the morning, I hop up to the starter's welcoming intro and I smash an absolute snot-bubbler of a drive, leaving me with little more than a flip-wedge to the green on this 445-yard hole.

My ball came to rest forty paces in front of their drives (*that's more like it*), and after waiting for them to knock their eight-irons on the green, I rest my sixty-degree wedge behind my ball. Perfect, steady, solid tempo, leading up to that deceptive distance paradox, when you swing so easy that the ball goes 20 percent farther. Ideal timing and a dash of adrenaline—it's great off the tee box, not so great into a green that's soft as aluminum siding. My ball bounds off the back fringe, one big hop into OB oblivion.

In this far-flung edge of civilization, is it really necessary to have OB stakes everywhere? Do the cows or the moose not want us tromping around behind this green, hunting for our golf balls in their forest? At length I debate the arbitrary nature of these stakes, then have a good loud moment of *FUCK, NOT AGAIN* . . . before deciding to take this new mess I've been handed and try to tie it back together.

A good hard pluck of the blue rubber hand, and no more blaming—no more blaming my swing, the superintendent, the Canadian Parliament. Drop another ball, choke the wedge down half an inch, and do it again. A golf ball jumping off the meat of the clubface, the ball hitting and checking, pin-high, about fifteen feet from the hole.

Players talk about knowing that they are going to make a putt just by taking one look at it. You hear the expression *That one just fit my eye.* As I approach the green, it isn't that I know the ball is going in, but it's like I have an inborn sense of the speed and line, as if this were my favorite putt in a former life. It would take an uncommon circumstance to keep this putt out of the hole—a bird or rock or a gust of wind—and maybe not even then. When it jumps off the back of the cup and happily hops into the darkness, Jorge is the first to speak.

"Great five, Tom," he says in his thick accent in which *Tom* still sounds vanilla compared with *Jorge.*

He doesn't have my scorecard, but he still knows I saved a spectacular five after taking the stroke and distance penalty. A bogey with a ball out-of-bounds is a ballsy show of golf toughness. And he called me by my name—insignificant, but appreciated.

A misbehaving putter is the rotten apple of the golfer's barrel. It infects every shot in the game. Ball-striking suffers when a player thinks he has to always hit it farther, hit it tighter, because he's got to get it inside two feet to keep from lipping out another effort. Similarly, hot-putting is as infectious as giggles in church. Believing you can roll anything home, it relieves all the pressures from a round of golf. No matter if you're hitting it crooked, if you couldn't hit a green from the fringe, no worries—you're going to get to that green eventually, and when you do, you're going to make the damn putt. One-putting can redeem almost any golf disaster, bring a quick death to a budding big number. And this is the case in my second round of the Canadian Fall Qualifying School—confident putting, capable playing. Funny how the shortest stick in your bag can change the way an entire golf course looks, feels, smells even—from a manure-stuffed patch of abandoned gray North, to a rosy, rolling frontier of bright possibility.

I demystify my putting routine. Much credit to Dr. Winters's techniques, and to my simply being tired of putting afraid. Standing behind every putt that afternoon, I wait until I see the line. Not until I *almost* see the line, not before I *guess* at a spot. I choose a target blade of grass that would put my golf ball in the dead center heart of the hole. Once I have the spot, I rehearse the required speed and length of the stroke, then step up to the ball and do exactly what I had rehearsed, counting down, *one, two, three, four,* the ball heading nowhere but that specific spot, at precisely the intended pace.

I often guess wrong. They don't all go in. But plenty of them do. I one-putt four times on the front, then three times more on the back nine. I turn double bogeys into bogeys, bogeys into pars, making two fancy birdies along the way. The best part about it, numbers aside, is that I have forgotten where I am on the scorecard. Granted, that can be the luxury of a player who has shot himself out of contention. Nonetheless, I feel as if I am actually playing real golf, participating in the Q-school not as a patron, but as a peer. I hold the honor for seven holes that day. While we're waiting on a par-three, I show them my new Mizuno MP-32's—*just got 'em, can't get them in the store yet, have a swing, if you want*—no longer embarrassed to be representing my brand. We bullshit about the setup—*brutal pins, eh?* We commiserate about the host hotel that is somehow twenty bucks more expensive (*twenty loonies, no way!*) than the Super 8 down the street.

I stumble a bit on my way in, splashing two balls over four brutal finishing golf holes, and I quick turn a possible 75 into a 79—not a bad number on a golf course that hadn't given up a score lower than 71 on day one (shocking among a field of professional tour players). My bumpy finish pushed me back from low man in my group to second lowest of the day, happy to be behind Jorge.

For my new friend Charles, who yesterday had divulged the pressures of the Q-school, it was as if he had written the first line of his own sad story. The three of us watched him crumble on the fifth tee, sniping three balls over a barbed-wire fence en route to a nine, finishing the day with an 83. If I said I wasn't tempted to ask him if this was *his* first Q-school, I would be a liar. And if I had gone ahead and asked him, I would surely be an asshole. Because, coming off the eighteenth, this tall, lanky man, he seemed to shrink inside his clothes. This thirty-year-old professional athlete, he looked like a kid on his way home to show Dad another shitty report card. It wasn't just a sadness in his face, there was a shadow of fear there just beneath his eyes, a guy who wasn't sure how he was going to make that phone call again.

I had thoroughly outplayed him that afternoon. If we were playing a match, I would have owned his house, when just twenty-four hours ago, he had written my game off as an impediment to his progress. Yet I don't feel an ounce of satisfaction in that turn of events. After a long season of gorging myself on heapings of crow, I just hand Charles his scorecard and wish him better luck tomorrow.

I had spotted Anthony from *The Big Break* bumping elbows on the driving range that week. The Golf Channel's *Big Break* had been my *American Idol* while living in Florida, so it was a little bit of a thrill to see this minor celebrity mulling about the clubhouse, a *Big Break* finalist beating balls on the range with the rest of us. While *Big Break* chat rooms (I fess up, I visited one on a lonely Florida evening) often challenge the worthiness of the contestants—they can look pretty mediocre in the golf challenges on TV—I, too, wondered if any of them could actually play, or if they were selected just for their screen tests. I didn't know I would get firsthand knowledge until I saw the pairings for day three.

Per the sheer tonnage of my opening 92, I was duking it out for not-last place. Anthony shot had 76-81, well safe of my caboose pairing, but one of the three players I would be tussling it out with is a young man named Scott. We're backed up on the second tee when he confirms the whispers I had been hearing around the driving range, that Scott is one of the lucky ten out of ten thousand applicants who is starring in season two of my favorite prime-time television show.

Scott can't talk about the results, as the show isn't airing until October (for those who haven't seen it yet, Scott would be eliminated third), but he does talk about how the show has already changed his life—he's doing interviews every afternoon, he's become a regular hometown hero.

"I'm hoping some sort of sponsorship comes out of it, but we'll have to wait and see. But first I need to not be playing in the last foursome," he laughs.

We all nod, commiserating over the troubles our group has shared together, even though we had found our big numbers in our own unique ways.

Twenty-three-year-old Scott has a great athletic swing, soft limbs, a long, languid Vijay-style swipe at the ball. His skills are a little more raw than the polished pros of yesterday's foursome, and his driver could get a little loose, but he's a gentleman through his struggles.

"My game is not ready for this right now," he confesses. "I was hoping I could put something together this week, maybe fight my way through it. But now I kind of wish I hadn't. I can't just shoot a big number and go home and forget about it. With the show and all, there are too many people who want to know what I shoot here. A lot of people are going to hear about it. You guys have no idea."

Actually, Scott, I kind of do.

I go around and make four birdies that afternoon, finishing with another 79—pretty weak for making four birds, but it's nice to know that some low numbers are in there, and might come out in bunches in competition.

The next morning, we're still grouped in the same final threesome, but I've distanced myself over the last two rounds, leaving Scott and Pat, a happy-go-lucky traveling pro from Arizona, to battle it out for the basement. The date is September 23. My thirtieth birthday. Turning thirty the last day of Q-school would be the perfect scenario for a career round, the lowest eighteen of the tournament where every wayward drive kicks back into the fairway, every iron is carried by the breeze, every putt catches the edge and curls into its shallow, plastic grave.

It would have been nice, but instead, for my birthday I fatten up my scorecard like it's the prized calf, gifting myself a nice plump 85.

Playing four days is tough, it is a whole other monster. At the Mizuno conference, one of the salesman had asked me if I ever played a four-banger before. Of all the responses I could have offered, "What's a four-banger?" was probably the lamest, though most truthful answer. Not only did it confirm that I had never played in a four-day tournament, it betrayed that I wasn't even player enough to know what they were called.

The fatigue of the four-day, it is real, and it is exhausting. I have a whole new appreciation for the PGA Tour player who takes a week off afterward, for Tiger not wanting to tee it up each and every Thursday. Granted, I had to carry my own bag, I was sleeping in an up-market jail cell, and my meals came wrapped in thin yellow paper. But the toll of three practice rounds and four full days of golf shots is far more severe than anticipated. I was in the shape of my life, and by the back nine of my final round, I am a zombie.

DQs and WDs included, I finish eleven places from the bottom. Of the players who post four scores, I almost hate writing it here, but Scott ended up bringing up the rear. I would have almost preferred it be me, because he had the Golf Channel and the tour officials putting him on interviews the minute he stepped off the golf course. For Scott and me, plenty more people than we would have liked are going to know precisely what we shot. And yet, as he came off eighteen and handed me my card, Scott had drawn a little birthday cake on it and has written *Happy Birthday to Tom.* To show a little humor and a lot of class after those four days says a lot. Scott's golf is going to be just fine.

I have earned a post-round beer, but I don't feel like stopping for it. I've done my damage here, left my messy tracks all over Ashburn, Ontario, and it's time to slip away. But on my way out the front door, I hear that accent.

"Tom, hold up."

Jorge ended up missing his card by just two strokes (shooting 75, 74, 73, 75). But that isn't why he stopped me. As busted as he must be feeling, he doesn't show a drop of disappointment. He has stopped to tell me that he thinks I am a fine player.

"You have a great golf swing," he says, pointing a finger at my chest. "You play very well. You are better than your scores this week. You are going to do very well."

There are moments when you don't look at all the other faces as ambition or work or talent, when you see more than the golfing machine. I go inside and buy Jorge a beer, and I find that Scott's in the grill, too, pointing at his scores amid good, hard belly laughs. It's a room crowded with people who just realized that, contrary to published reports, the sun was indeed going to rise tomorrow. Whether you made the cut or not, we were all *In Guys* now. If I were to come back next year, I'd look forward to seeing these faces on the range, maybe have a loud story or two to tell myself . . . *Do you remember that butcher job on number 12 . . .*

I stop in Syracuse and celebrate my thirtieth alone, toasting the news that I wasn't the only 92 that week at Royal Ashburn. Grant Fuhr finished his tournament with a 92, and he's in the Hall of Fame, so what did I have to feel bad about? Aside from the fact that I'm seated at a bar amid undergrads who make this birthday feel like my fiftieth.

It's a long drive home through rolling hills that were a lot more interesting the first time. Plenty of time to think about what lies ahead, just two more opportunities to qualify. In two weeks it will be Fort Lauderdale for the Tour de las Americas Qualifying tournament, another shot at redemption, a platform on which I might steady myself before heading to Georgia for Stage I.

Presents are waiting for me when I walk through the door. The best laser binoculars on the market, from Mom and Dad (vital accessory for any stick), and birthday cards from my brothers and sisters, all of them expressing fear and shock at their baby brother turning three-zero.

There's a thick letter from the PGA, and that's the gift I grab for first—finally, over a year since this all began, I get to see my own name in the Q-school pairings.

I'm ready for it. I've earned being ready. I have taken my beatings and learned from them. If Canada wasn't my virgin Q-school, who knows what I might have accomplished up yonder. Whatever names I find mine next to for Stage I, it will not matter. It will be *my time, my ball, my game.*

I rip open the envelope and I find a heavy stack of pages. They all look familiar, and I'm confused. These are the pages I had sent to them six weeks ago. My recommendations and tournament scores and my handicap, and here's my check, uncashed, for $4,500.

There is a cover letter attached to my original application. The letter reads:

YOUR APPLICATION FOR THE 2004 PGA TOUR QUALIFYING SCHOOL HAS BEEN DENIED FOR THE FOLLOWING REASON:

There is a long list of general reasons, and next to INSUFFICIENT TOURNAMENT RESULTS, there is a black check mark. The letter is not signed. There is no name or number to call.

I had included a personal letter to the PGA Tour with my application, explaining why my application for the Q-school might be considered an unconventional one. In the letter, I explain why I didn't have the four-day tournament results they were asking for— I was thirty years old, newly returned to competitive golf, that although I didn't have NCAA scores or results from the U.S. Amateur, I would nonetheless be a respectful, honorable, competitive member of the tournament field.

Please be assured, I wrote, *that I have prepared diligently and ceaselessly for competition in Qualifying school—with the help of my coach (please see attached reference from Dr. Jim Suttie), my psychologist, Dr. Robert Winters, and my trainers, I have brought my game to a level that we believe to be ready for tour school . . .*

I never expected to be reading this letter again. I'm shocked to see it here back on my kitchen table. But it knocks the air out of me to see that someone in the PGA Tour office took the time to uncap a pen and strike a long black line through the whole of my letter, then stuff it back in an envelope and send it back for me to see.

A year. Crossed off.

As it had been explained to me by the dozens of people I had met over the year who had been through Q-school, there was no handicap requirement for Q-schoolers—an arrangement that made sense, seeing as pros don't have handicaps, and the fact that the requirement of a USGA handicap, combined with the USGA's requirement that handicaps be issued through member clubs—it might raise an eyebrow about the PGA Tour and its entrance exam operating as something of a closed shop (mine would have probably been the lone eyebrow, but nonetheless). The five grand was explained to be the Q-school's only real admission standard, the tool with which they weeded out the not-so-serious entrants. My glowing recommendations from my head pro and my director of golf and the 2000 PGA national teacher of the year, accompanied by a smorgasbord of tourney results (from the Michelob tournaments to my one-day qualifiers to a charity event where I had carded a handy 69), capped off with a lengthy explanation of my personal commitment to the Qualifying School, *ALONG* with my check for five G's—I was sure it was application overkill, ounces more paper than I actually needed. I packed the envelope thick.

Still, it came back one sheet thicker.

It was as if they could smell me through the paper, those faces I had seen guarding the Q-school the year before, golf's secret service in sunglasses, feet propped up on their golf carts, walkie-talkies on their hips and wires in their ears. There are few professionals who take themselves more seriously than your typical tournament official. Umpires show a touch of flair and the occasional sense of humor; football referees have been known to mix it up on the sidelines; tennis umpires are regular stand-up comedians compared with the stone-faced crew of PGA officials I had found at the Q-school and the Nationwide Mondays. I'm sure they are all great people, I am sure they are a barrel of monkeys after a couple Manhattans on Sunday evening, but the weight of the game's rules and traditions and interpretations, the mass of so much legacy—it can sit right down on a beautiful, simple pursuit, and make this game for bored shepherds feel more grave than a meeting of the Joint Chiefs of Staff.

Is that a cheap shot? Absolutely. If I could conjure up a cheaper one, I would take it. Because the ultimate cheap shot was running a line through the explanation of my circumstances and tossing my application aside.

When I called the tour office to press the issue, the conversation didn't last three minutes.

"We didn't get your tournament results."

"They were there." I listed each one of them for her. "Somebody read them, they crossed them all out."

"Those scores don't count. We need two scores from USGA, PGA, or sanctioned section events. Minimum thirty-six holes each."

The tone of her voice said I wasn't going to get a chance to make the point that those sorts of tournaments are not readily available to most golfers in the world. Sure, I would have played the AT&T at Pebble Beach if somebody invited me, but I didn't quite make the guest list. If you've been on a mini-tour, or you're coming of an NCAA roster, this issue would never occur to you, but for someone coming at the game from deep left field, who is no less qualified to play in Stage I than the 600 other guys who aren't going to make it through, it gets a bit sticky.

The Michelob tour events didn't count. A local charity outing didn't count. A pro-am didn't count. Club tournaments, they certainly didn't count. The one-day USGA and PGA tournaments, none of them were going to be good enough. But to say they didn't even get them, as if the page of scores I sent them were invisible to their holy eyes, like they couldn't lower themselves to even read the numbers off these "other-man" events. The conversation was past pointless, there was no budge, it was as inflexible as everything in golf. Golf's unwillingness to yield to change, it's what has made the game great, timeless. But it has also made the game small and pedantic, paranoid, clammed up.

"So what do I do now?" I ask in vain, hoping there was some crack of hope or bribe to offer or string to pull.

"What do you mean, what do you do now?"

"I'm past the deadline. I got this letter back past the deadline. So what can I do now?"

"Nothing."

"So . . . I'm out?"

Of all the conversations this year where I had to go running for a pencil to scribble down a quote, I needed no help remembering the two words that ended this one.

"You're out."

I pursue every connection I have in golf, pleading to Mizuno and Titleist, with Dr. Suttie and *Golf Magazine* and the guy at my club who knew a guy whose brother who used to caddy for a guy who once played two days of a tour event . . . but the news all comes back the same. The PGA doesn't budge, and they are not actively seeking reasons to bend their rules and deadlines.

It is during a desperate Googling of "Q-school," hoping I might find some secret cyber back door, discover some legal precedent, some old case of Duffer versus PGA Tour, that the top item to pop back from my search is *PGA Tour Q-school*. But not the one from which I had already been banned, the tour that had carefully taped up and quarantined my tournament results. This was a different Q-school. For a different tour. One being held just around the corner.

There's something about a country built by convicts, a nation whose greatest hero is an Irish outlaw gunslinger, a place where you go when they don't want you anywhere else. A giant land with no memory, where I might reinvent my golfing self. Halfway around the world, in a whole new hemisphere, they don't know about the thirteens or the 92s or that Tom Coyne couldn't break 80 a year ago. If the PGA doesn't want me, I'll board a ship as millions had done before and take the long voyage searching out an opportunity Down Under.

The Australasian PGA Tour would also be a better fit for the status of my game. The competition will be more realistic, I won't be quite the dead money I would be in the PGA Tour. Let's face it—I might give Stage I a decent run, but the chances of being in that final thirty after fourteen rounds of golf—a whole squad of top golf psychologists couldn't coax me to embrace that possibility. A tour like the Asian, Australasian, or Canadian Tour—this is where a player who is trying to break into pro golf would first test the waters. The field will still be made of absolute talents, but it's a crowd where I won't shoot ten under and miss the cut. And in Australia, I'll have to play through only two stages and seven rounds of golf to get my qualifying card. Not to mention the nifty fact that I can actually get into the tournament (click on their user-friendly site, the Australasian application just about pops out of your printer).

I've come this far, what's 3,000 more miles?

In two days' time, my plans are laid. Application, flights, hotels, even a yardage guide for the host course. Crisis averted. The only problem left to consider was that Paddy, with two little girls and a real job (so he claims), can't make the twenty-day trek around the globe. Now I need a good caddy substitute, a good traveler who knows the game but can still keep me loose. Someone who can tell when I'm losing my shit, and tell me to get off my butt and go find it.

"It's a long way to go. I don't think too many loopers are making the trip from the States to carry a bag at the Australasian Q-school," I explain. "I understand if you can't make it."

"Australia? Seriously?"

According to Allyson, my being rejected from the American Q-school is forgettable to the point of total insignificance. Golf, shmolf—in her eyes, her plane ticket just got upgraded from South Carolina to Melbourne.

If there was anyone who was up for an adventure, it was Allyson. The world is always exciting to her—dinner out at the corner café, a weekend down the shore, *Pretty Woman* unexpectedly on TV. She can get ecstatic about the simplest things, every day is full of wonderful surprises. It isn't fake. It is joy, and she has it in spades.

"Are there kangaroos on the golf course?" she wants to know, as if it's her condition for caddying.

"It might be tough getting the time off," I explain. "It's two stages, one after the next. I'm talking two weeks in the beginning of December."

And without checking a calendar or asking anybody, she answers, "Okay."

"Are you sure? It's a long way to go to just watch me hit golf balls."

"Don't worry about me," she says. "Just worry about getting your yourself on that plane."

It was the first thought that had shot into my head as I considered Australia. The flight. My stomach had gone sour with nerves. The thought of air-tubing across the Pacific for fifteen hours nonstop . . . working up the guts would require its own year of dedicated work with a whole new team of consultants. I deserve the most remote Q-school in the planet. I can accept that on most any level. Yet if I only had known that my missed cuts would send me on a trans-Pacific flight, I might have been able to nerve myself through the whole U.S. Amateur, might have brought Tiger to his knees to keep me off that jumbo.

And yet, that is commitment—when you lie in bed believing that a 92 has put your life in grave jeopardy, and you accept your imminent death as just another part of the game.

I am searching for her plane ticket on the Internet, checking if Qantas offers heavy sedatives with any of their meal options, when I steer over to Google and I type in *engagement rings*.

There it is. And that's the moment. Who knew Some Day was just going to be some ordinary afternoon?

There are no angels or lightning or trumpets. The inspiration didn't come to me in a fortune cookie or coded in my Alpha Bits. It just suddenly occurred to me that researching cut and clarity and settings would be a good idea. Maybe it's not entirely romantic, but when you've been together nine years and you still think of an engagement ring as a very good idea, and you're as relaxed about doing it as you would be if you were picking a video—that's good enough for me. The stuff that requires cymbals and trumpets and pronouncements from God, all that stuff can vanish as quickly as it occurs to you. Epiphanies are overrated.

As a single man, you think about waiting and not getting married as if you are outsmarting all the other suckers. It is intelligent and sophisticated to be single and successful. You're one up on all the drips. And maybe it's a year of busted hopes or all the doctor visits, but I'm not really interested in outsmarting anyone anymore. I just want to be happy. And I suspect I might just now be making my first stroke of genius.

"If Paul makes it through Q-school, I am going to quit my job and divorce my wife, and I'm going to caddy for him on the PGA Tour."

Paul's caddy's eyes are heavy with Chardonnay, but his London accent remains boarding school crisp. Considering the assault he's put on his liver this evening, I am shocked to see how lucid and sincere he is when he explains, matter of factly, "Because I love golf more than I love my wife."

It is a timely bit of insight, seeing as I have just purchased a shiny pebble set on a simple platinum band. I was on the range at Edgmont when the call came from my mother: *I'm in the jewelry store right now, I've got the ring here. This is the one, the salesgirl and I are both beside ourselves. I've told her all about Allyson....*

As I wasn't doing anything that didn't involve softspikes and short grass, I had put Mom on diamond ring detail, and she delivered as usual. It was the one—simple, classic, one big honking rock that a friend said looked like a skating rink. Mom didn't trust me to keep it safe, so she hid it one of her shoe boxes. Though, with Mom turning seventy (not that she's losing it, but the cordless phone rang the other night and she actually tried to answer the remote control), and her being well past seventy in shoe boxes, I wasn't sure who would be the better guardian. Not only didn't she trust me to keep track of the ring myself, but she was convinced I had no idea how I might pass it along. *You know you can't just hand it to her at dinner, right? You do know that, don't you?*

With commitment sitting on the top shelf of my mother's closet back home, I am now listening to Rodney talk of his love for the game, how he had left his wife home and spent his vacation traveling from London to Florida to caddy for his best friend Paul in the Tour de las Americas Qualifying School. Rodney is thirty-nine years old and a solicitor (attorney) who seems just as well-off as, if a touch more modest than, a big-city lawyer here in the States. Rodney himself had struggled on the European mini-tours in his early twenties, a career he was fortunate enough to abandon for a training contract at a London law firm. He's more conversational than conceited when he mentions a Mercedes, a new getaway in the Swiss Alps, a zone-one flat with a front window that frames Big Ben. But with all his toys and money, I absolutely believe Rodney when he explains how he loved nothing in this life more than a good game of golf.

I have met Rodney and Paul on my first night back in Florida, at the bar of a host hotel that was convenient to nothing aside from the golf course. I had decided not to rent a car, so the understaffed and under-swept lobby lounge was my home base for breakfast, dinner, and the only alternative to a fuzzy television set. I had overheard their two accents talking golf, and judging by Rodney's tight pink Lendenberg slacks and thick white belt, I had taken him for a player with skills who had certainly come to this tournament from somewhere that wasn't America. In jeans, T-shirt, with a little extra anchor around his midsection, I had guessed that Paul was the typical caddy—pudgy, and at the bar.

But as Rodney soon pointed out, "He's the player, mate, I'm the fucking caddy," the words dribbling out of his mouth like he was doing his best Arthur for me.

"Are you from Australia?"

"Australia?" Rodney says, turning up his nose. "You think we'd come for this fucking tournament all the way from Australia?"

"We're from London," sober Paul jumps in, "and Rodney here is pissed."

"I am not pissed, you're pissed, mate. You're the one whose pissed," Rodney defends himself.

Because I know *pissed* means *shitfaced* instead of *enraged*, I can laugh instead of think I just walked into a pub brawl.

"You're bloody right we're here for the tournament. Paul here's the best golfer you have ever seen, and I don't even know who the hell you are," Rodney tells me, pointing at the middle of my chest.

"Sorry about my friend, he's enjoying his vacation a bit too much," Paul explains.

Rodney swallows down another mouthful of white. "Brilliant Chardonnays you have in this country. None of that French shit. Big, ballsy white wines. I love it."

"And there might not be any left by the time Rodney gets back on the plane," Paul says.

"I'm not planning on getting back on that plane. Because once Paul wins this tournament, he's going to win that Nationwide tournament next week, and then he's going to go through the PGA Q-School, and then I'll have a job. I'll be the caddy."

Paul shrugs at me, not entirely convinced if he's on board with his looper. But as Rodney seems to be Paul's financier for the moment—just what every golfer needs, a millionaire philanthropist for a caddy—Paul can't exactly fire him, no matter how many strangers he tries to offend along the way.

"You're going to the PGA Q-school?" I ask.

"Of course he is. Paul's exempt into Stage II."

I am green with exemption envy. "Really? How did that happen?"

"Paul made the cut at the Open. He played four days at Royal St. George's. This man here, this man played in the *British Open*," Rodney explains. He's on the verge of drunken tears when he continues, "Greatest fucking golf I ever saw."

Rodney spits bitterness about the European Tour and their Francophile tournament director who hands out exemptions to "bloody frogs" but wouldn't stoop to help out a limey.

"Paul finishes top forty at the Open—he's one of the best forty players in the whole world that week. And he can't get a single invitation to play in a single European tournament. It's a disgrace. It's bloody criminal." Rodney slaps the bar, and I can appreciate the frustration. Not too long ago, they're toasting a thirty-thousand-pound check at Royal St. George's, and tonight they're outside Fort Lauderdale at a crumbling, lonely hotel bar with the likes of me and a caddy who's about to be cut off by the cute Israeli bartender.

Rodney turns to me, inquiring about my handicap with the British expression, "What do you play off?"

I'm happy to give him the math—a handful of 69s at Edgmont, and a smattering of even rounds on tough golf courses, I have worked my way down to a plus-1, a handicap better than par that Rodney doesn't find impressive at all.

"Scratch is shit. Scratch can't play. You simply cannot play," he informs me, the gentle diplomat. "You might as well not even show up this week. Do you know what Paul here plays off of? He's bloody plus-six and he can't even get a spot on the bloody challenge tour. Scratch, plus-one, whatever, it's entirely ordinary."

"I apologize for my friend," Paul says.

"Don't worry about it. He's making me laugh," I say, because he is.

I'm sort of enjoying this soggy, skinny Brit barking at me about how the world really is, describing the game to me as if I've never met golf before, having no idea that we've actually been unhappily married for quite some time now. I explain what I'm doing here and what my last year has been like, and why, in my case, plus-one isn't exactly shit.

"So, are you a writer? Or are you a golfer?" Rodney is totally confused by this latest revelation. With his face bunched up, he asks, "Are you writing about the tournament? Or are you playing in the tournament?"

"Both, actually."

I do my best to explain, but my sentences seem to bounce off his face that's growing more rubbery by the sip. Paul and I decide that Rodney can decide for himself—we're going to play our practice round together the next morning, ten A.M. sharp.

"Are you going to join us, Rodney?" Paul sticks an elbow in his caddy's shoulder. "Talking an awful lot of shit tonight, mate. Are you going to back it up tomorrow?"

"You're bloody well right, I am," Rodney says with a big floppy nod of the head.

"Are you playing in the Q-school yourself, Tom?" Paul asks. "Is this a warm-up for you, or are you really interested in playing in South America?"

"Well, it's sort of a warm-up. I'd love to finish well and get an exemption, maybe play some of the events in the Caribbean," I explain. "But I'm not going to the American Q-school. After this, I'm going to go try to qualify for the Australasian Tour."

"So you're a writer?" Rodney asks, still trying to wrap his head around it. "Or are you a golfer?"

"Why would you go all the way down to Australia?" Paul asks. "Q-school here starts next week."

"Well, you know how you're exempt into Stage II? I'm not. In fact, I'm not exempt into Stage I, either."

Paul thinks for a moment. "But, everybody is exempt into Stage I."

"I know."

Dr. Jekyll was an Englishman, so I'm not surprised to meet an all-new Rodney the following morning. Overnight he has gone from surly golf hooligan to Jeeves, overly polite and endlessly apologetic. He's particularly sorry for the fact that he doesn't remember meeting me, or a single syllable from the evening before.

He leaves his bag in the car, takes a pack of cigarettes and a tall bottle of water, hydrating a hangover that I can see throbbing red behind his sunglasses. He drives Paul's cart and tapes each of Paul's swings on the video camera. For every swing that day, Paul doesn't pull the trigger until Rodney is precisely in the perfect spot to shoot his swing right down the line. It holds us up, but as a twosome we move along well enough. But as I watch Paul quietly go about his business, rewinding the tape of each and every pass, I see that he's the player I need to be—dedicated, deliberate, unconcerned if setting up a tripod behind every shot is annoying to his playing partners. And he is never satisfied the whole way around. I watch him pound drivers and pinch irons off the turf that are so center-of-the-clubface-pure that I want to weep, but each swing disappoints him.

"I've been working with a new coach," he explains as he takes his tenth practice swing on the fourth tee box, overexaggerating an over-the-top move to try to keep the clubface from falling behind his hands.

"You haven't missed a shot all day," I say.

He grimaces, shakes his head. "Nah, it's not there. I mean, I can get it around. I can still make a score. But it's not clicking yet."

Paul makes four birdies on the front nine, and I wonder what it must be like to watch when things are clicking. Rodney's seen it—maybe that's why he's ready to quit his job.

I am surprised how nervous I'm not, playing with a guy who cashed a check at the British Open, his gentle manners making me feel at home. He almost seems apologetic about hitting all these great shots, as if he didn't mean to show me up. I hold my own, making two bogeys and a double on the front, coming back with three birdies on the back. I know Paul has lapped me on the score-card, but it would have been plenty good to give Rodney a run for his euros.

We get a shot at Rodney's Black Card later when he treats us both to a steak dinner, where, after two bottles of big American white, he starts talking about his wife and how she ranks one peg below the Chelsea Football Club, and several notches below golf and Paul's career. He loves his wife, she's fine as far as wives go, but their union sounds like some detached British manor house marriage—*you take the west wing, I'll have the east.* She wasn't bad to have at dinner parties, didn't mind her company for a few hours in the evening, sipping brandy in the sitting room. But in the end, she was replaceable. A PGA Tour card was not.

When Paul is off in the bathroom, Rodney gets to talking about his friend, and he's not an over-served tourist bragging about his golfer buddy. He's a fan, not envious but a pure lover of the game whose eyes start to well up as he talks about the things his quiet friend can do.

"People watch him on the range, these old men, they're hitting balls next to Paul and they have no idea what they're looking at. They don't get it, and they can't. They cannot appreciate just how special he is. The way he can hit the ball, Tom, you've seen it," he says. "I don't know what it would even be like to play a round of golf the way Paul can. I'll never feel what it's like to hit the ball that way.

It's a gift. And he's got it. I just hope more people get to see it other than myself."

Paul returns from the bathroom, and we talk about footie until Paul and I have nursed enough waters, and we decide to call it quits (we both have early morning tee times). Rodney had already been cut off by the same Israeli bartender from the night before, even though he had tried to impress her by ordering Chardonnay in what he said was Hebrew but to me sounded like bad Spanish. On our way out the door, it occurs to Paul and I that Rodney either had too little steak or too much vino. He slips off the bottom step out of the lobby, doing a giant drunken pirouette in midair, arms and legs flying like a discarded puppet, thumping headfirst into the wooden decking below.

"Holy shit, I think he's dead," I inform Paul.

I'm not trying to be funny, but Paul is laughing for the first time since I met him.

I actually do think Rodney is dead—lying on his back, his hands and knees pointing upward like an expired kitchen bug. His eyes are wide open, staring at a spot just above his forehead. He's not speaking or moving, and I can't say if he's breathing. He's just smiling with this strange look on his face, like he was having a nice dream about carrying Paul's bag around Augusta.

"Paul, I think he's seriously fucked up," I say. "He could have cracked his skull. He could have a concussion."

"That would be unfortunate," Paul says.

He couldn't be less bothered, as if Rodney had committed a minor social faux pas, picking the wrong fork at a dinner party, as if slips and falls and cracked skulls were all part of a Londoner's good night out. And here I am again, the evening before a tournament, faced with a situation that reduces golf to a silly game of dirt and plastics, insignificant in comparison to the complexity of a cold slab of Britain laid out dead on the hotel hardwood. I imagine myself eulogizing this stranger in some damp English church, having to explain to his poor wife that his last thought of her was trading her in for the life of a golf hobo.

It feels like months, but it's probably a few seconds of Paul and I staring blankly at Rodney's blank stare, taking inventory of our survival skills—*if he says he knows CPR, I'll play dumb*—but before we can even think to ask Rodney if he's okay, a SWAT team of hotel staff descends upon us from above. It's the most action this dying hotel has ever seen on a Monday night, a swarm of hotel managers, security, paramedics, and one crying young barmaid from Jerusalem mumbling apologies to her boss in an accent that seems to be growing thicker, trying to explain how she just killed a hotel guest with a 1997 Clos du Bois.

"Are you with this man?" asks a squat man in a blazer as wide as it was long, beefy mustache befitting his walkie-talkie.

Paul and I look at each other. Then back at the guard. *Which man? Oh, you mean the one at our feet who's turning blue? Never seen him before in my life.*

"He's with me," Paul finally says, claiming his caddy as if he were picking up his kid from detention. "Stupid bastard. Won't remember any of this in the morning."

Rodney is stirring by the time the ambulance arrives, paramedics wheeling a stretcher through the hotel lobby. Propped up in a patio chair, Dr. Jekyll can't understand what all this fuss could possibly be about. He refuses any treatment.

"Of course I'm not going to the hospital, I'm absolutely fine," he tells the paramedic as he signs a release.

I'm not convinced he's fine myself, but I have a feeling he'll survive when he sees the bartender and says, "You should all be this attentive when somebody's trying to get a drink. Maybe your bloody hotel wouldn't be empty."

———

The following morning it was Tom Coyne taking the headfirst fall out the doorway, and at no point in the proceedings would I have tried to convince anyone that I was absolutely fine.

It was the ultimate round of *If I could only hit another one.* Not to make excuses—though I have made many, and will continue to do so—I am not a great fan of the punitive flavor of Florida golf. The way I grew up playing, it was okay to hit it left, hit it right—if you had enough imagination, and enough coordination, you could see your way out of all sorts of trouble. There was always the chance to save yourself with a good putter or a punch shot snaking through the sycamores. Yet there is not much imagination about a golf ball lying two feet beneath the surface of the agua. There is little creativity involved in raising your arm to shoulder's length, opening up your fingers, and dropping a new golf ball. Florida golf courses are 50 percent water, 50 percent land, because if you dig down ten feet—try to build up a green or just bury a bulb in Florida soil—you will find water lickety-split. Florida architects aren't sadists, they just have to dig ponds if they want to have soil to work with. So there needs to be water everywhere, and it was the everywhere water at the Bonaventure Country Club that got the best of me. Three marginal drives and one sniper that was so wrong, it would have found a water hazard if I was playing on the moon—and its four drops spoiling my trip.

The Tour de las Americas (TLA) Q-school has a different feeling from the Canadian, and I am sure it will be quite different in Australia. It was sort of like showing up for a job interview when nobody knows you're coming. The tournament directors were probably the warmest golf officials I have met in my whole twelve months, but the event didn't feel like too much of an event. We had to take carts, there were no caddies. Scores and standings were posted on a single sheet of paper by the locker room entrance. We paid for our range balls and practiced alongside the retirees from the community across the street. The course was still open for play to the public, so right behind the final group came a pissed-off foursome of beer drinkers wondering what the hell had their golf course all backed up. Canada at least had a smattering of spectators—at the TLA, it was like we were out there executing some covert golfing operation.

But I didn't wish it was more like a pro golf tournament, because this was exactly what a pro golf tournament was. Pro golf on TV, that's played by only 150 guys on the planet. Everyone else is playing in front of no crowds, no scoreboards, and nobody cares what they shoot aside from the hundred other guys who showed up to this Hooters Tour or Golden Bear or Challenge Tour event, hoping to bump their check from $476 to $621 if they are able to beat you out. I guess that's why everyone still takes their shot at the big tour—no matter how expensive, no matter how slim the margins. Because we don't grow up watching tournaments where the players' golf carts cost them $19 a day, where there's one marshal on the course for a hundred players, where the tournament scorecard is the same one they give to the tourists.

To say the tournament was unglamorous doesn't mean that the play wasn't accomplished and the prize not worthy. A TLA card doesn't just get you a long season of good purses throughout South and Central America (roughly sixteen events), but as the TLA cosanctions events with the European Challenge Tour (the European Tour's version of the Nationwide), the pros had come from England and France and Colombia and Chile. My first day, I am the only English speaker in my group. With my small amount of Spanish, I can confirm that the two Mexican players in the group did not take undue advantage of their opportunity to mock me in their native tongue. I don't have a partner to talk to until day three, when I'm paired with two Yanks, one of whom melts down on seventeen and drives straight off the golf course (I'm keeping his scorecard at the time, so I can't say that I blame him). On day four, I'm scrapping it out for the bottom of the barrel with a humorless hacker from Germany and an ex-motorcross champion from Guatemala who goes out and shoots 72. For four days, I turn opportunities into 84-80-87-81, for a whopping total of plus-44, tying my German friend in a tie for 37th, keeping my basement-free streak alive by two whole strokes.

The morning after the Curious Incident of the Dead Brit in the Nighttime, Paul was right: Rodney didn't remember a minute of it. He woke up with a suspicious bump on his head and asked Paul if he had fallen out of his bed in his sleep. Paul would go on to finish near the top of the leaderboard that week, ready for his upcoming run at the big tour.

For me, the tournament had been like one long night out with Rodney: Everything that happened the four previous mornings was a little hazy, difficult to recall. The golf had been, at best, forgettable.

Over the past fifteen months I have done my best to spread golf balls around the continent. I have been the Johnny Appleseed of Titleists, losing dozens in the ponds of Florida, the forests of Canada, the yellow fields of Indiana harvest. Deciding to stamp my full name on three dozen Pro V1's was a particularly poor idea—months later, the balls were still showing up on my doorstep, in my mailbox, giggling Bonita Springs golfers returning my lost golf ball in the middle of an otherwise pleasant afternoon.

But now I'm preparing to shed golf balls around a whole new continent in an unfamiliar hemisphere. And in my carry-on, there sits a sleeve of Titleist Pro-V1x that I absolutely must not lose, a threesome of golf balls that is more precious than most of my organs. Wrapped in white tissue and disguised as the third in a set of golf balls is a fuzzy black box full of every last bit of my personal worth.

The application to the Australasian Q-school went through with one simple fax. Credit card number, address, handicap—*G'day, mate, welcome to the tournament*—and my last chance was confirmed. I had managed this peripatetic year with a minimum of air travel, largely avoiding the unpleasantness of the airport terminal where I would typically wait pale-faced by my gate, contemplating the afterlife. But unless I wanted to play in *next* December's Aussie Q-school, there was no way to get Down Under that didn't include a 747.

We cheat fate again on that first flight to Los Angeles, some-how arriving safely in Bradley International Airport's terminal, where we'll wait for our nonstop flight to Melbourne. Fifteen hours in the air, one of the longest flights in the world. I had approached the prospect of fifteen hours in a 747 as if it were a mysterious conceit, an unintelligible performance art. *Flying, for a whole day? Fascinating.* But as we sit in cold, strange Bradley International's terminal, already groggy from our six hours to L.A., Allyson, red-nosed and clogged with a nasty head cold with half a day's flying still remaining—it's as close as I have come to putting the brakes on the whole entire deal and just saying *Fuck it, I'll be a farmer.*

The bogeys and the double bogeys and the double-digit scores had been tough. The letter from the PGA had been a sucker punch to the kidneys. But waiting in the L.A. airport, nothing but the early-morning blackness outside, a concrete-walled terminal with all the character of an interrogation room where nobody is speaking English and flights heading across the ocean to places I had never heard of, on airlines that sounded made up (*Cathay Pacific? I hope that plane floats*), on jets that were surely not up to the task of so much distance, heading to destinations where reaching Hawaii was not even halfway there—how the hell am I going to do this?

We get some McDonald's, a two-cheeseburger meal we nibble down, sharing the worst last meal of all time. I keep thinking about Qantas and *Rain Man*, how Dustin Hoffman informed the entire world that Qantas has never crashed, and how that record provided only an illusion of safety, that the law of averages guaranteed one was going down soon. Tonight seems as good a night as any.

But the flight to Melbourne isn't bad. It's quite good, in fact. After shooting off into the dark ocean night, a quick ding of the seat belt sign (much appreciated, always like the little nod of con-fidence from the cockpit), we were soaring on a well-oiled trans-Pacific machine. We both sleep as if drugged (I was, actually), and the individual movie screens with flight-track is all I need to realize that I am going to be one more in the billions of people who have walked off a plane into a warm, bright destination.

Today soon becomes yesterday—or rather tomorrow, or the day after, as we cross the date line, the equator, and wake up in a place where they told us it was now seven A.M. (for future reference, this trip adviser recommends breaking up the trip—Hawaii or L.A., Sydney is even quite a bit closer—east coast U.S. to Melbourne in one continuous go is a bit much, even for a carefree traveler). We were greeted by excited customs agents and a blond puppy as we disembark into the terminal. Jetlagged to the point of slap-happy, I assume that the dog is here to welcome us to the country, a little puppy welcome wagon or a showcase of some native wildlife. I stop to pet the cutesy sniffing dog—*good boy, you're a good dog*—the rapport is instant. The dog loves me. If I weren't visiting for two weeks I would have put him into my bag and taken him with me.

At immigration, we swear up and down that we aren't carrying food or plants or inferior American beer into their carefully balanced agricultural system. About an hour after touching down, we put together our bags and sleepwalk to our final check-out through customs.

After a capacity flight on the biggest air machine in existence, the mass of passengers trying to squeeze their way through line number one was enough to crush a traveler's tested spirit. After thirty hours, it was a sight just sad enough to finally break a traveler's heart. But as Allyson and I approach the queue, a smiling guard waves us over.

"Why don't you just head down line number three?" he tells us.

Number three being the line where there was no line at all.

Now, I don't consider myself a *huge* celebrity, but it's nice to be recognized from time to time, always rewarding to meet a fan of coming-of-age golf literature. I had heard that *A Gentleman's Game* did come out in Australia on DVD, and there was that ESPY nomination, after all. I can't imagine they get too many big names willing to come this damn far, so I can see why they would want to take extra care of those who make the trip. A little respect—I can't say it isn't nice. And I've been traveling too many hours to generate a drop of sympathy for anyone stuck in that line. *See ya, suckers, must be in the front row.*

We cruise down the long, snaking, empty hallway of line number three, whistling as we roll our bags along, giddy about our good fortune. *Some people just weren't meant for line number one,* we're both thinking—*some people are just line three people.*

And it was soon clear to me that I was correct. Some people *are* line three people. And those are the people who smuggle large quantities of narcotics across international borders.

At the end of our unimpeded walk down the hallway, we arrive at a team of customs agents with looks on their faces like they had been waiting for us their entire lives. Allyson has gone a little bit white, but I'm still amused by the situation in a *when in Aussie* sort of way.

There's nothing about this predicament that would usually concern me. On an ordinary day I would laugh my way through a DEA strip search. I ain't holding, as they say. No reptiles or vegetables, no drugs any stronger than Tylenol PM. But then . . . if my thoughts were being broadcast across the loudspeakers at Tullamarine Airport, you would have heard one long, loud *fuuuuuuuuuuuuuuuuuuuuuuuuuck.*

The diamond. The fucking diamond.

Can't a guy ever catch a break?

Agent number four—not the one who took my golf bag into a room with mirrored windows for further inspection, and not the one who took my spikes to be pressure-washed clean of foreign soil, and not the one who is currently going through my clothes as if they were the plastic foam packing surrounding his Christmas present—agent number four seems to be in charge. He's the one asking the questions, and he doesn't like it a little bit that I smile when he asks me if I'm carrying any coke.

"Coke?" I couldn't help but chuckle. It sounded so 80s, so Crockett and Tubbs. "No sir, I am not carrying any coke."

"Do your friends do coke?"

I am not quite sure the point of the question. Is he doing a background check, a public service survey, or is this just the shittiest icebreaker of all time?

"Not that I know of," seems like a fair response.

I'm trying to not laugh anymore, and Allyson looks like, after all these hours traveling with a hacking cough, that she is finally going to be sick. She looks at me like she only half-knows me, some stranger whom she goes to Australia with only to discover the dark truth: that her love was an international gangster.

"We have stopped you today because the dog that sniffed you as you departed the airplane, that was a narcotics dog. He paid special attention to your left pant pocket. So if you wouldn't mind, please turn out your pockets and empty the contents on the table here in front of you."

The fact that they knew the dog sniffed my left pocket an hour and half before on the other side of the airport and these people had, since that sniffing, been waiting to pull us into line three—it was Orwellian creepy. I show him my empty wallet and a vile of Dramamine that he sniffs like a wine snob breathing in a big Bordeaux, eventually accepting that I haven't manufactured cocaine in the form of motion-sickness pills. And then he turns his attention to my carry-on satchel, the one spot I was praying he would overlook.

I prepare myself. If he pulls out the sleeve of balls, if he opens the box and pulls out the ring, then I am getting engaged right here in the customs line at the Melbourne airport, and this narcotics agent who looks like Jean-Claude Van Damme, he's going to take our engagement picture, right after he gets through searching my colon for my friend's imaginary cocaine.

"What is the nature of your trip to Australia?" he asks as he picks through the pockets of the satchel.

"A golf tournament."

"Are you a professional golfer?"

"Yes. Well, no. Well, I'm a writer."

"You're a writer? I thought you said you were a golfer?"

"I'm a golf writer." Good God, don't make me explain this here while you whip out my fiancée-to-be's diamond here in the land of white walls and crew cuts and two-way mirrors.

He nods at my explanation with mild interest, as if the writer part only confirmed the dog's suspicions. I watch his hands run over my iPod, my notepads, tape recorder, then going for the secret, zipped-up side pocket where a lone sleeve of Titleists would surely arouse suspicion.

"We don't know why the dog pays more attention to some passengers than others. It is not uncommon to get false alarms."

He unzips the pocket, takes a look inside. "So you are a golfer," he says.

And out comes a sleeve of golf balls with a street value this narcotics agent can't possibly imagine.

I guess we'll have to invite him to the wedding now, I think as I get ready to take a knee. I'm a second away from snatching back that box of golf balls when he takes a look at the cellophane window, sees nothing of interest, drops the sleeve of Titleists back into the pocket, and zips the bag closed.

"What part of Australia will you be visiting?"

I can't speak.

Allyson saves me, piping up, "Cranbourne. He's playing in the tour school."

"Some good golf courses out that way," the agent informs us. "Good luck to you. Hope you play well. Enjoy Australia."

No wonder they're the number-one ball in golf. Titleist had yet to make a tour player out of me. But as a jewel smuggler, I was all-World.

There is plenty to love about Australia—the gambling (slots, horses, you name it, it's everywhere), the cricket I almost understand, the meat-and-starch diet. Chips come with absolutely everything—order a plate of French fries, they come with a side of fries. But I would trade every Bloomin' Onion in America for a regular supply of Aussie meat pies. They are the ideal male foodstuff—meat, in pie form. How could that not work? The filling is reminiscent of the dog food of my youth that, as a very young child whose only chore was to prepare the golden retriever's bowl, I was always tempted to sample (I did try a Gaines Burger once—*huge* disappointment). Brown, nonspecific, glorious meat mush, wrapped in pastry. It's almost worth the flight. Almost.

And yet, I found we have plenty of misconceptions about the nation continent. First, everybody isn't running around in striped prison digs. The toilets don't flush counterclockwise—they pretty much just suck the water straight down. And as for the giant beers, what a cruel mistruth. Most beer is served in small glasses, as it is delicious, yet far stronger than our pilsners here at home. I also didn't find any Outback Steakhouses, but that was okay. It was my expectation of the weather that turned out to be the most costly misconception of them all. You think of Australia and you think of surfers and sunburn and long, dry seasons in a dusty outback. When we step out of the car for my practice round, the Antarctic blast nearly blows me back into our Nissan.

The pins spread across this links course are pointing sideways, as if showing the way to the next tee. The rain is cold as needles and attacking from all directions. My spikes can't quite pierce the South Australian turf that has turned out to be soft as a pool table, and the weeds that line the fairways of this treeless golf course are chin-high and tangled in knots. It's not grass. It's like hitting a golf ball out of somebody's dreadlocks.

Ranfurlie. As carefully as Dr. Winters and I had discussed selecting the ideal PGA Tour qualifying site, Ranfurlie Golf Club is a cornucopia of all that my golf game isn't, a veritable top ten of everything I was hoping I wouldn't find. Down Under golf means keeping it down under the wind. And hitting it low, with all the hours and all the range balls, it was something I was never quite able to manage. As Dr. Suttie finally conceded, "You don't hit it under the wind. You hit it over it."

The course is hard and fast, and balls moving in the wrong direction continue to do so until they find a batch of weeds to interrupt them. In the age of miracle spinning golf balls and tender catcher's mitt greens, Ranfurlie is a throwback to when golf was played along the ground. Balls that struck the putting surface on the fly bound into oblivion, hopping through the green, cozying down into impossible lies.

It is a pretty golf course, a fair and good test of golf, if it was the kind of golf you felt capable of playing. It's not my dream golf course, but hoping for Edgmont isn't going to do much good. No matter that God continues to campaign against my golf career—I can look at Ranfurlie either as bad luck, or a big opportunity. This is supposed to be hard, and I decide that Ranfurlie is just one more chance to show how far my game has come.

The practice facilities are almost nonexistent. The course doesn't feel like it's ten years old—the clubhouse is still under construction, and yet, they built a giant golf course on a piece of former farmland, and didn't think to add anything more than a range where players have to shag their own balls. I'm disappointed that my tour school won't have a driving range, but I'm not surprised. My travels have shown me that we are driving-range-spoiled in the States. I don't know if it makes us better or worse, that we can beat a thousand balls a day of perfect, level lies, learning to launch gorgeous golf shots, but perhaps learning little else. I would tire of a range like Ranfurlie's very quickly, which would make me go figure it out on the actual golf course, which in the end might not be a bad way to learn after all.

The field is largely from Japan, Korea, Australia, and New Zealand. While many of the Aussie players seem to have come from college programs in the States, there is only one other native Yank in the field, a pro named Mike, who worked in the shop at his club all season long to save up enough bread for the trip over here in December to make his third run at Qualifying School. He has made it through on two occasions, playing for one, then two years before losing his card. If Mike makes it through this week, he's playing golf for a living. If not, he's back looking for a club job, selling shirts or teaching beginners. You have to love this kind of authentic journeyman golf pro, the sort of migrant cowboy you don't find in our 401(k) culture anymore. Rare to find an educated, qualified professional who works only when he needs money, then quits his job when it's time to be moving along, chasing tournaments like they're roaming buffalo.

When I ask Mike about that kind of pressure, selling his car to pay his airfare to Australia with no guarantees outside his tee time, he gives me a look like it never occurred to him to be anxious about such an arrangement, confirming my suspicion that there are some guys meant to grind this out for a living, and some guys meant to run the annual member-guest.

"I need the competition," he explains. "I need to feel like my back is up against it. I need to feel like I have to hit the perfect golf shot. That pressure gets me going. That's when I play my best, when I have no choice, put it in the hole or go home. I guess some people don't respond to that, but to play out here, when you're playing for money to pay that week's hotel bill, you've got to embrace those situations. You've got to seek it out."

Mike continues as we roll our golf balls across the practice green, "Last Q-school I was in down here, I started the last day on the cut line. I made two doubles on the front nine, but it was almost like I needed that challenge, to be out of it, to have to start clawing my way back. I shot thirty-two on the back and ended up making it by two shots. I would rather have not made it so close, but I think I sort of needed it, to get my blood going, you know? Someone might call it pressure, but I really think of it as fun."

Jack Lemmon once described the feeling of hitting off the first tee in front of a crowd to be like standing onstage with your back to a crowded auditorium, taking off your clothes, then slowly turning around. I agree with everything Mr. Lemmon said, but I would add that you do so while standing in a bucket of ice water, with an auditorium full of every girl who wouldn't talk to you since you were eight years old, and they all have camera phones, and slingshots.

"Now on the tee, from the United States, Tom Coyne."

Hearing my name in a classic Aussie accent, not to mention the fact that I was suddenly carrying not only my own personal burdens, but the baggage of 300 million prideful Americans—it only ratchets up the nerves. I could hear the heads turning and the necks craning. *Who's the Yank, must be a player . . . can't believe someone came all this way.* In Jack Lemmon's view, the room was full, and I was butt-ass-naked with a penis that had turned into an innie.

The evening before, I had gone over the many pages of Dr.

Winters's workbook. I had read his philosophies about the opening tee shot, reread and repeated so much of it that resonated with how I would like to play the golf course: *Will you be ready to play when you step onto the first tee—the answer must be YES. Will you step into each shot with a clear, decisive plan? YES. Will you address each shot with 100 percent commitment? YES. Will you swing with trust and emotional freedom on each and every shot? YES. Will you accept the results of each shot, and go into the next shot with renewed enthusiasm and confidence? YES. Always, you must get to YES, over each and every shot, to every question in your head, there can't be doubt, there can only be YES.*

I do my best to do all these things, but on that first morning, with the air going sideways and my not quite remembering where the fairway went on this blind opening hole, I only get to about Maybe. Mike and Jimbo and UK Paul, they wouldn't have hit a golf ball thinking Maybe, not if they had to stand there on that first tee all morning, holding back the hundred guys behind them.

But I step to my ball with a mind-set that would make my psychologist shoot one of his rubber bands at my eye, just hoping to get this one moment out of the way as quickly as possible.

Standing over the ball, the silence becomes deafening. I can hear the nerves swarming, buzzing in my skull, and I am once again just barely involved in what I am doing. I just hope that in a short while I'll be walking down the fairway instead of going back to my bag for another one. We're all the same on the driving range—in fact, my move looks better than most. But if there's a difference between me and the thems, I guess that mind-set pretty much sums it up.

As if for nostalgia's sake at the end of a long road, I lean back and crank the ball deep and long and dead right. The marshal up ahead turns to follow my ball, then turns back and gives my group that hopeless shrug of the shoulders that, from 200 yards away, looks just like a fat middle finger. I just couldn't help myself. On this opening drive I was going to find a way to get back in that golf bag, digging for a provisional, as if I were some sort of junkie and that airport puppy was right, my bag was stuffed with outlawed delights.

Number ten is a par-five with a long strip of nasty jungle weeds framing the fairway, a reverse Mohawk of a golf hole. My body had, in fact, made a genius adjustment as my hands approached my golf ball, knowing that if I was going to block it right, better to blow it right big-time, leaving my first drive propped up in the fairway of a golf hole to be played later.

My two partners were Johnny, a skinny kid from London who had a pale, street-tough look about him, like he had come from the Artful Dodger's Golf Academy. Next to him was a six feet three stick from central casting, an Australian named Adam Blyth, who was barely in his twenties and had just turned pro. I heard that he was one of the country's top juniors and amateur players, and his game seemed native to Ranfurlie. He didn't hit it a mile (for his size, pretty average distance, but my even noticing that as a point to critique betrays my misplaced golf sensibilities), but he could control his ball flight. Blyth could golf his ball. No matter that his tee ball didn't stretch to outrageous distances—he could hit stingers with his driver that didn't get more than ten feet off the ground but were sneaky long, leaping their way up the fairway.

His father was caddying for him, but Adam didn't seem the kind of kid who needed any pushing. Dad would hardly say a word, allowing Adam's intense focus to grind out hole after hole. Same routine over every shot, same number of practice strokes, deliberate to the point of slow. But when you don't hit the ball that many times, you can afford to take a few extra minutes. Halfway around the world, and I had found that there are sticks all over. And regardless of time zone or hemisphere, they look and walk and strike the ball the same way—solid as hell. Here or there, the sticks are all so lovely.

Today's mistakes are more dramatic than most, the track's sharp teeth bringing all my accidents into greater relief. Like on the short sixth hole, where I should have knocked a four-iron into the fairway instead of tugging a driver into the weeds. And when we're lucky enough to find the ball at the bottom of the cabbage, with no space to take a drop and an unplayable lie, I should have gone back to the tee and played again instead of hacking at the ball until it had disappeared again. After three tries with a sand wedge to rip my ball free, after it is too late to go back to the tee, I can do nothing but keep knifing the grass, taking my nine.

There is something especially brutal about tournament golf, where there are no gimmes and no stroke limits, where, in a split second, the game escapes you. That quickly, the game is playing you, you are no longer playing it. One swing, and suddenly it has nothing to do with qualifying or making par or getting to yes. All you're trying to do is keep moving forward, stay out of everyone's way, too busy wondering what everyone else is thinking to have any real swing thoughts of your own.

While this might make me something of a mental midget, allow me to remind you, I am not playing your Thursday afternoon four-ball. This is a Tour Qualifying School, being played for real money, where the players all around me are playing for their way of life. It's quite easy to start worrying about the effect you are having on their chances, especially when you're only pretending that this is your real job.

On a 142-yard par-three into the wind, I crush a six-iron into the breeze that, by the time it reaches the apogee of its flight, is actually retreating in the air, moving back toward us and crashing down like a busted kite, fifty yards short of the green. A round that I was slowly putting back together, on the easiest golf hole on the scorecard, I make triple bogey. On the day's final scoreboard, an abominable 90 puts me in second-to-last place, ahead of a young man from South Korea. When I returned home, I would get an e-mail from Paddy from that afternoon as he followed my progress on the Internet.

Tough luck. You did your best, and that was all you can do. At least you're not in last place. You really showed Satoshi Mizoguchi who's boss.

All the weeds and water hazards and wind in the world—
they could all conspire against me and none of it can stop
today from being my day. Finally, I know that there is
nothing they or I can do to give this round a sour ending.

It's all up to her now.

Low expectations, in this case, are my friend. My track record
for spoiling opportune moments for a proposal over the past nine
years has left her totally unsuspecting. There is no way she can possibly suspect that I had the time or the wherewithal to add a diamond to my tally over the past year. Whatever hopes she may have
had were no doubt dashed by the airport search; best part, she
has no idea that her ring is in the top pocket of the golf bag she has
been pulling around the course all week. I don't know when or how
the moment is going to come, but I am perfectly relaxed about it.
Right now, the prospect of asking a young woman to spend the rest
of her life with me seems infinitely easier than going back out to
Ranfurlie Golf Club for day two of Down Under Q-school fun.

I didn't think the weather could get worse, but day two of the
Q-school has me reminiscing about the rosy conditions of day one.
None of us has any business being outdoors on day number two. If
this were the United States, the wind and rain would have been as-
signed a category. We would have been curled up in our basements,
watching a Fox News crawler scream *Q-school golfers stranded in*

Hurricane Dingo—survivors doubtful. It was more golf rapture than golf tournament, pounding wind and icy rain that felt like a face full of daggers. It was a golfing End of Days, and I have been Left Behind.

I hit my opening drive down the middle of number one, and my caddy made it halfway to the fairway before turning over the reins to her pull cart.

"This is crazy. You can't play in this. I can't do this," she tells me, her clothes already soaked through to the skin. A young lady who could look happy going to the dentist, she has a ripe sort of misery in her eyes. "This is not a good idea."

And I agree. It isn't a good idea—to play in a windy rainstorm, to shoot 90 in the opening round, to be hanging three shots out of last place. Ranfurlie is full of bad ideas. The weather can wash you into a funk, or it can break you free from your crooked path. The conditions can tighten up your focus, make you play one shot at a time because you cannot possibly bear to think about having to hit another one.

So I decide to stop making stupid choices, the first of which would be to ask Allyson to caddy for me in forty-mile-an-hour winds and rain and a temperature we couldn't precisely translate from Celsius but was damn well cold enough. I encourage her to wait inside, to get some tea and read a book.

It didn't take too much arm-twisting—I think I got to "Why don't you . . ." when she did her about-face, sneakers sprinting back toward the clubhouse.

I cannot control the weather. I can't control all the results. All I can control is my plan, my effort, my attitude. I play one shot at a time until I make the turn by the clubhouse where I see Allyson cozy inside with a pot of tea. She pops out to hear that I'm making the turn at two-over, 38. It wasn't going to set any course records, it wasn't going to get me on the Aussie tour, but it showed some guts. With the rain blowing upward into our noses, and with the disaster from day one, it felt like I had walked out there and made nine birdies in a row.

On the back nine, things got a little loose—literally—when my driver slipped out of my hands on two occasions. Allyson picked a good day to sit one out, because on the back nine I did plenty of bitching at the most useless caddy in the Southern Hemisphere (i.e., myself), handing wet grips and wet gloves to a player trying to grind out a round in the 70s. On one attempt, the driver nearly left my hand altogether, the golf ball knuckle-balling off the heel into the gooey stuff. One swing, that awful *zip* of hairy reeds sucking up a Titleist, and it was welcome back to Triple Bogeytown. I shot 47 on the back to sully a solid round of golf, while young Adam Blyth continued to separate himself from the field. Any worries I had about holding back my playing partners were dismissed when Adam duplicated his opening 75, vaulting him to the top of the class in this maelstrom.

This was not a unique phenomenon. Looking back to my Nationwide events and USGA qualifiers, I was regularly partnered with either a qualifier or a medalist. I was no distraction at all, and worrying that I might have been a distraction was a colossal waste of time, not to mention a contradiction of just about everything Dr. Winters had tried to impress upon me. And I can't beat myself up too much about being intimidated from time to time—it's part of the nature of what I am doing, that at the end of the day, I am ultimately an observer. I will be going back to a keyboard, not to a golf tour. I am here for only a little while, visiting in this world of the seasoned and the serious.

Driven in a way that could have made him seem aloof, arrogant, I got the chance to become friendly with Adam over our two days together, and he was a pretty warm, level young man. He told me about his home up on the Sun Coast, not too far from Surfer's Paradise, which I believed to be the greatest name of any beach town in the world. I told him a little about Philadelphia—*Have you seen Rocky? I live five blocks from those steps he ran up*—and Adam found that to be pretty cool. I looked at Adam and wondered if I could have been that kid—I had almost the exact same build at his age, and at twenty years old, I think it would have been simpler for me to wear that singular focus that he wore now, each shot the only thing that mattered in his young world. It was beautiful the way he made it look effortless. It must have been a great feeling to string those numbers together when it mattered, to be in the hunt, to need to make birdies, then step out of the car that morning and go make them.

I felt it a few times this year myself. Whether it was in a big tournament, or standing on a driving range at twilight by myself, I knew what it was to be a player. I wasn't pretending, I was living it. But over time, and over enough holes, the game chooses you, you can't force yourself in. I hope it chooses Adam, and Jimbo and Paul, too. The game isn't going to give me a playing career, but it has made me honest with myself in a whole new way. And if you or anyone you know might be interested in making themselves a candidate for golf greatness, I have a few pieces of plain advice:

1. Have yourself born or adopted into a rich family. Or pick the Powerball. Whatever money you think you'll need to chase your dream, double it. Don't be naive about the real cost of trying to play this game.

2. Play with players better than yourself. Play every tournament you can get in, and always play with something at stake. Make your regular golf competitive golf. Like Nicklaus's dad said, get comfortable with being uncomfortable.

3. Don't just love the game. Don't just enjoy the game. Need the game. For a young man to rise above all the talent out there, it has to go beyond obsession.

4. And don't need the game. It's the paradox at this upper tier of golf—even though you might be trying to make golf your living, you must be willing to play it for what it is: a game. The best players I walked with this year were able to pass off their intensity as a near disinterest, a settled quality that went beyond confidence, arriving at a beautiful Zen sort of peace. At the end of the day, the real players aren't the best coached or the best funded or the most focused—they are the ones who still see the game for what it is, who tie up their shoes, walk out the door, and just go play.

My life has been easy. My friends and I have been coddled by the world, a group who have known only good times and getting-better times. We were born not just with the right to pursue a simple happiness, but to stretch for our ultimate joys and dreams. We grew up believing no one had the right to call us mediocre or not good enough, we were all special and precious and unique in our gifts. Get a D, the teacher was to blame. Miss the cut, get the coach fired. Don't get into a college, sue the admissions office.

But not on a golf course. There is no hand-holding over a five-footer. No one to coddle you in a sand trap. I wasn't going to get one thing I didn't deserve. Just honesty, often more than I wanted. No one has been as frank and unapologetic with me as the golf courses I have played, and in all my trying, in all this dreaming of another life, of looking at all these beautiful backyards all around mine—when you are forced to be honest, to add 'em up and sign the card, you start to realize the spot you're standing in might be pretty great.

It's not too hard to realize that a few years from now, I was going to be a pretty good six-handicap, but one that never has to hit another solid ball and wonder, *What if?* I took my shot. I took millions of them.

And going into my final round of the year of my life, it was time to take the biggest one.

By day three, there are a few curious abbreviations on the scoreboard that I believe ensure I'm safe from finishing last (three saves in a row, quite a streak). The letters they would use at home are DNF (Did Not Finish), or WD (Withdrew), but in Australia, they go with RT, for Retired, as if in the middle of the round the player decided to pack it in and begin collecting his pension then and there. Or my favorite, a handful of names that are NR, for No Return, forgotten players who went out and never came back. Perhaps they're still out there haunting the tall grass, lost souls roaming the weeds for their golf balls.

On my final round of the year, perhaps the final competitive round of my life, I am at peace, perhaps for a variety of factors. The sun has come out in all its glory, the rain has stopped, and I know that soon my Mizunos will be back in a travel bag and relocated to a closet where they will have a long, dark, well-deserved sleep.

After scrambling the groups for our final round, I am paired with Kim Woo of Japan, who does not speak a syllable of English. He has a short swing but a big turn, ripping at the golf ball. He smiles and nods a lot, and it is kind of nice to finish this way, with a partner I cannot attempt to small-talk, almost like Allyson and I are out there alone. Our spot at the bottom of the tee times puts us late off the tenth tee, and I birdie the first hole, leading to a round of some rather handsome golf shots, relaxed, my golf expectations abandoned, knowing that I do not need to play well to make this a great day. And it had been a while since I'd had a great day on the golf course. I walked the fairways with light feet, shoulders back, looking around at the expanse of Australian green that I had not bothered to notice until this morning.

I'm not scoring, but I'm making the best golf swings I've made in months. A few bad bounces keep my score fat for Christmas, but I throw in the occasional birdie to give Allyson something to laugh about, and if I'm twenty over or ten under—I really don't know. All I know is the number hole we are on: fifteen. Then we're on sixteen. When we get to seventeen, that will be one hole away from my getting on my knees and pulling out the best caddy tip since Tiger signed his Stevie.

On sixteen, I send Allyson off to snap some photos of a bird I tell her I think looks interesting (we will later have nine pictures at home of this ugly black crow), but it does the job of getting her away from the bag so that I can slip the ring into my Dockers. As the fuzz of the black box hits the bottom of my pocket, my stomach cinches up in some spontaneous gastric bypass. The blood is barreling through my veins, thumping into the back of my throat. Almost there. Almost eighteen, where in front of the scoreboard, in front of God and everyone, I might just trump the leaders.

Sixteen, I slop around a quick bogey. The whole afternoon seems to have taken on my mood, a cool purple sky stretching over the clubhouse, the smell of electricity and nerves on the summer air. My drive splits the penultimate fairway, but we are not halfway out to our golf balls when the eerie quiet is broken by a low rumble. And then a horn . . . in the middle of seventeen, with a diamond ring in my pocket, a goddamn blasting horn . . .

"What does that siren mean?" Allyson asks.

Kim Woo points at the sky, international golf language for lightning.

With one hole to go, I explain to her, "Weather. We have to go in."

Weather is a great leveler. It inconveniences both rich and poor, the mighty and the meek. Thunder has ruined many a perfect round of golf, laid waste to whole vacations—in the golf world, the elements have always been the real boss of the moss. But lightning at the end of a perfectly clear Australian summer day, 500 yards from my getting down on my knee and confusing the hell out of my partner from Japan, it all comes to a grinding, rumbling halt.

What remains of the field has packed into the clubhouse restaurant, watching lightning scratch at the farmland in the distance. We wait an hour without five words of conversation between Allyson and me—jingling platinum in my hand, I can't think of that many interesting things to say, and I'm afraid I'll faint or vomit, or both, if I try to say too much. Soon, it's two hours waiting. Two and a half. I understood that God didn't want me to be a golf pro, but the fact that he was weighing in so vociferously on this engagement issue was beginning to make me wonder. There are a lot of anxious golfers waiting out the storm, guys needing to go out there and squeeze out one more birdie to make it to next week's Stage II. But nobody seems quite as humorless as the white-faced American staring out the window, a look on his face like he's left his puppy out in a hurricane.

The updates arrive by the half hour. "We're following the storm on the radar, but tour rules won't allow us to send you back out until the area has been lightning free for thirty minutes," is what they kept telling us, until 6:30, when the skies finally cleared and the final ruling came down.

"I'm sorry, fellas, but we can't let you finish today. We're going to have to ask you to come back out tomorrow and finish your rounds first thing in the morning."

There's a collective whining sigh over the room, but from one member of the field, there comes a good, hard, head-turning, "No fucking way, mate!" in an accent that no one would mistake for Aussie.

We have big dinner plans with Allyson's Australian cousins and hotel reservations in Melbourne, a good hour from the golf course, and now we must unexpectedly return to Cranbourne in the morning, assuming our former positions on the golf course by seven A.M. I'm not surprised to see most of the bottom-dwellers withdrawing from the tournament. Kim Woo has a flight to Japan, and he wouldn't be returning tomorrow. If I plan on finishing, I'll have to match up with somebody else.

"If I were you, mate, I'd just take off. Go to Melbourne. Start seeing Australia, start enjoying yourself. You don't really need to come all the way back here, do you?" Adam asks me.

He certainly needs to come back—he's one hole away from winning the tournament. As for me . . .

"Adam, buddy, I have come a long damn way to do this, and I am going to finish. I am going to sign a scorecard and post a score, if it kills me."

It almost does. With a 4:30 wake-up call after a late dinner, stuffing our luggage back into the rental, and heading out of the city center on our way back to Cranbourne, I am too cranky and tired and pissed off about getting up at four to play one hole of golf to be even remotely nervous about giving Allyson this ring. I'm half-inclined to toss it to her and roll back over and go back to bed. But, instead, we pile out of our room and start trekking back to this most un-touristy part of Australia. I feel badly about Allyson coming all this way to see life in the average Australian suburb. There is nothing *Crocodile Dundee* about anything we have seen yet. It's like a foreigner coming all the way to the United States to spend a week in Fort Wayne—perfect, if you want to see real America, but not so hot if you're on vacation.

So I had one extra night as an non-engaged man. One more evening of being ostensibly single. And I didn't like it at all. It was supposed to be a big night for toasting and celebration and starting to plan the rest of our lives. But after nine years, fair play that I'm made to wait another eighteen hours.

When we get back to Ranfurlie at sunrise, I have to match up with three other players whose partners hopped on planes last night, two Japanese players and an Australian. Everybody is off watching Adam and his threesome fight their way up the final hole, but they should take a look at this foursome. They should take our picture coming up our last hole, and call it PERSEVERANCE. Four guys with one hole to play and nothing to play for, who can't bring themselves to quit.

Our finishing hole is number nine, a tricky par-four with two thick trees planted in the middle of the fairway, tangled goalposts at the end of an Aussie football pitch. I go to the bag and peel the cover off my three-wood.

"Last hole," I say to Allyson, who's busy swatting mosquitoes away from her ears.

"Last hole," she says. "Thank God."

The sun is low over the clubhouse to our left, the air damp but just steaming up with the day as I press my final Titleist into the spongy tee box, then step back, taking it all in, a high-arcing three-wood soaring over the trees, falling from left to right, dropping onto a flat patch of fairway not 150 yards from the green.

"Tom, wow," Allyson says, as if it had just occurred to her that for the past fourteen months I had actually been up to something. "Awesome shot," she whispers.

And it was a beauty—there were less then a dozen shots over the past year that had so precisely mimicked my vision of what they were about to be. It helped knowing that I would never hit another drive like this one, never have to stand on a tee box as a golf professional again, never have the chance to be playing partners with such rare and talented people.

It's not until that final hole, until there are no other shots or scores or holes to think about, that I can truly take Dr. Winters's advice and honestly say I am playing one shot at a time. There is a clarity, a trust, a personal investment with that ball that I wish I could bottle up and sip from time to time. No worries, just warm expectations: I knew I was going to pipe a perfect drive, that I was going to hit a solid eight-iron up the hill and onto the green—so solid that it hits pin-high and sucks back off the green, leaving me a tricky little chip back up to the pin.

There was no doubt that I was going to hit it well—but not too well, so that I leave myself a good five-feet par putt that slides from left to right. A putt that I had made my fair share of, and a putt I had missed a thousand times in the past year. The year can't end with a tap-in. And it shouldn't end with a bogey, or even a birdie. I would like to finish things with a hard-working par.

I stand over my ball, a twitch staring up in my palms. The nerves are coming now. *You can't end this year this way, another lip-out, another five. God, don't let me make bogey and walk over to my caddy and ask her to spend the rest of her life with me.*

At the end of a year of owed-me-ones, golf takes over for just a brief moment, and I just stand there, watching. The putter head drawing back straight and smooth and gently pushing my ball with a soft rising stroke, my Titleist riding on a gently bending rail that stops at the center cut.

That perfect plastic rattle.

"A par?" my caddy asks as I hand over my putter for the last time, my cheeks a little warmer than they should be for a ho-hum four.

"Par," I say. "This game is easy."

"That was a really good hole for you." She smiles.

"Do me a favor," I say, handing her my glove and tees and my golf ball, "put these in my bag and grab the keys and my wallet. I've got to sign my card over here, then we can get out of here."

It's a substantial bump in caddy responsibility. To this point I had not so much asked her to grab the flag, but she knows where I keep the wallet, and where the glove goes. She doesn't know that the wallet is already in my back pocket, and the keys are jingling in my fingers.

The scorer's table is ten paces from the final green, and a dozen players are milling about the scoreboard, debating the final cut, waiting for the leaders to finish their final hole. In the distance I see Adam walking up eighteen—he is still the leader, good for him, needing one more par to finish off another 69. But I am not entirely interested in seeing if he makes his birdie putt, because in front of the eighteenth green, just off to the side of number nine, I am watching Allyson dig through my bag, hunting for my wallet. I watch her stick her hand in one pocket and her whole body freezes, as if fingers inside the bag had grabbed her back. I'm guessing that for a young lady, there are few items with as distinctive a shape and texture as that black velvet box.

I sign my card and walk over to the bag, where Allyson is looking at her shoes, her face gone ashen—she looks like she got hold of a bad meat pie.

"Did you find my wallet?"

"There . . . it . . . wasn't there," she mumbles under her breath, wonderfully confused.

Committing to a golf shot, believing that you will hit a great shot when all the laws of physics are stacked against you, when all the available evidence says the odds are not in your favor—it is a great leap of faith and trust, maybe even an act of defiance. To expect greatness when there is nothing but trouble all around you, to expect joy when there is so much potential for sadness—you have to hand it to the great players. And you have to hand it to my parents.

And to every guy who had the guts before I did, to get down on his knee in front of a young woman and have the gumption to promise her happiness.

It has taken me fifteen-plus months. It has taken a million golf balls and nearly every penny to my name. But here, on the eighteenth green of the Ranfurlie Golf Club, in Cranbourne, Australia, as I get down on my knee and open that velvet box in front of her, I still somehow suspect that golf has given me more than I gave to it, now that *Tom Coyne from the United States* has finally gotten to Yes.

It is Adam Blyth, Q-school medalist, who takes our engagement picture beside the eighteenth green. Just a few moments after proposing in front of a small gallery of groggy golfers, Adam is there with our camera, snapping a shot of me, Allyson, and, of course, the Mizunos. Adam finished first, but with more class than you would expect from a young man his age, he doesn't mention it. He just congratulates us at length, shocked as most twenty-year-olds would be by what I just did—*You just proposed? To your caddy? On the eighteenth green?*

Allyson and I buy a few more souvenirs in the pro shop than we normally would have at a course where I didn't break 84, then we head out to the car park.

Placing the clubs in the trunk is like laying a body in a tomb. I am punching the time card for the final time, and it feels magnificent. I have worn nickel-sized dots into the heart of each of the clubfaces, and now they will be put away and might never see daylight again—and if they do, I will be lucky to ever find those nickel centers once more. Golf and I, we will be casual acquaintances passing in the hall from now on. In fourteen months, these clubs had never spent a night in the back of a car. They were always there next to me in the hotel room, always lugged upstairs to Allyson's city apartment, hardly ever out of eyeshot for one entire year. And closing the trunk on them now, I know they will be spending many cold nights in there, and I am more than okay with that. If I need to look at my sticks once in the next six months, I will be shocked.

We head out through Melbourne and down to the Great Ocean Road on our way to Lorne, a happening little surfer town on the south shore of Australia. As we drive, the car seems to float along, so much excitement at eight in the morning, halfway around the world and nobody to tell our news, no way to tell them—nobody at home knew how the world had changed while they'd slept, but it had.

We will be back in Australia someday. Now that I've retired my fear of flying with my other irrational anxieties (a distrust of first tees, wedding ceremonies, young golfers in snappy visors), I would hope to eventually return to Ranfurlie, maybe play a round of golf with my own son (an extra pair of eyes to hunt for my ball would be a big help).

But the biggest reason I think we'll need to come back is that for our whole next week of Australian touring (courtesy of my not making the cut to Stage II), Allyson would see almost zero of the Australian countryside. We work our way along an ocean-sprayed road, traversing cliffs and scooting around hairpin turns in a rental car for which I was ecstatic we had sprung for the insurance—but Allyson hardly looks out the window once. She is too busy looking at her lap, staring at the third finger on her left hand, with a smile on her face that makes her look ten years old. If I had known I was capable of making another human being this happy, I would have gotten around to doing this years ago. But I don't think back then that the smile would have been quite as beautiful as it is today, winding our way through an Australia that neither of us are looking at.

An hour into our trip along the Great Ocean Road, we pass signs for a golf club outside of Lorne, an arrow pointing to ANGLESEA GOLF CLUB.

"Up for a quick eighteen?" I laugh.

"Just what I was thinking."

"Don't worry. Those clubs are getting a long hibernation."

But Allyson reaches for the guide book.

"What was the name of that club?" And she finds a familiar page and reads one of the descriptions she had highlighted in yellow. "Anglesea Golf Club on the Great Ocean Road. That's the kangaroo course. There are supposed to be kangaroos all over the place," she says

The car goes quiet. The thought of the impossible floating in the air.

"Roos?" I ask.

"On a golf course."

U-turns down under are especially tricky, what with the flip-flopped steering wheels and backward traffic lanes, but we make our way back to the turn-off and follow the signs to Anglesea. By 9:30 A.M. on the morning I have proposed to my future wife, after playing golf for 545 days and vowing not to reach 546 for a very long time, we exhume my golf clubs from the trunk of our car and strap them to a golf cart for just nine more.

I didn't know how long it was going to take for me to start enjoying golf again. But as I look down the first fairway at number one and pick out my target—a five-feet kangaroo lounging in the fairway like he's waiting for the pizza man—I am happy to know that it isn't going to be very long at all.

My caddy rides along in the cart. She's been placed in charge of the important tasks of taking pictures and counting marsupials. I'm not keeping track of my strokes, I don't think about my swing, I have no idea what I might be shooting. I just play, and Allyson applauds and snaps pictures and laughs when another kangaroo goes hopping through my line. All the rounds were worth it, for nine holes like these.

There is a scorecard on our cart, and Allyson uses it to keep a careful record of how many roos we see on each hole. Some holes six, eight, sometimes twenty kangaroos lounging around the green, nibbling at the rough. She writes down her tally, hole by hole, and it's the best scorecard I have seen in a very long time, crowded from top to bottom with nothing but beautiful big numbers.

AUTHOR'S NOTE

This book describes the author's experiences while attempting to play professional golf and reflects his opinions relating to those experiences. Events and conversations may have been reorganized for the sake of the narrative. The names and identifying details of some individuals have been changed to protect the innocent. The golf scores, alas, have not.

Acknowledgments

I have always found overwrought acknowledgments pages to be the golf equivalent of a shot-by-shot account of a stranger's eighteen holes, as if no one in history has ever managed to fire an 83 before, or jot down three hundred pages. Yet I must indulge myself here and take the space to thank the dozens of rare and generous individuals to whom my gratitude is long overdue, so many outstanding folks who made this uncommon year of my life possible.

First, many thanks to super-agent Dan Mandel, the first fan of this idea, and an individual whose support and guidance continue to make me feel blessed. And endless gratitude to the wise and fine souls who said yes; Bill Shinker at Gotham Books, and my editor, Brendan Cahill, whose friendship, enthusiasm, and insight along the way proved more valuable than anything the sagest of Scottish caddies could have offered.

Special thanks to my golf dream's dream team: Dr. Robert Winters, who helped me to understand and experience the beautiful simplicity of this game's soul; the miracle worker Mike Willett at Body Balance for Performance, who was there every morning, even when I wished he'd overslept; Bill Lacy and Joe Gomes at Titleist/Foot Joy, who took an immediate interest in my adventure and made sure the number one ball in golf was never more than an e-mail away; and Bob Puccini, Dick Lyons, and especially Bruce Riccio at Mizuno USA, who not only provided me with the best equipment in the game, but provided me with so much confidence, going above and beyond to make me feel a part of their amazing company—you'll never find another golf club in my bag.

And to my dream team's coach, quarterback, and general manager, Dr. Jim Suttie—I am so thankful for the day I darkened Doc's doorway. There is no story here without Dr. Suttie, whose honesty, friendship, and generous wisdom inspired me well beyond the golf course. I could go on, but I'll keep it as short and sweet as Doc would—there are two kinds of people in the world: Doc Suttie kind of people, and everybody else.

So much support and tutelage wouldn't have meant much without a place to play. In a landscape of closed doors, I was fortunate enough to find some of the great and munificent people of this game who were not afraid to turn over their first tee to a redheaded stranger. Many thanks to Ed Weber and Jay Garrick at Raptor Bay in Bonita Springs; Moe Kent, Larry Kent, and Gene Fieger at the Hideout in Naples; Paul Celano at TwinEagles in Naples; Joe Allinder and the entire pro shop at Spring Run at the Brooks; and Paul Mariani, Pam Mariani, Harry Heagy, and all the members of Edgmont Country Club, who provided me with such a warm home back in Pennsylvania.

Thanks to Patrick Mulligan at Gotham Books, for so much quick and able assistance. Thanks to Bobby Grace and MacGregor Golf, Liz Coyne of Coyne Realty, and my warmest regards to Ursula Michel, Sandra Suttie, Mike Via, Bill Price, Dale Welker, Al Balukas, Jerry Quinlan, Brian Lipson, and Gray Coleman.

And as many such pages claim—and sincerely intend—I cannot thank my family enough. Thanks to my parents, Jim and Alice Coyne, who, along with everything else in my life, gave me golf and the freedom to love it, or to leave it. And to my wife, Allyson—my best man had the room laughing about how you carried my golf bag this year. But I hope you know that you have always carried my spirit and my heart. I am the most fortunate, failed golfer in the world.